AF714879

California Divorce Property Division

Victor VeVea & Bakersfield Paralegal

Victor VeVea
1706 Chester Ave, Suite 347
Bakersfield, CA 93301

Bakersfield Paralegal – (661) 489-3369
1412 17th St., Ste. 349
Bakersfield, CA 93301

Copyright © 2026 Legal Research Services
P.O. Box 81
Bakersfield, CA 93302
(661)Justice (587-8423)
All rights reserved.

Part of the royalties from this book are
used to help victims of domestic violence.

ISBN-13: 978-1-950418-05-3

TABLE OF CONTENTS

INTRODUCTION

Judges resolve legal disputes by applying statutes and case law, collectively known as legal precedent. Whether deciding issues involving property division, spousal support, child support, or other family law matters, courts rely on California statutes and published California appellate decisions for guidance. By following precedent, judges strive to apply the law consistently and reach results that align with prior decisions in similar circumstances.

This book contains many of the most significant California family law statutes, cases, and formulas used in dissolution (divorce) proceedings involving property division. To make effective use of this resource, review the authorities that relate to your situation and identify the statutes, cases, and formulas that support your position. If you are represented by counsel, discuss those authorities with your attorney. If you are representing yourself, you may bring the relevant authorities to the court's attention in accordance with applicable court rules and procedures.

As examples:

"Your Honor, Mr. Smith was convicted in a domestic violence case, so I ask the court to apply the *Family Code section 3044* presumption and deny him any custody or visitation."

"Your Honor, Ms. Jones has extensive real estate holdings as shown on her FL-160 disclosures. I respectfully request that the court consider those holdings under *Family Code section 4320(d)* and *In re Marriage of Cheriton* and order support at $10,000 per month. The citation for that case is 92 Cal. App. 4th 269."

This book is intended to provide accurate and authoritative information about the subject matter covered. Use of this book does not create an attorney-client relationship with any of the authors, and this book is distributed with the understanding that the authors, publishers, and distributors do not render legal advice through this book. If legal advice or other expert assistance is required, seek the services of a competent professional. Those using this book in dealing with specific legal matters should exercise their own independent judgment and conduct their own independent research. Because the law changes daily, this book, like almost every other law book, is out of date. An effort has been made to ensure the accuracy of this book on the day of printing, but there is simply no way the printed word can morph to keep up with an ever-changing legal system, and no one can predict with certainty what any given court will do on any given day.

Quotation and Citation Verification Note

Before use, every quoted excerpt in this book should be checked against the official reporter, enacted statutory text, or other authenticated source and should be accompanied by a reporter or statutory pinpoint citation where available. Quotations reproduced without pinpoint pages should be treated as research excerpts only until the exact wording, punctuation, ellipses, bracketed insertions, and omitted context have been verified against the source.

Significant Cases

1. Lucas Rule

Concept:

A spouse who uses traceable separate property to acquire property during marriage does not automatically retain a separate ownership interest when the spouses take title in joint tenancy or another form suggesting shared ownership. Under Lucas, unless there was an agreement or understanding preserving a separate interest or a right of reimbursement, the separate contribution was treated as a gift to the community or joint estate. The Legislature later modified this result through *Family Code sections 2581 and 2640.*

Citation:

In re Marriage of Lucas (1980) 27 Cal.3d 808

Quote:

"The act of taking title in a joint and equal ownership form is inconsistent with an intention to preserve a separate property interest."

"Unless the latter knows that the spouse contributing the separate property expects to be reimbursed or to acquire a separate property interest, he or she has no opportunity to attempt to preserve the joint ownership of the property by making other financing arrangements."

"Accordingly, the expectations of parties who take title jointly are best protected by presuming that the specified ownership interest is intended in the absence of an agreement or understanding to the contrary."

Explanation:

Lucas is the historical starting point for many California characterization disputes involving separately sourced funds placed into jointly titled marital property. The key distinction is between tracing and characterization. Tracing identifies where the money came from; characterization determines what legal estate owns the property. Lucas made clear that, under then-existing law, tracing alone did not defeat the significance of taking title in a form that showed shared ownership.

Lucas held that the form of title presumption could not be overcome merely by tracing the source of the acquisition funds. When spouses acquired a residence in joint tenancy during marriage, the contributing spouse needed evidence of an agreement or understanding that the separate contribution would remain separate or be reimbursed. Without that evidence, the contribution was presumed to be a gift and the property was divided according to its community or joint character. Lucas also approved use of the Aufmuth apportionment approach where a separate ownership interest was actually preserved.

The practical effect of the original Lucas rule was harsh for the contributing spouse. A spouse could contribute a separate property down payment, take title jointly with the other spouse, and later receive neither a separate property share nor reimbursement unless the spouse could prove an agreement or understanding. The Legislature responded by adopting the statutory joint-title presumption now reflected in *Family Code section 2581* and the separate property contribution reimbursement right now reflected in *Family Code section 2640*. Modern practice therefore requires attention to the acquisition date, the form of title, any writing satisfying the transmutation statutes, and any *section 2640* waiver.

Lucas remains useful because it explains why title matters, why tracing is not always enough, and how appreciation may be allocated when a separate ownership interest is preserved. It is not, however, the final answer in a modern dissolution case. For acquisitions and divisions governed by current law, the court must also consider the statutory community property presumption, the joint-title presumption, the transmutation statutes, and the statutory reimbursement scheme.

Examples:

Separate down payment with joint title: Husband uses $100,000 of premarriage savings to make the down payment on a residence during marriage. Title is taken in both spouses' names as joint tenants, and community earnings pay the mortgage. Under the historical Lucas rule, if Husband cannot prove an agreement or understanding that his $100,000 remains separate or reimbursable, the contribution is presumed to be a gift. Under modern law, the property would usually be treated as community property at dissolution under *Family Code section 2581*, but Husband may have a *Family Code section 2640* reimbursement claim unless there is a written waiver.

Separate interest preserved by agreement: Wife contributes a traceable separate property down payment and the spouses sign a writing stating that Wife will retain a separate property percentage interest equal to her down payment contribution. In that circumstance, the issue is not merely reimbursement. Wife may claim an ownership share and a corresponding share of appreciation under a proportional apportionment formula, rather than only a dollar-for-dollar reimbursement.

Formula:

Lucas does not create a single mandatory formula for every case, but it is associated with the Aufmuth-style proportional apportionment formula when a separate property ownership interest is preserved rather than treated merely as a reimbursement claim.

Separate Property Percentage = Separate Property Acquisition Contribution / Purchase Price.

Community Property Percentage = Community Acquisition Contribution or Community Loan Component / Purchase Price.

Separate Property Share = Separate Property Acquisition Contribution + (Separate Property Percentage x Appreciation). Community Property Share = Community Equity Contribution + (Community Property Percentage x Appreciation).

Example calculation: Assume a residence is purchased for $500,000 with a $100,000 separate property down payment and a $400,000 community loan. At division, the residence is worth $700,000 and the loan balance is $360,000. Appreciation is $200,000. If the separate ownership interest was preserved, the separate percentage is 20 percent and the community percentage is 80 percent. The separate estate receives $100,000 plus $40,000 of appreciation. The community receives the principal reduction it paid plus $160,000 of appreciation, subject to the actual remaining equity and any other adjustments. If the claim is only a modern *Family Code section 2640* reimbursement claim, the separate estate generally receives the dollar amount of the contribution, without interest or appreciation, before the remaining community equity is divided.

Caveat:

(1) *Family Code section 2581*: *Section 2581* now provides a special dissolution presumption for property acquired during marriage in joint form. Unless the parties have a clear written statement in the deed or other documentary evidence of a separate property

agreement, the property is presumed community property for purposes of division at dissolution.

(2) *Family Code section 2640*: *Section 2640* reverses the no-reimbursement aspect of Lucas in many modern cases. When a spouse contributes separate property to acquisition of community property, that spouse generally receives reimbursement of the separate contribution, without interest or appreciation, unless the right has been waived in writing.

Further Reading:

Family Code sections 2581 and 2640.

In re Marriage of Aufmuth (1979) 89 Cal.App.3d 446: Aufmuth supplied the proportional apportionment method used when separate and community interests both contribute to acquisition of property and appreciation must be allocated between estates. The formula looks to the ratio of each estate's acquisition contribution to the purchase price and assigns appreciation accordingly.

In re Marriage of Walrath (1998) 17 Cal.4th 907: See *In re Marriage of Walrath (pg. 14).*

2. MacDonald Express Declaration Test

Concept:

A transmutation must be made in writing by an express declaration of the spouse whose interest is adversely affected. A writing that merely consents to a beneficiary designation, estate plan, or transaction is not enough unless the writing expressly states that the spouse is changing the character or ownership of the property.

Citation:

Estate of MacDonald (1990) 51 Cal.3d 262.

Quote:

"Following the approach elucidated in Bennett, we conclude that a writing signed by the adversely affected spouse is not an "express declaration" for the purposes of *section 5110.730 (a)* unless it contains language which expressly states that the characterization or ownership of the property is being changed."

"There is certainly no language in the consent paragraphs, or the adoption agreements as a whole, expressly stating that decedent was effecting a change in the character or ownership of her interest."

"We do not hold that *section 5110.730 (a)* requires use of the term "transmutation" or any other particular locution."

Explanation:

MacDonald established the express declaration standard for statutory transmutations. The Supreme Court held that the writing must contain language which expressly states that the characterization or ownership of the property is being changed. Extrinsic evidence may not be used to supply the missing declaration. The writing does not need magic words, but it must show on its face that the adversely affected spouse intended to change property rights.

MacDonald is the leading case on what counts as an express declaration. The rule is intentionally formal. California law treats spouses as capable of changing property character during marriage, but it requires a clear written act so that major property rights are not altered accidentally, informally, or through ambiguous estate-planning paperwork.

The distinction in MacDonald is between consenting to a transaction and transferring ownership. A spouse may sign a form acknowledging a beneficiary designation or approving an estate-planning step, but that does not necessarily mean the spouse has given away a community property interest. The writing must do more than permit the other spouse to act. It must say, in substance, that the signer gives, transfers, changes, converts, or relinquishes the property interest at issue.

The case is central in both probate and dissolution settings. In probate, it can determine whether property passes through an estate plan or remains subject to surviving-spouse rights. In dissolution, it determines whether a claimed separate property agreement, deed, beneficiary form, trust document, account form, letter, or memorandum actually changed the character of property.

Examples:

Beneficiary consent form: Husband has retirement benefits funded during marriage. Wife signs a form consenting to Husband's designation of a trust or children as beneficiaries. The form states that Wife understands the beneficiary designation but does not say that she gives up, transfers, or changes her community property interest. Under MacDonald, the form is not a valid transmutation.

Express transfer language: Wife signs a dated writing stating, "I give to Husband all of my community property interest in the funds in account number 1234, and those funds shall be Husband's separate property." That language is much more likely to satisfy MacDonald because it expressly declares a change in ownership and character on the face of the document.

Further Reading:

Family Code sections 850 and 852.

In re Marriage of Benson (2005) 36 Cal.4th 1096: See *In re Marriage of Benson (pg. 12).*

In re Marriage of Starkman (2005) 129 Cal.App.4th 659: See *In re Marriage of Starkman (pg. 22).*

In re Marriage of Barneson (1999) 69 Cal.App.4th 583: Barneson illustrates that informal writings can sometimes satisfy the statute if they expressly direct a change in ownership, but the writing must still satisfy the face-of-the-document requirement.

3. *In re Marriage of Valli*

Concept:

Property acquired during marriage with community funds is community property unless a statutory exception or valid transmutation applies. A policy, account, or asset titled in one spouse's name is not separate property merely because title or ownership documentation identifies that spouse as owner.

Citation:

In re Marriage of Valli (2014) 58 Cal.4th 1396.

Quote:

"During a marriage the husband used community property funds to purchase an insurance policy on his life, naming his wife as the policy's only owner and beneficiary. Upon dissolution of the marriage, is the life insurance policy community property or the wife's separate property? We conclude that, unless the statutory transmutation requirements have been met, the life insurance policy is community property."

"To satisfy the requirement of an "express declaration," a writing signed by the adversely affected spouse must expressly state that the character or ownership of the property at issue is being changed."

Explanation:

Valli is a modern anchor case for the proposition that title is not the whole analysis between spouses. The husband bought a multi-million-dollar life insurance policy during marriage using community funds. The policy listed the wife as owner and beneficiary. The wife argued that the title documents made the policy her separate property. The Supreme Court rejected that argument because no valid transmutation had occurred.

Valli held that a life insurance policy purchased during marriage with community funds was community property even though the wife was named as the policy owner and beneficiary. The Supreme Court held that California's transmutation requirements apply to interspousal property characterization disputes even when the asset is acquired from a third party. Title documentation alone did not satisfy *Family Code section 852*, and the *Evidence Code section 662* title presumption did not override the Family Code community property and transmutation rules.

The case is especially important because it rejected a narrow view that the transmutation statutes apply only to direct transfers between spouses. The Court reasoned that the statutes are designed to prevent spouses from inadvertently changing the character of property and therefore apply when one spouse uses community funds to acquire an asset from a third party in the other spouse's name.

For characterization analysis, Valli creates a disciplined sequence: identify the acquisition date, identify the source of funds, apply the Family Code presumptions, then ask whether there is a writing satisfying *section 852*. If the property was acquired during marriage with community funds, the asset is community unless separate property tracing, gift or inheritance, post-separation acquisition, or valid transmutation changes that result.

Examples:

Life insurance policy: During marriage, Husband uses community funds to buy a life insurance policy on his own life. Wife is listed as owner and beneficiary. At dissolution, Wife argues the policy is her separate property because the insurer's records list her as owner. Under Valli, the policy is community property unless a written express declaration satisfies *Family Code section 852*.

Vehicle or account in one spouse's name: Spouses use community earnings to purchase a vehicle, but title is placed only in Wife's name for convenience or financing reasons. The title certificate may be evidence, but it is not by itself a valid transmutation. The vehicle is presumptively community property absent a valid writing or separate property source.

Further Reading:

Family Code sections 760, 770, 850, and 852; *Evidence Code section 662*

In re Marriage of Haines (1995) 33 Cal.App.4th 277: See Haines Presumption of Undue Influence (pg. 17).

Speier v. Brace (In re Brace) (2020) 9 Cal.5th 903: Brace later reinforced the limited role of *Evidence Code section 662* in disputes between spouses where the

Family Code community property presumption and transmutation statutes control.

In re Marriage of Brooks and Robinson (2008) 169 Cal.App.4th 176 and *In re Marriage of Summers* (1984) 159 Cal.App.3d 1028: Valli rejected the reasoning of decisions that treated some third-party acquisitions in one spouse's name as outside the transmutation statutes.

4. *In re Marriage of Benson*

Concept:

An oral agreement to transmute property is ineffective, even if one spouse has partly performed in reliance on the oral agreement. *Family Code section 852* requires a written express declaration by the spouse whose property interest is adversely affected.

Citation:

In re Marriage of Benson (2005) 36 Cal.4th 1096.

Quote:

"Family Code section 852, subdivision (a) (section 852 (a)) provides that a "transmutation," or an interspousal transaction changing the character of community or separate property (id. at § 850), "is not valid unless made in writing by an express declaration" approved by the adversely affected spouse."

"Even assuming Husband's transfer of the deed constituted part performance of Wife's promise to transmute the retirement accounts, section 852 (a) requires such agreements to be both written and express, and seeks to prevent transmutations under circumstances like those present here."

"By insisting upon a special writing expressly changing the character of the disputed property, MacDonald all but decided that section 852 (a) is not satisfied where no such writing exists at all."

Explanation:

Benson held that the doctrine of part performance does not create an exception to *Family Code section 852.* The husband claimed that he transferred his community interest in the family residence to the wife because she orally agreed to waive her community interest in his retirement plans. There was no written express declaration by the wife changing the character of her interest in the retirement plans. The Supreme Court held that the retirement plans remained community property.

Benson treats the transmutation statute as more than a statute of frauds. It is a substantive rule for changing marital property character. Because the statute was enacted to reduce unreliable testimony and litigation over alleged oral understandings, the Court refused to allow part performance to substitute for the required writing.

The case is often used when one spouse argues fairness, reliance, or bargain-based expectations. Those arguments may support other remedies in an appropriate case, but they do not change characterization unless the statutory writing requirement is satisfied. A deed, transfer, or payment by one spouse does not automatically prove the other spouse gave up a different property right.

Benson therefore complements MacDonald. MacDonald defines what the writing must say; Benson explains that the court cannot bypass the writing requirement because the parties acted as though an oral agreement existed. Together, the cases push practitioners toward written marital agreements, settlement agreements, deeds with express transmutation language, and other formal documents.

Examples:

Home-for-retirement trade: Husband signs a deed giving Wife his interest in the family home. Husband contends Wife orally promised that, in exchange, she would waive any community interest in his pension and retirement accounts. Unless Wife signed a writing expressly changing her interest in those retirement assets, the retirement assets remain community property under Benson.

Informal settlement discussions: Spouses exchange text messages saying, "You can keep the house and I will keep my 401(k)," but the messages are not signed formal declarations and do not expressly transmute the identified property interests. Those communications may show negotiation history, but they may fail as transmutations unless they satisfy *section 852* and other agreement requirements.

Caveat:

Family Code section 721: Even when a writing exists, spousal fiduciary duties may create separate issues of disclosure, fairness, undue influence, and burden shifting. Benson addresses the threshold writing requirement, not every possible fiduciary-duty issue.

Further Reading:

Family Code sections 850 and 852.

Estate of MacDonald (1990) 51 Cal.3d 262: See MacDonald Express Declaration Test (pg. 8).

In re Marriage of Campbell (1999) 74 Cal.App.4th 1058: Campbell is a pre-Benson Court of Appeal case sometimes discussed in relation to part performance and transmutation. Benson controls and rejects part performance as a substitute for the statutory writing.

5. *In re Marriage of Walrath*

Concept:

A *Family Code section 2640* reimbursement claim for separate property contributions to community property can be traced through refinancing proceeds and into later-acquired community assets. The right is not limited to the first asset acquired with the separate property contribution.

Citation:

In re Marriage of Walrath (1998) 17 Cal.4th 907.

Quote:

"In the absence of a written waiver, a spouse who contributes separate property to a community property acquisition is reimbursed upon dissolution of the marriage."

"Therefore, it seems unlikely that the Legislature intended a contributing spouse would lose the right to reimbursement merely because the specific property to which the money was contributed was refinanced. Rather, the right to reimbursement should follow the assets to which the contribution can be traced."

"The community is entitled to any appreciation in these assets above the amount necessary to reimburse the parties for their separate property contributions to the Lucerne, Utah, and Nevada properties, and the joint bank account."

Explanation:

Walrath held that the contributing spouse could seek reimbursement under *Family Code section 2640* for separate property contributions that were traceable through loan proceeds from the original community property asset into other community property assets. The Supreme Court rejected a narrow rule limiting reimbursement to the original property. It also emphasized that *section 2640* reimbursement is generally limited to the dollar amount of the contribution, without interest or appreciation, and is capped by the net value of the property to which the contribution is traced.

Walrath is a reimbursement case, but it is important in characterization and tracing analysis because it explains how a separate property contribution can retain legal significance even after the asset changes form. A spouse may contribute separate property to a community asset, the community may refinance that asset, and the loan proceeds may be used to acquire or improve other community assets. If the separate contribution can be traced into the later assets, the reimbursement claim follows the trace.

The case distinguishes reimbursement from ownership. *Section 2640* does not automatically give the contributing spouse a separate ownership share in appreciation. Instead, it provides reimbursement of the separate property contribution before the remaining community estate is divided. That is different from Moore/Marsden or Aufmuth apportionment, where separate and community estates may each receive a proportionate share of appreciation because each estate owns part of the asset.

Walrath also matters because it rejects a purely asset-by-asset view of *section 2640*. In a real marital estate, equity is often moved through refinances, sales, payoffs, improvements, and purchases. The court permitted tracing through those transactions so long as the evidence connects the original separate contribution to the later community property.

Examples:

Refinance proceeds used to buy another property: Wife contributes $150,000 of separate property to purchase a community residence. The spouses later refinance the residence and use a portion of the loan proceeds as the down payment on a vacation property titled as community property. Under Walrath, Wife may trace a *section 2640* reimbursement claim into the vacation property if the evidence shows that the proceeds used for the vacation property carried part of her original separate contribution.

Loan proceeds used for improvements: Husband contributes separate property to acquire a community home. The home is refinanced, and proceeds are used to remodel another community property. If the tracing is adequate, Husband may claim reimbursement from the net value of the improved property, not only from the original residence.

Formula:

Walrath uses a tracing approach rather than a universal formula, but a practical calculation often proceeds in three steps.

Step 1 - Determine the reimbursement contribution: Identify the separate property contribution that qualifies under *Family Code section 2640*, such as a down payment, principal reduction, or improvement payment.

Step 2 - Trace the contribution into later property: If the original asset was refinanced or sold, determine what portion of the loan proceeds or sale proceeds is attributable to the separate contribution and where those proceeds went. A common tracing ratio is: Separate Contribution / Equity in Original Property at Refinance or Sale = Separate Contribution Ratio.

Step 3 - Apply the ratio to the later use of proceeds: Traceable Reimbursement in Later Asset = Separate Contribution Ratio x Proceeds Applied to Later Asset, subject to the net value cap and without interest or appreciation.

Example calculation: Assume Wife contributed $100,000 of separate property to a community residence. At refinance, the residence has $400,000 of equity, so Wife's contribution ratio is 25 percent. The spouses use $80,000 of refinance proceeds to improve a different community property. Wife can argue that $20,000 of the improvement money is traceable to her separate contribution (25 percent x $80,000). That amount may be reimbursable under *section 2640* if the proof is adequate and the net value cap allows it.

Further Reading:

Family Code section 2640: *Section 2640* authorizes reimbursement for separate property contributions to acquisition of community property, including down payments, payments for improvements, and payments reducing principal on acquisition debt. It generally excludes interest, taxes, insurance, and maintenance.

In re Marriage of Lucas (1980) 27 Cal.3d 808: See Lucas Rule (pg. 5).

In re Marriage of Witt (1987) 197 Cal.App.3d 103 and *In re Marriage of Tallman* (1994) 22 Cal.App.4th 1697: These cases are often discussed with *section 2640* tracing and reimbursement issues, including how reimbursement applies when the contributed value can be identified in later property.

In re Marriage of Aufmuth (1979) 89 Cal.App.3d 446: When a residence is acquired during marriage using both one spouse's traceable separate-property contribution and community credit or community funds, the property may contain both separate and community interests. The spouse's separate-property down payment does not become a gift to the community merely because the home is titled in both spouses' names, if the separate source is adequately traced. Conversely, a loan obtained during marriage is presumed community property unless the evidence shows the lender relied on one spouse's separate property.

6. Haines Presumption of Undue Influence

Concept:

When an interspousal transaction advantages one spouse, the law presumes undue influence and places the burden on the advantaged spouse to prove the transaction was fair, voluntary, fully informed, and understood. In family law characterization disputes, this fiduciary-duty framework can override ordinary title presumptions.

Citation:

In re Marriage of Haines (1995) 33 Cal.App.4th 277.

Quote:

"When an interspousal transaction advantages one spouse, "[t]he law, from considerations of public policy, presumes such transactions to have been induced by undue influence.""

"This confidential spousal relationship imposes a duty of the highest good faith and fair dealing on each spouse, and neither shall take any unfair advantage of the other."

"We conclude that application of *section 662* is improper when it is in conflict with the presumption of undue influence that emanates from former *section 5103*, subdivision (b) (Fam. Code, *§ 721*, subd. (b))."

Explanation:

Haines held that *Evidence Code section 662*'s title presumption should not be applied in a manner that defeats the protections arising from the confidential and fiduciary relationship between spouses. When the wife executed a quitclaim deed that advantaged the husband, the husband bore the burden of rebutting the presumption of undue influence. The court concluded that the trial court applied the wrong burden and that the deed could be set aside.

Haines is the leading California family law case on the interaction between title and spousal fiduciary duties. The ordinary title presumption says that record title is presumed to reflect beneficial ownership. But spouses are not ordinary arm's-length contracting parties. They owe each other duties of highest good faith and fair dealing, and neither may take unfair advantage of the other.

The practical rule is that an interspousal transaction giving one spouse an advantage creates a rebuttable presumption of undue influence. The advantaged spouse must show that the disadvantaged spouse acted freely and voluntarily, with full knowledge of the facts and complete understanding of the transaction's effect. This is especially important for quitclaim deeds, interspousal transfer deeds, refinance paperwork, and estate-planning documents signed without independent advice.

Haines should be analyzed alongside the transmutation cases. A writing may be clear enough to satisfy *Family Code section 852*, but it can still be challenged under *Family Code section 721* if it resulted from undue influence or breach of fiduciary duty. Conversely, a deed may create title evidence, but it will not necessarily control characterization if the advantaged spouse cannot meet the fiduciary-duty burden.

Examples:

Quitclaim for refinance: Husband tells Wife she must sign a quitclaim deed so he can refinance the home. Wife signs without independent advice and without understanding that she is giving up ownership. Husband later claims the residence is his separate property because title is in his name alone. Under Haines, Husband has the burden to rebut the undue influence presumption because the transaction advantaged him.

Independent advice and full disclosure: Wife transfers an interest in property to Husband after both spouses exchange financial disclosures, Wife consults independent counsel, and the written agreement clearly explains the property consequences. Those facts may help Husband rebut the Haines presumption, though the court still examines the entire transaction.

Caveat:

Family Code section 721: *Section 721* codifies the fiduciary duties between spouses and incorporates duties comparable to those of nonmarital business partners, including access to information, disclosure, and fair dealing.

Further Reading:

Family Code section 721; *Evidence Code section 662.*

In re Marriage of Delaney (2003) 111 Cal.App.4th 991: Delaney applied the undue influence framework to an interspousal transaction and emphasized the burden on the spouse who gained an advantage.

In re Marriage of Fossum (2011) 192 Cal.App.4th 336: See *In re Marriage of Fossum*: Undue Influence and Mandatory *Section 1101(g)* Fees (pg. 66).

Bonvino v. Bonvino (2015) 241 Cal.App.4th 1411: See *Bonvino v. Bonvino (pg. 19).*

7. *Bonvino v. Bonvino*

Concept:

When property acquired during marriage is funded by both traceable separate property and community property, and there is no valid transmutation, the property may be apportioned between separate and community interests. *Section 2640* reimbursement applies only after separate property has become part of the community estate; it does not automatically convert a preserved separate ownership interest into a mere reimbursement claim.

Citation:

Bonvino v. Bonvino (2015) 241 Cal.App.4th 1411.

Quote:

"In the published portion of the opinion, we hold that if property is acquired during marriage with both separate and community funds, the transmutation requirements of *section 852* must be satisfied before the reimbursement provisions of *section 2640* apply."

"The documents in this case do not contain an express transmutation of husband's separate property, and therefore, husband's separate property contributions remained husband's separate property."

"He held a separate property interest in the property proportionate to the separate property funds that he contributed."

Explanation:

Bonvino held that the husband's traceable separate property contributions to the acquisition and loan payoff of a residence remained separate property because there was no written transmutation satisfying *Family Code section 852*. The court rejected treating those contributions only as *Family Code section 2640* reimbursement claims because the property had not first been validly transmuted into community property. The court required apportionment of the residence between the husband's separate property interest and the community property interest.

Bonvino is a useful modern bridge between tracing, transmutation, title, and reimbursement. The residence was acquired during marriage, but the husband used separate property for the down payment and later used additional separate property to pay off the acquisition debt. Some community funds or community credit were also involved. The trial court treated the home as community property with a *section 2640* reimbursement. The Court of Appeal held that this skipped a step: separate property does not become community property unless there is a valid transmutation or other legal basis for that change.

The case is important because it distinguishes a separate property ownership interest from a statutory reimbursement right. If the spouse's separate property was transmuted into community property, *section 2640* may provide dollar-for-dollar reimbursement without appreciation. If there was no transmutation, however, the separate property contribution may retain its character and receive a proportionate ownership share, including a share of appreciation or depreciation.

Bonvino also reinforces that loan characterization matters. Loan proceeds obtained during marriage are generally presumed community, but that presumption may be overcome by evidence of the lender's intent to rely primarily on separate property. The characterization of the loan affects the respective separate and community ownership shares.

Examples:

Separate down payment plus community loan: Husband buys a home during marriage using $300,000 from the sale of his premarital property and a purchase-money loan that is community in character. Title paperwork does not contain an express transmutation. Under Bonvino, Husband may retain a separate property ownership percentage based on his separate contribution, while the community owns the portion attributable to the community loan and community principal payments.

Later separate payoff: Wife acquires a mixed-character property during marriage. Years later, she uses inherited funds to pay off the remaining acquisition loan. If the inheritance is traceable and no valid transmutation occurs, Wife may have an additional separate property acquisition contribution, not merely a reimbursement claim, depending on how the payoff affects ownership under the applicable apportionment rules.

Formula:

Bonvino generally calls for an apportionment analysis rather than a pure *section 2640* reimbursement calculation. The exact formula depends on the timing and character of acquisition contributions, but the working approach is as follows.

Step 1 - Identify acquisition contributions: Separate property down payments, separate property principal payoffs, community loan proceeds, and community principal payments must be identified and traced. Interest, taxes, insurance, and maintenance are usually treated differently from acquisition principal.

Step 2 - Determine ownership percentages: Separate Property Percentage = Traceable Separate Acquisition Contributions / Total Acquisition Basis. Community Property Percentage = Traceable Community Acquisition Contributions / Total Acquisition Basis.

Step 3 - Allocate equity and appreciation: Each estate receives its contributed acquisition principal plus its proportionate share of appreciation or depreciation, subject to refinements required by Moore/Marsden, Aufmuth, loan characterization, and the actual facts.

Section 2640 distinction: If the separate contribution was validly transmuted into community property, the spouse ordinarily receives a dollar-for-dollar *section 2640* reimbursement without interest or appreciation unless waived. If there was no transmutation, Bonvino supports preserving a proportionate separate property ownership interest rather than collapsing the claim into *section 2640* reimbursement.

Example calculation: Assume a $1,000,000 residence is acquired during marriage with $400,000 traceable separate property and a $600,000 community loan. Ignoring later principal payments for simplicity, the separate estate owns 40 percent and the community owns 60 percent if no transmutation occurred. If the residence later has $500,000 of net appreciation, the separate estate receives $400,000 plus $200,000 of appreciation, and the community receives its equity contribution plus $300,000 of appreciation. If the $400,000 had instead been transmuted into community property, *section 2640* would usually reimburse $400,000 without appreciation before the remaining community equity is divided.

Further Reading:

Family Code sections 760, 770, 850, 852, and 2640.

In re Marriage of Valli (2014) 58 Cal.4th 1396: See *In re Marriage of Valli (pg. 10).*

In re Marriage of Moore (1980) 28 Cal.3d 366 and *In re Marriage of Marsden* (1982) 130 Cal.App.3d 426: See Moore Formula (pg. 24) and Marsden Adjustment for Premarital Appreciation (pg. 27).

In re Marriage of Grinius (1985) 166 Cal.App.3d 1179: Grinius is often cited for the rule that the characterization of loan proceeds turns on the lender's intent and the property or credit on which the lender primarily relied.

In re Marriage of Aufmuth (1979) 89 Cal.App.3d 446: When a residence is acquired during marriage using both one spouse's traceable separate-property contribution and community credit or community funds, the property may contain both separate and community interests. The spouse's separate-property down payment does not become a gift to the community merely because the home is titled in both spouses' names, if the separate source is adequately traced. Conversely, a loan obtained during marriage is presumed community property unless the evidence shows the lender relied on one spouse's separate property.

In re Marriage of Marsden (1982) 130 Cal.App.3d 426 and *In re Marriage of Valli* (2014) 58 Cal.4th 1396: See Marsden Adjustment for Premarital Appreciation (pg. 27) and *In re Marriage of Valli (pg. 10).*

8. *In re Marriage of Starkman*

Concept:

Estate-planning trust language does not transmute separate property unless the writing expressly and unambiguously changes the property's character or ownership. General trust provisions describing trust property as community property are not enough if they can reasonably be read as administrative or descriptive rather than transmutative.

Citation:

In re Marriage of Starkman (2005) 129 Cal.App.4th 659.

Quote:

"The express declaration must unambiguously indicate a change in character or ownership of property."

"A party does not "slip into a transmutation by accident.""

"In deciding whether a transmutation has occurred, we interpret the written instruments independently, without resort to extrinsic evidence."

Explanation:

Starkman held that revocable trust documents and a general assignment did not validly transmute the husband's separate property into community property. The documents did not expressly declare that the husband's separate property was changed, converted, or transmuted into community property. The court applied MacDonald and refused to rely on extrinsic evidence to create a transmutation not stated clearly in the writing.

Starkman is frequently cited in cases where estate-planning documents are later used in dissolution to argue that one spouse changed the character of substantial separate property. Many trusts use broad language for probate avoidance, management convenience, tax planning, or classification of assets within the trust. Starkman warns that such language is not automatically a transmutation.

The writing must unambiguously show that the adversely affected spouse intended to change ownership or character. Language saying that property "is" community property may be insufficient if the document's purpose and structure do not clearly show that existing separate property is being converted. Stronger language includes words such as "transmute," "convert," "change," "transfer," "give," or "becomes," paired with identification of the property and the spouse whose interest is affected.

The case also shows why extrinsic evidence is limited. The court will not use testimony from lawyers, spouses, or estate-planning history to supply an express declaration missing from the document. The writing must stand on its own.

Examples:

General revocable trust clause: Husband transfers his premarital investment accounts into a joint revocable trust. The trust states that property transferred to the trust is community property unless listed separately, but it does not expressly say Husband's identified separate property is converted or transmuted. Under Starkman, that clause may not be enough to change characterization.

Separate transmutation agreement: Husband signs a trust amendment and a separate written agreement stating, "Husband hereby transmutes the assets listed on Exhibit A from Husband's separate property to the community property of Husband and Wife." The assets are identified, the change in character is express, and the affected spouse signs. That type of language is much more likely to satisfy *Family Code section 852*.

Further Reading:

Family Code sections 850 and 852.

Estate of MacDonald (1990) 51 Cal.3d 262: See MacDonald Express Declaration Test (pg. 8).

In re Marriage of Holtemann (2008) 166 Cal.App.4th 1166 and *Marriage of Lund* (2009) 174 Cal.App.4th 40: These cases show circumstances in which estate-planning documents or related agreements can satisfy the transmutation requirements when the language is sufficiently express.

In re Marriage of Barneson (1999) 69 Cal.App.4th 583: Barneson demonstrates that informal written directions may qualify when they expressly change ownership, but Starkman confirms that ambiguity will defeat a claimed transmutation.

In re Marriage of Barneson (1999) 69 Cal.App.4th 583: A document transferring property into a spouse's name is not enough. The writing must clearly show that the adversely affected spouse is giving up or changing a property interest, such as by saying the property is being given to the other spouse, transferred as the other spouse's separate property, or otherwise changed in character or ownership. The court noted that language such as giving the stock to the wife or transferring it to her "as her sole and separate property" would have been much stronger.

9. Moore Formula

Concept:

The Moore Formula (now known as Moore / Marsden) is a rule governing community property contributions to a separate property asset.

When community funds reduce principal on real property acquired by one spouse before marriage, the community acquires a pro tanto interest in that otherwise separate property. The community interest is based on principal reduction and the corresponding share of appreciation; interest, taxes, insurance, and maintenance do not increase the ownership share.

Citation:

In re Marriage of Moore (1980) 28 Cal.3d 366.

Quote:

"Where community funds are used to make payments on property purchased by one of the spouses before marriage "the rule developed through decisions in California gives to the community a pro tanto community property interest in such property in the ratio that the payments on the purchase price with community funds bear to the payments made with separate funds.""

"Since such expenditures do not increase the equity value of the property, they should not be considered in its division upon dissolution of marriage."

"The community property percentage interest is found by dividing the amount by which community property payments reduced the principal by the purchase price."

Explanation:

Moore is the foundational California real property contribution case. It addresses a common fact pattern: one spouse owns a residence before marriage, the parties live in the residence during marriage, and community earnings are used to make mortgage payments. The residence does not become community property merely because community funds are used. Instead, the owning spouse retains a separate property interest, and the community receives a proportionate interest reflecting its contribution toward acquisition of the asset. Moore focuses on acquisition value, not the total cost of occupancy. A payment that reduces principal increases equity and helps acquire the property. A payment for interest, taxes, insurance, or maintenance preserves the use of the property, but it does not increase the ownership equity being divided. For that reason, Moore excludes those expense items from the apportionment percentage. The practical result is a hybrid asset. The separate estate receives credit for the separate contributions and the corresponding appreciation. The community receives credit for the community principal reduction and the corresponding appreciation. Each spouse then receives one-half of the community portion, unless a separate equalization rule or reimbursement statute changes the result.

In Moore, wife purchased the Menlo Park residence before marriage, made a separate down payment, and obtained a purchase loan. During marriage, community payments reduced principal by $5,986.20. The Supreme Court concluded that the community percentage equaled that community principal reduction divided by the purchase price. The resulting community share included both the principal reduction and the corresponding percentage of appreciation.

The Supreme Court held that the community obtained an interest in the residence because community funds were used during marriage to reduce the principal balance of a loan secured by a residence purchased by Wife before marriage. The court rejected Husband's argument that the community percentage should include the full amount of mortgage payments, including interest, taxes, and insurance. Those items did not increase equity and therefore were not capital contributions. The court treated the premarital down payment and premarital purchase loan as separate property contributions because the loan was based on separate credit and separate assets. The community percentage was calculated by dividing the principal reduction paid with community funds by the purchase price.

Examples:

Premarital purchase with community mortgage payments: Husband buys a home before marriage for $500,000 with a $100,000 down payment and a $400,000 loan in his name. During marriage, community earnings reduce the loan principal by $50,000. At trial, the home is worth $800,000. Under Moore, the community percentage is $50,000 divided by $500,000, or 10 percent. The community receives the $50,000 principal reduction plus 10 percent of the $300,000 appreciation, for a total community interest of $80,000. Each spouse receives one-half of that community interest. Husband retains the separate property balance.

Expense payments do not change the ownership percentage: Assume the same home, but the community also paid $90,000 in interest, property taxes, and insurance. Moore does not add those expense payments to the numerator of the ownership formula because they did not reduce principal or increase the capital investment in the home. They may matter for cash flow, support, reimbursement, or equitable arguments, but they are not part of the Moore ownership percentage.

Formula:

The basic Moore formula is used when separate real property is acquired before marriage and community funds reduce the purchase loan principal during marriage. Define P as the purchase price, C as the principal reduction paid with community funds during marriage, and A as the appreciation allocated under the Moore analysis.

Community percentage = C / P.

Community interest = C + (Community percentage x A).

Each spouse's share of the community interest = Community interest / 2.

Separate property percentage = 1 - Community percentage, subject to separate credits for the down payment, purchase loan treated as separate, premarital principal reduction, and other traceable separate contributions.

Excluded from C: interest, property taxes, insurance, maintenance, and ordinary carrying costs.

Further Reading:

Family Code § 770 (separate property owned before marriage).

Family Code § 760 (community property acquired during marriage).

In re Marriage of Marsden (1982) 130 Cal.App.3d 426: See Marsden Adjustment for Premarital Appreciation (pg. 27).

In re Marriage of Branco (1996) 47 Cal.App.4th 1621: See *In re Marriage of Branco* (1996) 47 Cal.App.4th 1621 (pg. 29).

In re Marriage of Aufmuth (1979) 89 Cal.App.3d 446: When a residence is acquired during marriage using both one spouse's traceable separate-property contribution and community credit or community funds, the property may contain both separate and community interests. The spouse's separate-property down payment does not become a gift to the community merely because the home is titled in both spouses' names, if the separate source is adequately traced. Conversely, a loan obtained during marriage is presumed community property unless the evidence shows the lender relied on one spouse's separate property.

In re Marriage of Lucas (1980) 27 Cal.3d 808: See Lucas Rule (pg. 5).

10. Marsden Adjustment for Premarital Appreciation

Concept:

Marsden refines Moore when the separate property was acquired and appreciated substantially before marriage. The separate estate receives credit for premarital appreciation, and only the appreciation during marriage is apportioned between separate and community interests according to the Moore percentage.

Citation:

In re Marriage of Marsden (1982) 130 Cal.App.3d 426.

Quote:

"The community property percentage interest is found by dividing the community property payments on the loan principal by the purchase price."

"Husband proposes a modification of the above formula. He contends, and we agree, that he should have the benefit of approximately nine years of appreciation in the value of the property before the marriage in 1971."

"We think it is equitable to credit the separate property interest with this prenuptial appreciation."

Explanation:

In Marsden, the court agreed that the community had an interest in a Husband's separate property house because community funds reduced the principal balance on property Husband acquired before marriage. The trial court erred by allocating appreciation based on the ratio of community principal payments to separate principal payments only. The court held that the separate estate must receive credit for the property's premarital appreciation. The proper analysis first identifies the separate contribution and the community contribution under Moore, then allocates only the appreciation during marriage. Marsden also confirmed that post-separation principal payments made with the owner spouse's separate funds are separate property contributions, not community contributions.

Marsden is often paired with Moore because it supplies the adjustment needed when the property was not purchased shortly before marriage. If a spouse buys real property many years before marriage, the value at the date of marriage may be far higher than the original purchase price. That premarital increase occurred before the community came into existence. Marsden prevents the community from sharing in appreciation that was already realized before marriage. The case therefore separates time periods. First, the court identifies the separate property position at the date of marriage, including premarital equity and premarital appreciation. Second, the court identifies community principal reduction during marriage. Third, it apportions marital appreciation using the Moore percentage. The separate estate receives all premarital appreciation, the separate share of marital appreciation, and any post-separation principal reduction paid with separate funds. The community receives the community principal reduction and the community percentage of marital appreciation. Each spouse receives one-half of the community share.

Examples:

Property purchased long before marriage: Wife buys a property for $300,000 ten years before marriage. On the date of marriage, the property is worth $500,000, subject to a $200,000 loan. During marriage, community funds reduce principal by $60,000. At trial, the property is worth $800,000. The premarital appreciation from $300,000 to $500,000 belongs to Wife's separate estate. If the Moore percentage is $60,000 divided by $300,000, or 20 percent, the community receives $60,000 plus 20 percent of the $300,000 marital appreciation from $500,000 to $800,000, for a community interest of $120,000. Each spouse receives one-half of that community interest.

Post-separation payments: Husband owns the property before marriage. The parties separate in 2022, and Husband alone pays principal from his post-separation wages until trial in 2026. Under Marsden and later Mohler, those post-separation principal reductions ordinarily do not increase the community's Moore/Marsden percentage because the payments are made with separate property earnings after separation.

Formula:

Marsden uses the Moore formula, but it separates premarital appreciation from marital appreciation. Define P as the original purchase price, C as principal reduction paid with community funds during marriage, M as fair market value at marriage, and V as fair market value at the valuation date used by the court.

Premarital appreciation = M - P, adjusted as necessary for debt and equity facts.

Community percentage = C / P.

Marital appreciation = V - M.

Community interest = C + (Community percentage x Marital appreciation).

Separate interest includes premarital equity, premarital appreciation, the separate percentage of marital appreciation, and separate principal reductions made before marriage or after separation.

Further Reading:

Family Code § 770 (separate property owned before marriage).

Family Code § 771 (post-separation earnings and accumulations as separate property).

In re Marriage of Moore (1980) 28 Cal.3d 366: See Moore Formula (pg. 24).

In re Marriage of Mohler (2020) 47 Cal.App.5th 788: See Mohler Pro Tanto Rule (pg. 34).

11. *In re Marriage of Branco* (1996) 47 Cal.App.4th 1621

Concept:

A community refinance that pays off a premarital purchase money loan can create a Moore/Marsden community interest in the separate property. For acquisition purposes, the community loan proceeds used to retire the separate purchase debt may be treated like community payments reducing principal.

Citation:

In re Marriage of Branco (1996) 47 Cal.App.4th 1621.

Quote:

"In the present case, the parties did not, as in Moore and Marsden, make payments on the original mortgage with community property funds but rather paid off the original mortgage in full with proceeds from a community property loan."

"We can discern no meaningful difference, for purposes of determining whether the community acquires an interest in real property, between the use of community funds to make payments on one spouse's preexisting loan and the use of proceeds from a community property loan to pay off the preexisting separate loan."

"The Moore rule, however, is not a presumption that can be rebutted but a rule to be applied when community funds are used to acquire a residence by reducing the principal owed on the loan by which the property was purchased."

Explanation:

The Court of Appeal reversed the trial court's refusal to recognize a community interest in Wife's premarital residence. During marriage, the parties obtained a community loan secured by the residence and used part of the proceeds to pay off Wife's premarital mortgage. The court held that, for Moore/Marsden purposes, there is no meaningful difference between making community payments on a separate purchase loan and using proceeds from a community loan to pay off that purchase loan. The Moore rule is not merely a rebuttable presumption. It is an apportionment rule applied when community funds contribute to acquisition by reducing or retiring purchase debt. The court also held that loan proceeds used for purposes unrelated to acquisition did not, merely because they were secured by the separate residence, create a community ownership interest in the property.

Branco addresses a refinance variation of Moore/Marsden. In many marriages, the parties do not simply make monthly payments on a premarital mortgage. They refinance, borrow against the property, consolidate debt, or use the home as security for multiple purposes. Branco separates the acquisition component from the debt component. To the extent a community loan pays off the original purchase money obligation on separate real property, the community has contributed to acquisition and receives a pro tanto interest. To the extent the same loan proceeds pay unrelated debts, living expenses, vacations, credit cards, or obligations of either spouse, those funds may create community debt or reimbursement issues, but they do not automatically become an ownership contribution to the real property. This distinction is critical. A loan secured by a separate home is not, by itself, a community purchase contribution. The use of proceeds matters. The portion used to retire purchase debt can be counted in the Moore/Marsden numerator. The portion used for other purposes must be characterized separately.

Examples:

Refinance used partly for purchase debt: Wife owns a home before marriage. The original mortgage balance is $90,000. During marriage, Wife and Husband obtain a $250,000 community refinance secured by the home. The refinance uses $90,000 to pay off the premarital mortgage and $160,000 to pay credit cards, buy a vehicle, and fund living expenses. Under Branco, the $90,000 payoff may be treated as a community contribution toward acquisition for Moore/Marsden purposes. The remaining $160,000 does not create a real property ownership interest simply because the home secured the loan.

Community loan with no acquisition use: Husband owns a premarital rental property free and clear. During marriage, the spouses borrow $100,000 against the property to pay unrelated community expenses. No proceeds buy the property, improve it, or retire purchase debt. Branco would not treat the loan as a Moore/Marsden acquisition contribution merely because the debt is secured by the property.

Formula:

Branco adapts the Moore/Marsden formula to a refinance. Define P as the purchase price, C1 as community principal reductions on the original purchase debt, and C2 as the amount of community refinance proceeds used to retire separate purchase money debt. Amounts used for nonacquisition purposes are excluded from C2.

Community acquisition contribution = C1 + C2.

Community percentage = Community acquisition contribution / P.

Community appreciation share = Community percentage x appreciation during the relevant marital period.

Community interest = Community acquisition contribution + Community appreciation share, subject to debt allocation and any later adjustments ordered by the court.

Excluded from the acquisition contribution: refinance proceeds used for unrelated debts, consumption, noncapital expenses, or obligations not tied to purchase or improvement of the property.

Further Reading:

Family Code § 760 (community property).

Family Code § 770 (separate property).

In re Marriage of Branco (1996) 47 Cal.App.4th 1621: See *In re Marriage of Branco* (1996) 47 Cal.App.4th 1621 (pg. 29).

In re Marriage of Moore (1980) 28 Cal.3d 366: See Moore Formula (pg. 24).

In re Marriage of Marsden (1982) 130 Cal.App.3d 426: See Marsden Adjustment for Premarital Appreciation (pg. 27).

In re Marriage of Nelson (2006) 139 Cal.App.4th 1546: Nelson is useful contrast authority. A home equity loan unrelated to acquisition does not necessarily confer a Moore/Marsden interest merely because it is secured by the property.

12. *In re Marriage of Geraci* (2006) 144 Cal.App.4th 1278

Concept:

A spouse claiming a separate property contribution, reimbursement, or separate equity interest must prove the actual contribution and trace it to a separate property source. Fair market value alone is not enough where the record does not show equity, encumbrances, financing, loan purpose, or the source of funds used to acquire or improve the property.

Citation:

In re Marriage of Geraci (2006) 144 Cal.App.4th 1278.

Quote:

"Because of this crucial evidentiary gap the trial court found John had failed to carry his burden of identifying his separate property contribution to the Manhattan Beach property."

"there was an absence of evidence concerning the crucial issue of John's actual contributions of separate property to acquisition of the house"

"What was crucial was evidence of his actual equity in the house at the time."

Explanation:

In Geraci, the Court of Appeal affirmed the trial court's refusal to award Husband the separate property reimbursement or separate equity claim he sought from sale proceeds of the Manhattan Beach residence. Husband had purchased the property before marriage, razed the original structure, built a new residence before marriage, and then refinanced or borrowed against the residence multiple times during marriage. Although he presented evidence of fair market value around the time of marriage, he did not prove the critical facts: how the rebuilding was financed, the amount of debt secured by the property at marriage, the amount of his actual equity at marriage, or the source of funds used for acquisition and improvement. Because he failed to carry his tracing burden, the trial court could enforce the parties' pretrial division of sale proceeds. The court also rejected an argument that transfer into a family trust transmuted the residence into community property, because the trust instrument did not contain the required express declaration of a change in character or ownership.

Geraci is a proof case. It does not reject Moore/Marsden or *Family Code § 2640*; it shows why those doctrines cannot be applied without evidence. A party can own real property before marriage and still fail to prove the value of the separate property interest at dissolution. This happens when the property has been rebuilt, refinanced, encumbered, paid down, or improved over time without records that distinguish separate contributions from community contributions. The key point is that a reimbursement or apportionment claim requires equity evidence, not just market value evidence. A residence may be worth $400,000 at marriage, but if it is subject to large loans or if improvements were financed by debt later paid by the community, the separate equity may be far less. The court will not speculate. The spouse asserting the separate interest must supply documents, credible testimony, loan histories, escrow records, construction records, appraisals, and tracing evidence sufficient to calculate the contribution. If that spouse cannot trace, the court may deny the reimbursement or confirm an equitable division based on the available record.

Examples:

Failed tracing after reconstruction: Husband buys a lot and small home before marriage. Before marriage, he demolishes the home and builds a new residence, but he cannot prove whether he paid cash, used a construction loan, used insurance proceeds, or borrowed against the property. During marriage, the parties refinance several times. At divorce, Husband proves only that the home was valuable at marriage. Under Geraci, that is not enough. The court needs evidence of his actual equity and the source of acquisition and improvement funds.

Successful tracing contrast: Wife buys a premarital home for $600,000, pays a $150,000 separate down payment, and has a $450,000 loan at marriage. She produces the closing statement, premarital mortgage balance, appraisals, refinance records, and payment history. The community later pays $80,000 of principal. Unlike Geraci, the court has enough evidence to calculate a Moore/Marsden apportionment and any separate reimbursement that applies.

Formula:

Geraci does not create a new apportionment formula. It supplies a proof rule for applying Moore/Marsden or *section 2640*. The calculation begins only after the claimant proves the facts necessary to trace separate contributions and community contributions.

Proven separate reimbursement under *Family Code § 2640* = traceable separate down payments + traceable separate payments for improvements + traceable separate payments reducing principal on a loan used to purchase or improve the property.

The reimbursement is without interest or adjustment for changes in monetary value and cannot exceed the net value of the property at division.

For a Moore/Marsden claim, the claimant must prove purchase price, value at relevant dates, principal reductions, loan balances, sources of payment, and the purpose of each refinance or loan.

If the evidence does not establish actual equity and traceable contributions, the court may deny the claimed reimbursement or apportionment.

Further Reading:

Family Code § 2640: *Section 2640* reimbursement depends on tracing separate property contributions to acquisition of community property. Contributions include down payments, improvements, and principal reductions, but not interest, maintenance, insurance, or taxes.

In re Marriage of Branco (1996) 47 Cal.App.4th 1621: See *In re Marriage of Branco* (1996) 47 Cal.App.4th 1621 (pg. 29).

In re Marriage of Moore (1980) 28 Cal.3d 366: See Moore Formula (pg. 24).

In re Marriage of Marsden (1982) 130 Cal.App.3d 426: See Marsden Adjustment for Premarital Appreciation (pg. 27).

In re Marriage of Walrath (1998) 17 Cal.4th 907: See *In re Marriage of Walrath (pg. 14).*

13. Mohler Pro Tanto Rule

Concept:

Moore/Marsden apportionment is based on community funds used to build equity. When community payments stop at separation, post-separation payments by the owner spouse from separate income do not increase the community's Moore/Marsden percentage. If the owner spouse exclusively occupies the hybrid property after separation, the community's partial interest may instead be compensated through proportionate Watts charges.

Citation:

In re Marriage of Mohler (2020) 47 Cal.App.5th 788.

Quote:

"The Moore/Marsden rule applies only insofar as community funds are used to build equity in an asset, a situation which often terminates, as it did here, upon separation."

"The community's equity interest in the Lomello property thus no longer increased under the Moore/Marsden approach once community assets were no longer paying down the property's principal."

"We hold, as a matter of first impression, that Watts charges may be levied against a spouse for his or her post-separation occupation of a property where the property is not entirely community property, but rather is treated as partially community property due to the Moore/Marsden rule."

Explanation:

In Mohler, the Court of Appeal vacated the judgment because the trial court incorrectly increased the community's Moore/Marsden percentage based on Husband's post-separation mortgage payments made from his separate income. The parties agreed that, through separation, the community held a 33.66 percent beneficial interest in Husband's premarital residence. The trial court treated Husband's post-separation principal payments as if they were additional community contributions and increased the community interest to 64.9 percent. The appellate court held this was error. Moore/Marsden applies only to community funds used to build equity. Post-separation occupancy may create a benefit to the occupying spouse, but the proper analytical tool is Watts, not an expanded Moore/Marsden percentage. The court held, as a matter of first impression, that Watts charges may be imposed where the community owns only a partial beneficial interest in the property under Moore/Marsden.

Mohler is important because it keeps two doctrines separate. Moore/Marsden measures ownership acquisition. Watts measures post-separation use. If the owner spouse uses post-separation earnings to pay the mortgage, those payments usually come from separate property under *Family Code § 771*. They should not be treated as community principal reduction. Otherwise, the nonoccupying spouse would receive an ownership increase funded by the other spouse's separate post-separation earnings. At the same time, the occupying spouse may be receiving a post-separation benefit by using a property in which the community has a partial beneficial interest. Mohler solves that problem through a proportionate Watts charge. The charge is not based on principal reduction or appreciation. It is based on the community's share of the net rental value during the period of exclusive occupancy. The trial court retains equitable discretion to decide whether to impose the charge and how to calculate it, but the basic approach discounts the net rental benefit by the community percentage.

Examples:

Post-separation payments do not increase ownership percentage: Husband owns a home before marriage. During marriage, community payments create a 30 percent Moore/Marsden community interest. After separation, Husband remains in the home and pays principal with post-separation wages for five years. Under Mohler, those post-separation payments do not raise the community interest from 30 percent to a larger percentage. They are not community acquisition contributions.

Hybrid Watts charge: Assume the same 30 percent community interest. The home would rent for $4,000 per month, and monthly expenses for mortgage interest, taxes, insurance, maintenance, and repairs are $2,500. Net rental benefit is $1,500 per month. A proportionate Mohler/Watts charge would start at $1,500 x 30 percent, or $450 per month owed to the community for the period of exclusive post-separation use. Because the charge belongs to the community, the nonoccupying spouse effectively receives one-half of that community charge in the property division, subject to equitable offsets.

Formula:

Mohler uses two calculations. The first is the Moore/Marsden ownership calculation through the date community acquisition payments stop, usually separation. The second is a proportionate Watts calculation for post-separation exclusive use of a hybrid asset.

Moore/Marsden community percentage = community principal reduction during marriage / applicable purchase price or adjusted denominator.

Moore/Marsden community interest = community principal reduction during marriage + (community percentage x appreciation allocated under Moore/Marsden).

Post-separation separate principal payments by the occupying owner are not added to the Moore/Marsden community percentage merely because they reduce the mortgage.

Possible Watts starting point = reasonable rental value for the period of exclusive use × the community's beneficial ownership/use percentage, subject to the trial court's equitable discretion.

Do not mechanically subtract every ownership expense from rent or double-count expenses already addressed through Epstein credits or other reimbursements. Mohler permits proportionate Watts charges for hybrid property, but the court must account for offsets and fairness on the facts.

The resulting Watts charge is owed to the community and is divided through the overall property division, subject to the court's equitable discretion.

Further Reading:

Family Code § 771 (post-separation earnings and accumulations)

Family Code § 2552 (valuation timing)

In re Marriage of Moore (1980) 28 Cal.3d 366: See Moore Formula (pg. 24).

In re Marriage of Marsden (1982) 130 Cal.App.3d 426: See Marsden Adjustment for Premarital Appreciation (pg. 27).

In re Marriage of Watts (1985) 171 Cal.App.3d 366: See Watts Charges (pg. 52).

In re Marriage of Jeffries (1991) 228 Cal.App.3d 548: See Jeffries Credits (pg. 113).

Family Code section 771 (post-separation earnings and accumulations)

Family Code section 2552 (valuation of assets)

14. Mix Direct Tracing Method

Concept:

A spouse can overcome the community property presumption for property acquired during marriage from a commingled account by tracing the acquisition to separate property. Commingling alone does not change the character of separate funds if the separate component can be identified.

Citation:

In re Marriage of Mix (1975) 14 Cal.3d 604.

Quote:

"The presumption that all property acquired by either spouse during the marriage is community property may be overcome."

"Generally speaking, there are two methods of carrying the burden of showing property purchased during the marriage to be separate rather than community property."

"Whether separate funds so deposited continue to be on deposit when a withdrawal is made from such a bank account for the purpose of purchasing specific property, and whether the intention of the drawer is to withdraw such funds therefrom, are questions of fact for determination by the trial court."

Explanation:

Mix is the principal California family law tracing case. It explains that the community property presumption is powerful, but not conclusive. A spouse who deposits separate funds into an account that also contains community earnings does not automatically make the separate funds community property. The separate character survives if the spouse can identify the separate source and connect that source to the acquisition or payment at issue.

The court held that property acquired during marriage is presumed community property when purchased from a disputed or commingled source. The presumption may be overcome by tracing. Mix identifies two tracing methods: direct tracing and family expense tracing. Direct tracing asks whether separate funds were still on deposit when the withdrawal was made and whether the drawer intended to withdraw separate funds. Family expense tracing asks whether community funds had been exhausted by family expenses at the time of acquisition, leaving only separate funds available for the purchase. Esther Mix did not rely on the family expense method. She relied on direct tracing through a chronological schedule of separate property receipts and expenditures, supported by her testimony. The Supreme Court held that the schedule alone would have been inadequate, but the schedule plus credited testimony constituted substantial evidence supporting the trial court finding that the disputed property was separate.

The case is also a warning about proof. The issue is not merely whether separate funds existed somewhere during the marriage. The party asserting separate property must show that separate funds were available at the relevant time and were actually used, or that community funds were exhausted at the relevant time. The court accepted Esther Mix's tracing because the trial court believed her testimony and because her schedule reconstructed separate receipts and separate expenditures in chronological order. That holding should not be read as permission to rely on general estimates. Later cases, especially Frick and Braud, emphasize that detailed account records are usually necessary.

In current practice, Mix is used to structure bank tracing, brokerage tracing, inheritance tracing, and tracing of acquisition payments into real property. The lawyer or expert should begin with the source of separate property, follow each deposit and withdrawal, and show the character of funds at the moment the challenged asset was acquired or the challenged payment was made.

Examples:

Inheritance used to buy stock: Wife receives a $120,000 inheritance and deposits it into a checking account that also receives community wages. Two weeks later, $80,000 is withdrawn to buy stock in Wife's name. If the statements show that the inherited funds remained in the account, that the community wages were separately spent on household expenses, and that Wife intended the stock purchase to use inheritance funds, Mix supports a separate property characterization.

Available funds without tracing: Husband sells separate property during marriage and later buys a rental property from a joint account. He proves that he once had enough separate money to buy the rental, but he cannot show account balances, deposits, withdrawals, or the source of the funds used at purchase. Mix does not support separate property characterization because availability is not the same thing as tracing.

Family expense tracing: A commingled account receives $10,000 of community wages and $50,000 of inheritance. Before a $40,000 purchase, the account pays $12,000 in family expenses. If the evidence shows the community wages were exhausted by those expenses before the purchase, the remaining funds can be treated as separate funds under the family expense method.

Formula:

Direct tracing method: Traceable separate balance at acquisition equals beginning separate balance plus separate deposits minus separate expenditures and withdrawals before the disputed acquisition. If the traceable separate balance at acquisition is at least the disputed payment, and the evidence shows an intent to use separate funds, the payment may be characterized as separate.

Family expense method: Community funds available at acquisition equals community income and deposits through the acquisition date minus family expenses and other community expenditures paid before that acquisition. If community funds available at acquisition are zero or less, and traceable separate funds remain, the acquisition may be traced to separate property.

These are evidentiary tracing models rather than statutory formulas. They only work if the underlying records and testimony establish the source, timing, amount, and purpose of the relevant transactions.

Further Reading:

Family Code section 760 (community property)

Family Code section 770 (separate property)

Hicks v. Hicks (1962) 211 Cal.App.2d 144. The court in Hicks addressed whether assets acquired or improved during marriage were community property or the husband's separate property when both separate and community funds had been deposited into the same bank account. The court held that commingling alone does not destroy separate-property character if the separate funds can still be identified or traced.

See v. See (1966) 64 Cal.2d 778: See *See v. See*: Family Expense Tracing Rule (pg. 40).

In re Marriage of Frick (1986) 181 Cal.App.3d 997: See *In re Marriage of Frick*: Strict Proof for Direct Tracing (pg. 42) and In re Marriage of Braud: Records, Intent, and Partial Tracing (pg. 47)

In re Marriage of Braud (1996) 45 Cal.App.4th 797: *In re Marriage of Braud*: Records, Intent, and Partial Tracing.

15. *See v. See*: Family Expense Tracing Rule

Concept:

When separate and community funds are commingled, property acquired during marriage is presumed community property unless the spouse claiming separate property traces the acquisition at the time it occurred. A marriage ending recapitulation of total income and expenses is generally insufficient.

Citation:

See v. See (1966) 64 Cal.2d 778.

Quote:

"The character of property as separate or community is determined at the time of its acquisition."

"A husband who commingles the property of the community with his separate property, but fails to keep adequate records cannot invoke the burden of record keeping as a justification for a recapitulation of income and expenses at the termination of the marriage that disregards any acquisitions that may have been made during the marriage with community funds."

"Once he commingles, he assumes the burden of keeping records adequate to establish the balance of community income and expenditures at the time an asset is acquired with commingled property."

Explanation:

In See, the husband had commingled accounts containing separate property funds and community earnings from his employment with See's Candies entities. The trial court accepted his theory that, because total community expenses during the marriage exceeded total community income, no community property existed at separation. The Supreme Court rejected that theory. The character of property is determined at the time of acquisition. To trace by the family expense method, the spouse must show that community income was exhausted by family expenses when the asset was acquired. Only when it is impossible through no fault of the spouse to determine the balance at the time of acquisition may a broader recapitulation be used. Because the husband did not prove deficits at the times the disputed assets were acquired, the community property presumption controlled. The court also rejected a general reimbursement claim for separate property used for community living expenses absent an agreement.

See is the foundation for exhaustion tracing in California community property law. It protects the community's present interest by preventing one spouse from waiting until dissolution and then arguing that all assets are separate because the marriage as a whole was expensive. The inquiry is asset specific and date specific. Each acquisition must be examined at the time it occurred.

The decision assigns the record keeping burden to the spouse who commingles. If the spouse mixes community income and separate property in the same account, that spouse must keep records adequate to show the balance of community income and expenses at the time each asset was acquired. If the source cannot be traced and no community deficit is shown at the acquisition date, the asset remains community property under the presumption.

See should be read carefully in modern reimbursement disputes. Its rejection of reimbursement for separate property used for family expenses predates the current statutory reimbursement scheme. *Family Code section 2640* now permits reimbursement for certain traced acquisition contributions, but See remains controlling on the tracing point: proof must focus on the relevant transaction, not a generalized end of marriage accounting.

Examples:

Investment account purchased during marriage: Husband buys mutual funds from a mixed account on June 1. At trial, he proves that community living expenses exceeded community income over the entire twenty year marriage. That does not prove the mutual funds are separate. He must show that community funds were exhausted on or before June 1, or he must directly trace the purchase to separate funds.

End of year deficit is not enough: Wife uses a mixed account to buy a vehicle in March. By December, the family spent more than it earned. See does not allow Wife to treat the March vehicle as separate unless the evidence shows the community funds were exhausted at the time of the March purchase.

Separate funds used for ordinary living expenses: A spouse uses inherited funds to pay groceries, utilities, and vacations because community income is insufficient. Without an agreement or a specific statutory basis, See does not create a general reimbursement right for those ordinary family expenses.

Formula:

Community funds available at the acquisition date equals community deposits and income in the commingled source through that date minus family expenses and other community expenditures paid before that date.

If community funds available at the acquisition date are greater than zero, the community presumption remains unless the claimant proves direct tracing. If community funds available at the acquisition date are zero or less, and separate funds are present, the acquisition may be traced to separate property by exhaustion.

A total marriage recapitulation is not a substitute for this calculation unless the balance at the time of acquisition cannot be determined through no fault of the party relying on tracing.

Further Reading:

Family Code section 760 (community property)

Family Code section 770 (separate property)

In re Marriage of Mix (1975) 14 Cal.3d 604: See Mix Direct Tracing Method (pg. 37).

In re Marriage of Cochran (2001) 87 Cal.App.4th 1050: See *In re Marriage of Cochran*: Sequential Exhaustion and *Section 2640* *(pg. 45)*.

16. *In re Marriage of Frick*: Strict Proof for Direct Tracing

Concept:

Direct tracing from a commingled account requires account specific proof. Evidence that separate income was deposited and that a payment was made around the same time is not enough if the court cannot determine the actual character and balance of funds when the payment was made.

Citation:

In re Marriage of Frick (1986) 181 Cal.App.3d 997.

Quote:

"In the case at bar, Jerome provided evidence he received a specific amount of separate property income each month which he deposited in a particular personal account. He also made loan payments from this account. However, he made no other showing of the activity that occurred in this account during this month. We are merely provided an isolated portion of the account's activity."

"As the court properly found, "...petitioner [Jerome] commingled community and separate funds so that no separate property funds could be found to be the source of the payments on the real estate after marriage." Moreover, we are not satisfied Jerome presented sufficient evidence to demonstrate it was his intent to use only separate property funds to make loan payments. As such, Jerome did not meet his burden of tracing the monthly loan payments to his separate property income."

"While we recognize post-separation earnings of a spouse are that spouse's separate property. (Civ. Code, *§ 5118.*), the same tracing difficulties discussed above compel us to reject Jerome's contention. Jerome did not present sufficient evidence establishing the amount and nature of the funds in the account during this period and the types of transactions that were made. We do not believe evidence of only an isolated portion of the account's activity is enough to meet the requirements of tracing."

Explanation:

Jerome Frick owned the Mikado Hotel and Restaurant real property before marriage. During marriage, the business and real property remained his separate property, but payments reducing the real property debt were made from an account containing both separate rents and community salary. Jerome argued that the loan payments were traceable to separate rents because the rent deposits and loan payments were contemporaneous. The Court of Appeal rejected the argument. He showed an isolated part of the account activity but did not prove other deposits, other withdrawals, account balances, the nature of funds in the account, or intent to use separate funds for the payments. The court also rejected his postseparation tracing argument because he still failed to establish the amount and nature of funds in the account during that period. The community therefore received credit for the principal reduction in the Moore and Marsden apportionment.

Frick is a practical limitation on Mix. It holds that direct tracing requires more than a plausible source and a nearby payment. The court must be able to determine the exact amount of separate property in the account when the withdrawal occurred. If the account includes community salary, separate rents, business transfers, living expense payments, and loan payments, the tracing party must reconstruct the account activity rather than present only the favorable deposits and payments.

The case often appears in real property contribution disputes because principal payments from community funds can give the community a pro tanto interest in a spouse's separate property real estate. If the owner spouse wants to prevent a community credit, the owner spouse must trace the principal payments to a separate source. Frick shows that separate rents retain separate character under the law, but they can become practically unprovable once they are mixed with community funds without adequate records.

For forensic accounting, Frick means that a tracing report should not simply match same month deposits to same month payments. It should show beginning balances, each deposit, each withdrawal, characterization of each transaction, and the resulting separate and community balances at the time of each disputed payment.

Examples:

Same month deposit and payment: Husband deposits $9,000 of separate rent into a personal account and pays a $5,000 mortgage payment from the same account later that month. The account also receives community wages and pays household bills. Without a complete ledger, Frick would treat the payment as untraced and presumptively community.

Complete ledger: Wife deposits separate rent into an account that also receives community wages. Her tracing expert shows every transaction for the month, proves the community wages were spent on family expenses before the mortgage payment, shows a sufficient separate balance remained, and establishes intent to use separate rent for the payment. That evidence addresses the proof problems identified in Frick.

Postseparation earnings issue: A spouse may argue that payments after separation came from separate earnings. Frick shows that the legal character of postseparation earnings is not enough by itself. If the earnings are placed into a mixed account, the spouse must still trace the payment from the account.

Formula:

No new mathematical apportionment formula arises from Frick. The case supplies an evidentiary requirement for applying direct tracing.

Traceable separate amount at payment equals prior separate balance plus separate deposits before payment minus separate withdrawals before payment. The ledger must also account for community deposits, community withdrawals, and uncharacterized transactions so the court can determine the actual balance at the time of payment.

An incomplete model that shows only separate deposit amount and disputed payment amount fails because it does not establish what funds were actually in the account when the payment was made.

Further Reading:

Family Code section 760 (community property)

Family Code section 770 (separate property)

Family Code section 771 (classification after separation)

See v. See (1966) 64 Cal.2d 778: See *See v. See*: Family Expense Tracing Rule (pg. 40).

In re Marriage of Frick (1986) 181 Cal.App.3d 997: See *In re Marriage of Frick*: Strict Proof for Direct Tracing (pg. 42).

In re Marriage of Mix (1975) 14 Cal.3d 604: See Mix Direct Tracing Method (pg. 37).

In re Marriage of Braud (1996) 45 Cal.App.4th 797: See *In re Marriage of Braud*: Records, Intent, and Partial Tracing (pg. 47).

17. *In re Marriage of Cochran*: Sequential Exhaustion and *Section 2640*

Concept:

A spouse may establish a traced separate property reimbursement claim when the source amounts in a mixed account are known and the sequence of payments shows that community funds were exhausted before the disputed acquisition or improvement payments were made.

Citation:

In re Marriage of Cochran (2001) 87 Cal.App.4th 1050.

Quote:

"Under *section 2640*, a spouse has a right to receive reimbursement at the time of dissolution for any separate property payments for improvements to community property, unless there has been a written waiver."

"Then, by process of elimination (there being no community property funds left in the bank account), we conclude that husband's remaining separate property funds were used for the construction loan and school fees."

"The judgment is reversed as to the trial court's ruling that husband was not entitled to reimbursement for $22,950 in earnest money and $9,258 for the school fees."

Explanation:

In Cochran, husband liquidated a profit sharing plan and deposited the proceeds into a Chino Bank account. The parties stipulated that $43,061.24 was husband's separate property and $34,405.51 was community property. The first check, $34,192.15, paid a community debt related to a wind turbine generator. The court presumed that community funds were used first for the community debt, leaving only about $213 of community funds. The next payment, $32,950, was earnest money for a home construction loan. By process of elimination, the remaining community funds were applied first, and the balance was traced to husband's separate property. The $9,258 school fee payment was also traced to separate property. For reimbursement, the court allowed $22,950 of the earnest money because it was allocated to funds for improvements, disallowed the $10,000 interest reserve because husband did not prove it was used for improvements, and allowed the $9,258 school fees because they were mandatory to obtain a building permit and were not taxes.

Cochran is a tracing case and a statutory reimbursement case. Tracing answered the first question: did the payments come from a separate property source? *Family Code section 2640* answered the second question: were the traced payments reimbursable contributions to acquisition or improvement of property? The claimant had to satisfy both.

The case is useful because the account was not a typical messy household account. The source amounts were stipulated, only three checks were relevant, and the sequence showed that the first community obligation almost entirely exhausted the community funds. That allowed the court to use a process of elimination even though the usual tracing cases demand detailed records. Cochran should not be treated as eliminating the record requirement. It works because the record gave the court reliable numbers and a reliable sequence.

Cochran also clarifies the scope of *section 2640* in construction settings. Payments for improvements and payments that reduce principal on a loan used for purchase or improvement may be reimbursable. Interest, maintenance, insurance, and taxes are excluded. A cost not listed in the statute may still qualify if it is closely tied to acquisition or improvement, as with mandatory school fees required for the building permit.

Examples:

Sequential account tracing: A mixed account contains $60,000 of separate property and $40,000 of community property. The first check pays a $39,500 community debt. The next check pays a $25,000 construction deposit. Under Cochran, the remaining $500 of community funds is applied first to the construction deposit, and $24,500 may be traced to separate property if the construction deposit otherwise qualifies for reimbursement.

Interest reserve problem: A $35,000 construction deposit includes $12,000 set aside as an interest reserve and $23,000 designated for improvements. If the claimant cannot prove that the interest reserve was actually used for improvements rather than interest, Cochran supports reimbursement only for the improvement portion.

Permit fee: A city or school fee that must be paid to obtain the building permit for construction of the family residence may qualify as a reimbursable improvement related expense when it is not a tax and is paid in furtherance of construction.

Formula:

Sequential exhaustion model: Remaining community funds after first community obligation equals community component in the account minus the community obligation paid.

Separate portion of the next payment equals the next payment minus remaining community funds, assuming the record shows the next payment occurred after community funds were exhausted and separate funds remained.

Cochran numbers: $34,405.51 community component minus $34,192.15 community debt left about $213 of community funds. The next $32,950 payment was therefore treated as community to the extent of about $213 and separate as to the balance. Reimbursement then depended on whether the traced portion was a qualifying *section 2640* contribution.

Section 2640 reimbursement cap: Reimbursement equals the lesser of the traced separate contribution, the qualifying acquisition or improvement amount, and the net value of the property at division. Interest, maintenance, insurance, taxes, and unproven interest reserves are excluded.

Further Reading:

In re Marriage of Cochran (2001) 87 Cal.App.4th 1050: See *In re Marriage of Cochran*: Sequential Exhaustion and *Section 2640 (pg. 45).*

Family Code section 2581: (joint property presumption)

In re Marriage of Walrath (1998) 17 Cal.4th 907: See *In re Marriage of Walrath (pg. 14).*

Family Code section 2640: The statute requires tracing to a separate property source and limits reimbursement to the amount contributed, without interest or adjustment for changes in monetary value, and not exceeding the net value of the property at division.

In re Marriage of Braud (1996) 45 Cal.App.4th 797: See *In re Marriage of Braud*: Records, Intent, and Partial Tracing (pg. 47)

In re Marriage of Frick (1986) 181 Cal.App.3d 997: *In re Marriage of Frick*: Strict Proof for Direct Tracing.

18. *In re Marriage of Braud*: Records, Intent, and Partial Tracing

Concept:

A party claiming a separate property interest in commingled funds must present specific records showing deposits, withdrawals, balances, and use of funds. Intent testimony and general recollection are insufficient, but adequate records can support a partial separate property finding.

Citation:

In re Marriage of Braud (1996) 45 Cal.App.4th 797.

Quote:

"But if the separate property and community property interests have been commingled in such a manner that the respective contributions cannot be traced and identified, the entire commingled fund will be deemed community property pursuant to the general community property presumption of *section 760*."

"Under the "direct tracing" method, the disputed asset (in this case the improvements to the community property home) is traced to the withdrawal of separate property funds from the commingled account. This method requires specific records reconstructing each separate and community property deposit, and each separate and community property payment as it occurs."

"Separate property status cannot be established by mere oral testimony of intent or by records that simply total up all separate property funds available during the relevant period and all the separate expenditures during that period; such records do not adequately trace to the source of the purchase at the time it was made."

Explanation:

Daniel Braud inherited funds from his grandmother. The trial court credited him with a separate property reimbursement for a mortgage payoff, which was not disputed on appeal, and also awarded him $10,000 for alleged improvements to the family home. The Court of Appeal reversed the $10,000 improvement reimbursement because the tracing ran through a main household checking account and Daniel did not provide records proving the amounts spent on labor or materials, the beginning balance, community deposits, withdrawals, or depletion of community income during the remodeling period. His intent testimony was insufficient. The court separately upheld a $20,734 separate property interest in a later $25,000 withdrawal because bank records supported that calculation. Records showed a $30,734 separate deposit remaining after the mortgage payoff, two $5,000 withdrawals, $6,050 of later community deposits, and $10,030 of family living expenses that exhausted those community deposits.

Braud is a leading case on the evidentiary rigor of tracing. It states that direct tracing requires specific records reconstructing each separate and community deposit and each separate and community payment as it occurs. It also states that separate property status cannot be established by mere oral testimony of intent or by records that simply total up separate funds available during a period and separate expenditures during that period. The trace must connect the source to the actual payment at the time it was made.

The case is especially useful because it contains both a failed tracing and a successful partial tracing. The home improvement claim failed because the funds passed through the parties' main checking account and there were no documents proving what was paid, when it was paid, or whether community funds were exhausted. The investment account claim succeeded in part because the court had records from which it could reconstruct the separate balance and account for community deposits and family expenses.

Braud is often cited in *section 2640* disputes. A spouse may be entitled to reimbursement for separate property contributions to acquisition or improvements, but only to the extent the contribution is traced to a separate source. The word "extent" matters. The result may be all, none, or a partial amount depending on the proof.

Examples:

Failed improvement tracing: Husband deposits $10,000 of inherited funds into the parties' main checking account during a remodel. The parties also deposit wages into the account, pay ordinary expenses, and pay contractors from the same account. Husband testifies that he intended the inheritance to pay for the remodel, but he has no bank records, invoices, or account reconstruction. Under Braud, the claim fails.

Successful partial tracing: Wife deposits $50,000 of inherited funds into a brokerage account later made joint. Bank records show a $50,000 separate deposit, $8,000 of later community deposits, $10,000 of family expenses, and then a $40,000 withdrawal. Because the community deposits were exhausted by family expenses and the separate balance remained, the withdrawal can be traced at least in part to separate property.

Partial reimbursement: A spouse proves that $18,000 of a $25,000 payment came from separate funds, but cannot trace the remaining $7,000. The court can award a *section 2640* reimbursement only for the traced $18,000 if the payment was an acquisition or improvement contribution and no waiver applies.

Formula:

Partial tracing model: Traceable separate amount equals proven separate deposits remaining in the account minus proven separate withdrawals before the disputed transfer, adjusted for any community funds that have not been shown to be exhausted.

Braud successful tracing numbers: $30,734 remaining separate inheritance minus two $5,000 withdrawals equaled $20,734. Community deposits of $6,050 were more than exhausted by $10,030 of family living expenses, so the court could uphold a $20,734 separate property component in the later $25,000 withdrawal.

Braud failed improvement claim: No formula could be applied to the $10,000 remodel claim because the necessary inputs were missing. The court lacked proof of account balances, community deposits, family expenses, actual labor and material payments, and the link between the inherited funds and the improvements.

Further Reading:

Family Code section 760 (community property)

Family Code section 2640 (reimbursement of contributions)

See v. See (1966) 64 Cal.2d 778: See *See v. See*: Family Expense Tracing Rule (pg. 40).

In re Marriage of Frick (1986) 181 Cal.App.3d 997: See *In re Marriage of Frick*: Strict Proof for Direct Tracing (pg. 42).

In re Marriage of Mix (1975) 14 Cal.3d 604: See Mix Direct Tracing Method (pg. 37).

19. Epstein Credits

Concept:

"Epstein Credits" refers to the reimbursement to a spouse who used separate property to pay community debts.

Citation:

In re Marriage of Epstein (1979) 24 Cal.3d 76

Quote:

"a spouse who, after separation of the parties, uses earnings or other separate funds to pay preexisting community obligations should be reimbursed therefor out of the community property upon dissolution."

"However, there are a number of situations in which reimbursement is inappropriate, so reimbursement should not be ordered automatically."

"Reimbursement should not be ordered if payment was made under circumstances in which it would have been unreasonable to expect reimbursement."

Explanation:

Epstein Credits are a form of reimbursement one spouse can claim when they use their own separate funds after separation to pay community expenses or debts. Each spouse is generally responsible for half of the community's obligations, so if one spouse covers more than their share post-separation, they may be reimbursed for the other spouse's half. Courts examine the circumstances to decide if reimbursement is fair. These credits may be denied if the paying spouse intended the payments as a gift, received an offsetting benefit (like exclusive use of a property), or if there was an agreement waiving reimbursement.

Examples:

Spouse A pays $10,000 from separate savings to settle a joint credit card debt post-separation. The court may award a $5,000 Epstein Credit to reimburse half of that payment.

Spouse B lives in the community home after separation and pays the $2,000/month mortgage using post-separation income. Because B had exclusive use of the home with rental value equal to the mortgage, the court denies the Epstein Credit due to offsetting benefit.

Formula:

Step 1: Identify community debts paid after separation using separate funds (e.g., mortgage principal, credit cards).

Step 2: Identify the amount of the qualifying post-separation payment and account for it as a reimbursement or credit in the community-property division. The practical net effect often equals one-half of the qualifying payment after equal division, but the claim should not be described as automatically limited to one-half at the threshold stage.

Step 3: Analyze Epstein exceptions and related offsets separately, including whether the payment was intended as support or a gift, was made under circumstances making reimbursement unreasonable, was covered by agreement, or overlaps with a Watts charge for exclusive use.

Step 4: Apply the credit through the overall property division, subject to the court's equitable discretion and any statutory or case-law limitations.

Further Reading:

Family Code §2626 states, "The court has jurisdiction to order reimbursement in cases it deems appropriate for debts paid after separation but before trial."

In re Marriage of Jeffries (1991) 228 Cal.App.3d 548: See Jeffries Credits (pg. 113).

In re Marriage of Garcia (1990) 224 Cal.App.3d 885: Epstein Credits were denied where mortgage payments were treated as support; the wife was not charged for home use and no credit was awarded to the husband.

In re Marriage of Boblitt (2014) 223 Cal.App.4th 1004: The wife received Epstein Credits for post-separation payments on community real estate, confirming the continued use of the doctrine in modern property division.

20. Watts Charges

Concept:

The community may be reimbursed for the reasonable value of one spouse's exclusive post-separation use of a community asset, with the net benefit allocated through the property division.

Citation:

In re Marriage of Watts (1985) 171 Cal.App.3d 366.

Quote:

"The trial court found that John had the "use of" both the family residence and the medical practice between the date of separation and the date of trial."

"We hold that the trial court erred in concluding that it had no authority to reimburse the community for the value of John's exclusive use of the family residence and the medical practice between the date of separation and the date of trial."

"Upon remand, the trial court will determine whether John should be required to reimburse the community for the value of his use of community assets after the date of separation in accordance with its findings."

Explanation:

The Watts rule originates from Watts, where the court held that a spouse's exclusive post-separation use of community property could result in a reimbursement to the community. Subsequent cases (like Jeffries) clarified that such reimbursements (often called "Watts charges") are to be factored into an equal division of property, and confirmed the court's discretion to order them when fair. No statute explicitly uses the term "Watts charge," but California courts have embraced the concept through case law, and Family Code provisions (e.g., *§ 2626*) acknowledge the courts' power to order reimbursements in appropriate circumstances.

A Watts charge is a financial reimbursement in California divorces that is applied when one spouse has exclusive use of a community property asset after the date of separation and before the division of property (typically at trial or settlement). In plain terms, it means the spouse who gets the sole benefit of a community asset during separation may owe the "community" (and effectively the other spouse) money for that benefit. The classic example is one spouse living in the family home (a community asset) alone after separation. The court can assign a reasonable rental value to that exclusive use and require reimbursement. The purpose of a Watts charge is to ensure fairness in property division: it prevents one party from getting an unfair head start or extra benefit from a community asset. By charging for the post-separation use, the value of that use is added back into the community pot so it can be split equally. Watts charges most often apply to substantial assets like real estate (homes, rental properties) but can apply to any valuable community asset with a use value (for instance, a vehicle, boat, or even a business or piece of equipment, if one spouse had sole use of it). Importantly, the imposition of a Watts charge is not automatic; it is within the family court's equitable discretion. The court will consider all the circumstances, including whether there were any agreements between the spouses about the asset, whether the asset's value was factored into any support payments, and whether the spouse's exclusive use was offset by other payments. For example, if the occupying spouse was also paying the mortgage, property taxes, or other community expenses on that asset (often giving rise to an "Epstein credit" for paying community debt), the court might offset the Watts charge by those amounts. Likewise, if the spouses agreed that one could stay in the house in lieu of paying rent or in exchange for lower support, a Watts charge might be reduced or waived. In summary, a Watts charge ensures that when community property is divided, both parties share equally in the benefit of any community asset, even if one of them enjoyed that benefit alone during separation, thereby maintaining the principle of equal division under California law.

Examples:

Exclusive use of family home: After separation, Wife remains in the community-owned family residence for 12 months while Husband moves out. The home has no mortgage and a fair rental value of $3,000 per month. The gross use value is $36,000. A court may charge Wife with a $36,000 Watts reimbursement to the community for her exclusive use. Because the charge belongs to the community and the community is divided equally, the practical equalization effect is ordinarily that Husband receives one-half of the charge, or $18,000, through the property division, subject to any offsets or equitable adjustments.

Car or other asset usage: Suppose the spouses own two community cars outright (no loans). After separation, Husband takes one car and Wife takes the other. If both cars are similar in value, usually no issue arises. But if, for instance, there was only one community vehicle (say a high-value car) and Husband kept exclusive use of it after separation, the Wife might request a

Watts charge for the car's use value. For example, if the reasonable monthly lease or rental value of the car is $500, and Husband used it alone for 10 months before the divorce, the court could assign a Watts charge of $5,000 (10 × $500) to Husband's side of the ledger. This would effectively credit Wife with $2,500 (half of that amount) upon division to equalize the benefit. Another scenario: imagine a vacation cabin owned as community property. After separating, one spouse moves into the cabin or uses it every weekend while the other spouse can't use it. If the cabin has a market rental value (say $1,000 per month), the spouse using it exclusively may be charged that amount per month as a Watts charge, so that the other spouse gets compensated for the lost opportunity to use or rent out the cabin.

Formula:

A Watts calculation is an equitable accounting framework, not a mandatory formula. The court usually begins with the reasonable rental value or use value of the community asset during the period of exclusive post-separation use, then applies the relevant community ownership or use percentage and considers appropriate offsets.

Possible framework: Watts charge to the community = reasonable rental/use value × relevant community percentage × period of exclusive use, subject to equitable offsets and avoiding double counting with Epstein credits.

Expenses paid by the occupying spouse may be relevant, but they should be analyzed carefully. Mortgage principal, interest, taxes, insurance, repairs, and maintenance may create different reimbursement or offset issues. A court should not automatically subtract every expense from rental value if doing so duplicates a separately awarded Epstein credit or other reimbursement.

Example of calculation: Suppose a community home has a fair rental value of $2,000 per month and one spouse lives in it alone for six months after separation. The gross use value is $12,000. If the court finds no offsetting payments or other equitable adjustment, it may credit the community with a $12,000 Watts charge. Because the charge belongs to the community, the nonoccupying spouse's practical net benefit is generally one-half of that amount, or $6,000, through the property division. If the occupying spouse also paid mortgage, taxes, insurance, or necessary repairs from separate funds, the court should analyze those payments separately as possible Epstein credits or equitable offsets rather than automatically subtracting them in a way that double counts the same expense.

Further Reading:

Family Code § 2626 (authority for post-separation reimbursements)

In re Marriage of Jeffries (1991) 228 Cal.App.3d 548: See Jeffries Credits (pg. 113).

In re Marriage of Braud (1996) 45 Cal.App.4th 797: See *In re Marriage of Braud*: Records, Intent, and Partial Tracing (pg. 47).

In re Marriage of Boblitt (2014) 223 Cal.App.4th 1004: This is a more recent case where Watts charges were significant in a complex property dispute. In Boblitt, after separation the husband had sole use of a piece of community real estate (referred to as the "Hedge Avenue property") for an extended period. The parties actually stipulated that the fair rental value of that property was $3,000 per month. At trial, the court imposed a Watts charge requiring the husband to reimburse the community $3,000 per month for each month of his exclusive use. The total came to 22 months × $3,000 = $66,000 that he owed to the community. The wife contended on appeal that the trial court should continue charging him even after trial (since he remained in the property post-trial), but the Court of Appeal held that Watts charges are generally limited to the period between separation and the division of property at trial. Key points: Boblitt reaffirms that the purpose of Watts charges is to compensate the community for the reasonable value of exclusive use of a community asset during the separation period. It also explicitly noted that ordering a Watts charge is within the trial court's broad equitable discretion: meaning the judge can decide if and how much to charge based on fairness (the decision cited that imposing such a charge is not mandatory but an equitable call). In a footnote, the court pointed out that after property is divided (or after trial), continuing to assess Watts charges is not typical unless perhaps agreed to, because at that point the asset usually belongs to one party. In sum, Boblitt illustrates a straightforward application of Watts (with a large dollar amount) and emphasizes judicial discretion and the cutoff at property division.

In re Marriage of Mohler (2020) 47 Cal.App.5th 788: See Mohler Pro Tanto Rule (pg. 34).

21. Haines Presumption of Undue Influence

Concept:

When spouses transact with each other, they do not deal at arm's length. If an interspousal transaction gives one spouse an advantage over the other, *Family Code section 721* raises a presumption of undue influence. In a family law characterization dispute, that fiduciary presumption prevails over *Evidence Code section 662* when the two presumptions conflict.

Citation:

In re Marriage of Haines (1995) 33 Cal.App.4th 277.

Quote:

"When an interspousal transaction advantages one spouse, "[t]he law, from considerations of public policy, presumes such transactions to have been induced by undue influence.""'

"This confidential spousal relationship imposes a duty of the highest good faith and fair dealing on each spouse, and neither shall take any unfair advantage of the other."

"We conclude that application of *section 662* is improper when it is in conflict with the presumption of undue influence that emanates from former *section 5103*, subdivision (b) (Fam. Code, *§ 721*, subd. (b))."

Explanation:

Judy Haines quitclaimed her interest in the family residence to Clarence Haines in exchange for his cosignature on an automobile loan. The trial court applied *Evidence Code section 662* and required Judy to rebut legal title by clear and convincing evidence. The Court of Appeal reversed. The court held that, where a title presumption conflicts with the fiduciary presumption arising from an advantaging interspousal transaction, the title presumption must yield. Clarence, as the advantaged spouse, had the burden to rebut undue influence by showing that the transfer was freely and voluntarily made, with full knowledge of the facts and complete understanding of its effect.

Haines is the foundational California family law case for fiduciary duty in interspousal property transfers. The case recognizes that spouses may transfer property between themselves, including by deed, but the transfer is not analyzed as an ordinary commercial transaction. Because spouses occupy a confidential relationship, the law scrutinizes a transfer that benefits one spouse at the expense of the other.

The key point is the interaction between two presumptions. *Evidence Code section 662* generally protects record title by presuming that the holder of legal title owns the beneficial title. *Family Code section 721* imposes a fiduciary standard between spouses. Haines holds that, in a dissolution dispute between spouses, the fiduciary presumption controls when record title would otherwise validate a transaction that advantaged one spouse.

The burden shift matters in practice. The disadvantaged spouse does not have to prove actual fraud as an initial matter. Once the transaction and the advantage are shown, the advantaged spouse must prove that the disadvantaged spouse acted freely and voluntarily, knew the material facts, and understood the legal effect. A deed signed during marriage is therefore not the end of the analysis. It is the beginning of a fiduciary inquiry.

Haines is most useful when a spouse relies on title to characterize property as separate after a midmarriage deed, quitclaim, refinance, or other document changed ownership. The case frames the issue as one of fairness and fiduciary accountability rather than simply one of title mechanics.

Examples:

Quitclaim to complete a refinance: During marriage, Husband asks Wife to sign a quitclaim deed so he can refinance the residence in his own name. He tells her the document is only for loan qualification and that she will remain an owner. At dissolution, Husband claims the property is his separate property because title is in his name. Under Haines, the court asks whether Husband gained an advantage and, if so, whether he can prove Wife signed freely, knowingly, and with a complete understanding of the legal effect.

Transfer in exchange for credit help: One spouse agrees to sign away an interest in real property so the other spouse will cosign a car loan or other obligation. The advantaged spouse cannot rely solely on the deed. The court evaluates whether the disadvantaged spouse understood that the transfer affected ownership, not merely financing or convenience.

Settlement or title change in a confidential relationship: A spouse who controls finances prepares documents transferring a valuable asset into that spouse's name alone. The disadvantaged spouse signs without meaningful explanation. If the transfer gives the controlling spouse an advantage, Haines places the burden on that spouse to rebut undue influence.

Formula:

Undue influence framework: interspousal transaction plus an advantage to one spouse equals a rebuttable presumption of undue influence.

Rebuttal showing: the advantaged spouse must prove that the disadvantaged spouse acted freely and voluntarily, knew all material facts, and completely understood the legal effect of the transaction.

Practical result: if the advantaged spouse does not rebut the presumption, the court may disregard the title change for characterization purposes or otherwise restore the disadvantaged spouse's community interest.

Further Reading:

Family Code section 721: Haines should be read together with *Family Code section 721*. *Section 721* states that spouses are subject to the rules governing fiduciary relationships in transactions between themselves and imposes a duty of the highest good faith and fair dealing.

Haines also remains important when title evidence appears strong. It teaches that record title promotes stability in many settings, but it does not override the fiduciary protections that govern marital property disputes between spouses.

Later cases, including Fossum, rely on Haines to hold that the form of title presumption does not control when a deed or title change resulted from an advantaging interspousal transaction that has not been shown to be free from undue influence.

Evidence Code section 662 (ownership presumption of real property)

Civil Code section 1575 (fraud)

In re Marriage of Baltins (1989) 212 Cal.App.3d 66: Baltins is one of the authorities Haines relies on for the *Family Code section 721* undue-influence presumption. Baltins supplies two key propositions: marriage alone is not enough to presume undue influence where the transaction is fair, but when one spouse gains an advantage over the other in an interspousal transaction, the confidential/fiduciary relationship shifts the burden to the advantaged spouse to show the transaction was fair, voluntary, informed, and not the product of abuse of the marital relationship. Haines later applies that principle to hold that the spousal fiduciary/undue-influence presumption prevails over the *Evidence Code section 662* title presumption in marital property disputes.

22. *In re Marriage of Feldman*: Disclosure Duties and Monetary Sanctions

Concept:

During dissolution, spouses owe affirmative, ongoing fiduciary duties to disclose material financial information, including information affecting the existence, characterization, valuation, and disposition of assets and liabilities. A spouse cannot wait for the other spouse to discover the information through litigation.

Citation:

In re Marriage of Feldman (2007) 153 Cal.App.4th 1470.

Quote:

"This duty includes the obligation to make full disclosure to the other spouse of all material facts and information regarding the existence, characterization, and valuation of all assets in which the community has or may have an interest and debts for which the community is or may be liable, and to provide equal access to all information, records, and books that pertain to the value and character of those assets and debts, upon request."

"The disclosure requirements are designed to achieve the policy of ensuring a full and accurate disclosure of all assets and liabilities in which one or both parties may have an interest."

Explanation:

Aaron Feldman controlled privately held business entities and failed to disclose several transactions and assets, including a personal residence purchased through a company, an Israeli bond, a 401(k) account, and new business entities. The trial court found that he breached his fiduciary disclosure duties, intentionally sought to circumvent disclosure, and frustrated settlement policy. The Court of Appeal affirmed $250,000 in sanctions and $140,000 in attorney fees. The court held that sanctions under *sections 2107 and 271* do not require proof of separate financial injury and do not require the requesting spouse first to pursue lesser procedural remedies.

Feldman is the leading sanctions case for fiduciary nondisclosure in a dissolution proceeding. It applies the statutory disclosure scheme as an affirmative duty, not merely a response duty. A spouse who has superior access to business, investment, or account information must disclose material information even if the other spouse could eventually uncover it through discovery.

The case is especially important for closely held businesses and complex holdings. Aaron had superior access to information about the Sunroad entities and related transactions. The court treated that superior access as part of the fiduciary analysis. The spouse who controls or manages financial information must disclose it in a meaningful way, not simply produce scattered records and force the other spouse to piece together the case.

Feldman also clarifies the function of sanctions. Sanctions under *Family Code section 2107* are designed to enforce disclosure obligations and deter future noncompliance. Sanctions under *Family Code section 271* are designed to promote cooperation and settlement. Neither sanction depends on proof that the other spouse suffered a separate monetary loss from the nondisclosure.

For case analysis, Feldman should be used whenever the issue is a pattern of incomplete disclosure, delayed disclosure, strategic nondisclosure, or shifting the burden of investigation to the less informed spouse. It is not limited to hidden bank accounts. It applies to material information about business entities, real estate transactions, retirement accounts, liabilities, and any financial matter that affects property division or settlement.

Examples:

Closely held business entities: A spouse owns or controls multiple limited liability companies. During dissolution, the spouse discloses the main company but fails to disclose newly created affiliates, loans among entities, or real property held by an entity. Feldman supports sanctions because the omitted information affects valuation, characterization, and settlement.

Retirement or investment account omission: A spouse lists some accounts but fails to disclose a 401(k), bond, restricted stock account, or other investment. The other spouse later discovers the account through subpoenas. Feldman supports the argument that the duty was affirmative and did not depend on successful discovery by the other spouse.

Document production without explanation: A spouse produces large volumes of business records but does not identify material transactions, newly formed entities, or asset transfers. Feldman helps show that document dumping is not a substitute for full and accurate disclosure when the producing spouse understands the material facts and the other spouse does not.

Formula:

Section 2107 sanctions framework: disclosure violation plus no substantial justification and no unjust circumstances equals mandatory money sanctions.

Sanction amount: the amount should be sufficient to deter repetition of the conduct and may include reasonable attorney fees, costs, or both.

Section 271 sanctions framework: conduct that frustrates settlement or cooperation plus ability to pay without unreasonable burden equals discretionary sanctions after notice and an opportunity to be heard.

No separate injury requirement: under Feldman, sanctions under *sections 2107 and 271* do not require proof of independent financial harm from the nondisclosure.

Further Reading:

Feldman should be read with *Family Code sections 2100, 2102, and 2107*. These provisions create a policy of full disclosure, impose continuing disclosure duties, and require sanctions for failure to comply unless substantial justification or unjust circumstances are shown.

Feldman also connects fiduciary duties to litigation conduct under *Family Code section 271*. A disclosure violation may both breach fiduciary duties and frustrate settlement by increasing litigation cost and reducing cooperation.

The case is useful for distinguishing a mere accounting disagreement from conduct that obstructs disclosure. The focus is on whether the spouse failed to provide material information that the statutory scheme required the spouse to provide.

23. Rossi 100 Percent Remedy

Concept:

A spouse who intentionally conceals a community asset during dissolution violates fiduciary duties of disclosure. If the concealment amounts to fraud, oppression, or malice under *Civil Code section 3294*, *Family Code section 1101*, subdivision (h), authorizes an award of 100 percent of the undisclosed asset to the other spouse.

Citation:

In re Marriage of Rossi (2001) 90 Cal.App.4th 34.

Quote:

"The court found that Denise intentionally concealed her lottery winnings during the dissolution proceedings and that her conduct constituted fraud, oppression, and malice within the meaning of Civil Code section 3294 and Family Code section 1101, subdivision (h). On that basis, it awarded Thomas 100 percent of the winnings."

"Remedies for the breach of the fiduciary duty by one spouse when the breach falls within the ambit of Section 3294 of the Civil Code shall include, but not be limited to, an award to the other spouse of 100 percent, or an amount equal to 100 percent, of any asset undisclosed or transferred in breach of the fiduciary duty."

"The strong language of section 1101, subdivision (h) serves an important purpose: full disclosure of marital assets is absolutely essential to the trial court in determining the proper dissolution of property and resolving support issues."

Explanation:

Denise Rossi won a lottery prize shortly before filing for dissolution, used her mother's address to receive information, and did not disclose the winnings in the marital settlement agreement, judgment, schedules, or declarations of disclosure. The trial court found intentional concealment, breach of fiduciary duty, and fraud, oppression, and malice within the meaning of *Civil Code section 3294*. The Court of Appeal affirmed an award of 100 percent of the lottery winnings to Thomas Rossi under *Family Code section 1101*, subdivision (h).

Rossi illustrates the severe consequence of intentional concealment in dissolution. The spouse did not merely undervalue an asset or delay production. She concealed the existence of a major asset while the parties entered judgment. The court treated that conduct as a fiduciary breach and as conduct sufficient to trigger the highest statutory remedy.

The case is important because it ties the fiduciary disclosure statutes to *Family Code section 1101*, subdivision (h). Subdivision (g) provides a 50 percent remedy and fees for many breaches. Subdivision (h) applies when the breach falls within the ambit of *Civil Code section 3294*. In that situation, the remedy may be the entire undisclosed or transferred asset, or an amount equal to the entire asset.

Rossi also rejects the idea that a spouse may conceal an asset because the spouse believes it is separate property. A party may assert a characterization position, but the party still must disclose the asset. Disclosure permits the court and the other spouse to test characterization. Concealment prevents that process and strikes at the core of the fiduciary scheme.

For analysis, Rossi is best used when the evidence shows intentional secrecy: use of another address, false disclosures, omission from schedules, failure to list the asset in settlement documents, or postjudgment discovery of a significant asset. It is the key case for the 100 percent remedy.

Examples:

Hidden lottery or bonus: A spouse receives a lottery prize, employment bonus, stock payout, or settlement payment during marriage or before judgment and omits it from disclosure schedules. If the concealment is intentional and meets the *Civil Code section 3294* standard, Rossi supports awarding the entire asset to the other spouse.

Secret account: A spouse opens a separate account and diverts community earnings or sale proceeds into it while completing disclosure forms that omit the account. Rossi supports a fiduciary breach claim and, if the concealment is fraudulent, the 100 percent remedy.

Separate property claim with disclosure: By contrast, a spouse who lists the asset and claims it is separate property has preserved the dispute for adjudication. Rossi is aimed at concealment, not at a disclosed characterization dispute.

Formula:

Section 1101(h) remedy: undisclosed or transferred asset plus breach of fiduciary duty plus conduct satisfying *Civil Code section 3294* equals an award to the other spouse of 100 percent of the asset or an amount equal to 100 percent of the asset.

Section 1101(g) comparison: undisclosed or transferred asset plus breach without fraud, oppression, or malice equals 50 percent of the asset, or an amount equal to 50 percent, plus attorney fees and court costs.

Characterization point: a disclosed asset may be litigated as community or separate; a concealed asset exposes the concealing spouse to statutory remedies regardless of the spouse's asserted characterization theory.

Further Reading:

Family Code section 721 (fiduciary duty)

Family Code section 2100 (asset disclosures)

Civil Code section 3294 (punitive damages)

Rossi should be read with *Family Code section 1101*, subdivisions (g) and (h). Subdivision (g) addresses breaches resulting in a 50 percent award plus fees and costs. Subdivision (h) addresses breaches involving fraud, oppression, or malice and authorizes the 100 percent remedy.

The case reinforces that declarations of disclosure are central to the integrity of dissolution judgments. A marital settlement agreement depends on full disclosure of material assets and liabilities.

Rossi is frequently paired with Feldman. Feldman addresses sanctions for nondisclosure even without proof of separate injury. Rossi addresses the more severe remedy when concealment of an asset is intentional and fraudulent.

24. *In re Marriage of Brewer & Federici*: Incomplete Disclosure and Judgment Set Aside

Concept:

A spouse who is in the better position to obtain valuation information for a community asset must acquire and disclose it. Incomplete or inaccurate disclosure of major assets can support relief from a stipulated judgment based on mistake, even without intentional concealment.

Citation:

In re Marriage of Brewer & Federici (2001) 93 Cal.App.4th 1334.

Quote:

"Brewer's argument overlooks the fact that the Family Code imposes fiduciary obligations on both parties. One obligation is to make full, accurate, and complete disclosure, including the continuing duty to update and augment information."

"It reasonably follows that a spouse who is in a superior position to obtain records or information from which an asset can be valued and can reasonably do so must acquire and disclose such information to the other spouse."

"As long as such agreement is based upon a complete and accurate understanding of the existence and value of community and separate assets that are material to the agreement, the parties are free to decide on an unequal distribution."

Explanation:

Brewer listed the value of an NBC pension as unknown and used outdated information for another retirement plan. The plans were major community assets and the valuation information was reasonably available to her through her employer. The Court of Appeal affirmed the order setting aside the marital settlement agreement and judgment based on Federici's unilateral mistake. The court explained that a spouse in a superior position to obtain records or information from which an asset can be valued must acquire and disclose that information to the other spouse.

Brewer & Federici applies fiduciary duties to the settlement process. A marital settlement agreement is not an ordinary arm's length bargain between strangers. It is negotiated by spouses who owe each other statutory duties of full and accurate disclosure. Those duties include material valuation information, not just the bare existence of an asset.

The case is important because the disclosure failure did not have to be framed as intentional fraud. The omitted or inaccurate information caused a material mistake concerning the value of significant community retirement assets. That mistake supported relief from judgment under the Family Code set aside statutes.

The practical rule is that a spouse with superior access to asset records cannot disclose an asset as unknown when the value can be reasonably obtained. The spouse must make a good faith effort to secure the information and provide it. This is particularly important for pensions, deferred compensation, businesses, equity compensation, and employer controlled benefits.

For analysis, Brewer & Federici should be used where one spouse entered into a judgment or settlement without reliable valuation information and the other spouse had the ability to obtain or disclose that information. The remedy is not automatic relief from an unfavorable bargain. The moving spouse must still show that the disclosure problem materially affected the original outcome and that relief would materially benefit the moving spouse.

Examples:

Pension listed as unknown: Wife works for an employer that maintains a pension. She lists the pension but writes unknown for value and does not obtain available benefit information. Husband signs a settlement based on incomplete retirement information. Brewer & Federici supports set aside analysis based on mistake if the missing valuation materially affected the judgment.

Outdated account value: A spouse uses an old statement for a savings plan, deferred compensation account, or stock plan even though current information is available. If the stale value materially distorts settlement, the case supports relief based on incomplete disclosure.

Business records controlled by one spouse: A managing spouse discloses the existence of a business but fails to provide financial statements, tax returns, buy sell data, or other valuation information within that spouse's control. Brewer & Federici supports the argument that existence alone is not enough when valuation information is material and reasonably available.

Formula:

Set aside framework for mistake: incomplete or inaccurate disclosure of a material asset plus resulting unilateral or mutual mistake plus material effect on the original outcome plus material benefit to the moving party equals potential relief from a stipulated or uncontested judgment under *Family Code sections 2121 and 2122.*

Disclosure adequacy test: identifying an asset is not enough if valuation information is material, reasonably available, and controlled or readily obtainable by the disclosing spouse.

Further Reading:

Brewer & Federici should be read with *Family Code sections 2121 and 2122.* Those statutes govern relief from judgment and require both a qualifying ground, such as mistake, and a showing that the alleged facts materially affected the original outcome and that the moving party would materially benefit from relief.

The case also reinforces the policy stated in *Family Code section 2100.* Dissolution should be resolved with full disclosure and reduced adversarial cost. Incomplete disclosure undermines that policy even when the nondisclosing spouse did not set out to commit fraud.

Brewer & Federici is a strong companion to Feldman. Feldman addresses sanctions during ongoing litigation. Brewer & Federici addresses the consequences when incomplete disclosure produces a materially mistaken judgment.

In re Marriage of Feldman (2007) 153 Cal.App.4th 1470: See *In re Marriage of Feldman*: Disclosure Duties and Monetary Sanctions (pg. 58).

25. *In re Marriage of Fossum*: Undue Influence and Mandatory *Section 1101(g)* Fees

Concept:

Fossum applies both strands of fiduciary duty analysis. First, an interspousal deed that advantages one spouse may be set aside or disregarded when the advantaged spouse fails to rebut the presumption of undue influence. Second, when a spouse breaches fiduciary duties concerning community property, but the conduct does not rise to fraud, oppression, or malice, *section 1101*, subdivision (g), makes attorney fees and costs mandatory.

Citation:

In re Marriage of Fossum (2011) 192 Cal.App.4th 336.

Quote:

"Edward contends the trial court erred when it refused to award him attorney fees, which are mandated under section 1101, subdivision (g), for Sandra's fiduciary violation. On this point, we conclude Edward is correct."

"Prior to the parties' separation, Sandra took a cash advance on a credit card of $24,000, but never disclosed the transaction to Edward. The trial court found Sandra had breached her statutory fiduciary duty to her spouse."

"the spouse who was advantaged by the transaction must establish that the disadvantaged spouse's action was freely and voluntarily made with a full knowledge of all the facts and with a complete understanding of the effect of the transaction."

Explanation:

The Fossums acquired a residence during their marriage. Sandra signed quitclaim deeds so Edward could obtain or refinance loans in his name, and she testified that Edward promised to restore her to title. The Court of Appeal held that the form of title presumption did not control because the *section 721* presumption of undue influence applied. Edward failed to prove that Sandra acted with full knowledge and complete understanding of the effect of making the property his separate property, so the house remained community property. The court also held that Sandra's undisclosed $24,000 cash advance breached her fiduciary duty and that, once the breach was found, Edward was entitled to attorney fees and costs under *section 1101*, subdivision (g).

Fossum confirms the continuing force of Haines. A spouse may not rely on a quitclaim deed or form of title alone when the deed resulted from an interspousal transaction that advantaged that spouse. The question is whether the advantaged spouse can rebut the presumption that the transaction was the product of undue influence.

The residence analysis is straightforward but powerful. The house was acquired during the marriage and was community property. Sandra's later quitclaim deed placed title in Edward's name alone. That transaction advantaged Edward, so he had the burden to prove that Sandra understood she was making the property his separate property and did so freely and voluntarily. The trial court found he did not meet that burden, and the appellate court affirmed.

The second part of Fossum concerns remedies for fiduciary breach. Sandra incurred an undisclosed $24,000 cash advance. The trial court ordered reimbursement of one-half of the amount but denied attorney fees. The Court of Appeal held that *section 1101*, subdivision (g), required attorney fees and court costs once a fiduciary breach was found and the conduct did not fall under *section 1101*, subdivision (h) or *section 271*.

Fossum is useful because it links characterization and remedies. It can support a community characterization claim when title was changed through an advantaging interspousal transaction, and it can support mandatory fees when a fiduciary breach concerning community property is established.

Examples:

Refinance quitclaim: Husband asks Wife to quitclaim the residence to him so he can refinance. Wife believes the deed is only temporary or only for lender purposes. At dissolution, Husband claims the house is his separate property. Fossum supports applying the undue influence presumption and placing the burden on Husband to prove Wife fully understood the ownership effect.

Promise to restore title: One spouse signs title away based on the other spouse's promise that title will later be restored. The advantaged spouse later relies on the deed. Fossum supports the argument that the court should examine the fiduciary context and not treat record title as conclusive.

Undisclosed cash advance or debt: A spouse incurs a significant credit card advance or similar obligation without disclosure. If the court finds a breach of fiduciary duty but not fraud, oppression, or malice, Fossum supports an award of the appropriate reimbursement plus mandatory attorney fees and court costs under section 1101, subdivision (g).

Formula:

Undue influence framework: interspousal transaction plus advantage equals a presumption of undue influence. The advantaged spouse must rebut the presumption by a preponderance of the evidence with proof of free and voluntary action, full knowledge of facts, and complete understanding of effect.

Section 1101(g) remedy: undisclosed or transferred asset in breach of fiduciary duty multiplied by 50 percent, plus mandatory attorney fees and court costs. The value of the asset is measured at the highest value among the date of breach, the date of sale or disposition, and the date of award by the court.

Debt variation from Fossum: when the breach concerns an undisclosed debt, such as a cash advance, the practical reimbursement may be the nonbreaching spouse's one-half share of the concealed debt, plus mandatory fees and costs.

Further Reading:

Evidence Code section 662 (property ownership presumption)

Fossum should be read with Haines on the conflict between the form of title presumption and the fiduciary presumption of undue influence. Both cases emphasize that family law characterization disputes between spouses require fiduciary analysis.

Fossum should also be read with *Family Code section 1101*. Subdivision (g) provides the 50 percent remedy plus attorney fees and costs for fiduciary breach. Subdivision (h) provides the 100 percent remedy when the breach falls within *Civil Code section 3294*.

The case is particularly helpful when one fact pattern includes both a title change and nondisclosure of a debt or transaction. It shows that fiduciary duty can affect both characterization and remedy.

In re Marriage of Mathews (2005) 133 Cal.App.4th 624: Mathews confirms that a quitclaim deed or interspousal transfer that advantages one spouse triggers the Haines undue-influence presumption, but the transaction can still be upheld if the advantaged spouse proves, by a preponderance of the evidence, that the other spouse knowingly, voluntarily, and intelligently made the transfer.

In re Marriage of Haines (1995) 33 Cal.App.4th 277: See Haines Presumption of Undue Influence (pg. 17).

26. Brown Rights

Concept:

Retirement benefits earned during marriage are community property even when they are nonvested, unmatured, contingent, or not yet payable.

Citation:

In re Marriage of Brown (1976) 15 Cal.3d 838.

Quote:

"Pension rights, whether or not vested, represent a property interest; to the extent that such rights derive from employment during coverture, they comprise a community asset subject to division in a dissolution proceeding."

"We have concluded, however, that the French court's characterization of nonvested pension rights as expectancies errs."

"Fortunately we can appropriately reflect the realistic situation by recognizing that the husband's pension rights, a contingent interest, whether vested or not vested, comprise a property interest of the community and that the wife may properly share in it."

Explanation:

Brown is the foundation case for California retirement characterization. The Supreme Court rejected the earlier rule that nonvested pension rights were only expectancies. The court held that pension rights are a form of deferred compensation and a contingent property interest. To the extent the right is earned by employment during marriage, it is a community asset subject to division on dissolution. The court also recognized practical methods for division: present valuation and offset where feasible, or retained jurisdiction and division of each payment if uncertainty makes present valuation unfair.

Before Brown, California law treated a nonvested pension as too uncertain to divide. Brown changed the analysis. The important question is not whether the employee spouse can demand payment immediately. The important question is whether the employee spouse earned a contractual or employment-related right during marriage. If the answer is yes, the community has an interest, even if the right may later be forfeited or never mature. This treatment reflects the economic reality that pensions are part of the compensation package earned by labor. The community supplies that labor during marriage and should not lose the asset merely because vesting or retirement occurs after separation. Brown also separates characterization from valuation. Characterization asks whether the community acquired an interest. Valuation and division ask how to fairly divide a right that may be difficult to value. A trial court may value the community interest at dissolution and offset the nonemployee spouse with other property, but Brown allows a court to reserve jurisdiction and divide payments if and when they are received. That approach spreads the risk of forfeiture between the parties rather than making either spouse bear it alone. In modern practice, Brown supports the treatment of pensions, defined benefit plans, deferred compensation rights, and other employment benefits as divisible community assets when earned during marriage.

Examples:

Nonvested defined benefit pension: Husband works for a utility company for 18 years during marriage. His pension will vest after 20 years. The parties separate after year 18. Under Brown, the court should not ignore the pension simply because two more years of service are needed. The portion earned during the 18 community years is a divisible community asset. The court may reserve jurisdiction and later divide payments if Husband actually vests and retires.

Uncertain future benefit: Wife participates in an employer retirement plan that may be lost if she leaves employment before a stated date. The uncertainty affects valuation and method of division, not characterization. If the right was earned by community labor, the court can divide the risk by ordering each spouse to receive the appropriate share of any future payment when paid.

Formula:

Brown does not impose a single mathematical formula. It identifies two principal methods. First, the court may determine the present value of the community interest and divide or offset it with other assets. Second, if present valuation is too uncertain, the court may reserve jurisdiction and divide each payment if and when paid.

A common time-rule implementation for a defined benefit plan is: Community share of each retirement payment = monthly benefit x (service during marriage before separation / total service used to calculate the benefit). Nonemployee spouse share = 1/2 x community share.

Example of calculation: The employee spouse receives a $4,000 monthly pension after 25 years of service. Fifteen years occurred during marriage before separation. The community fraction is 15 / 25, or 60 percent. The community share of the monthly pension is $4,000 x 60 percent = $2,400. The nonemployee spouse's one-half share is $1,200 per month. If the pension never vests or is never paid, the reserved jurisdiction method prevents either spouse from being forced to pay for a benefit that never materializes.

Further Reading:

Family Code section 2550 (equal division presumption).

Family Code section 2610: Current California law authorizes orders necessary or appropriate to ensure that each party receives the party's full community property share in a retirement plan, including survivor and death benefits where applicable. Brown supplies the characterization principle; the Family Code supplies procedural authority for effective division.

In re Marriage of Skaden (1977) 19 Cal.3d 679: See *In re Marriage of Skaden*: Termination Benefits as Deferred Compensation (pg. 80).

27. Gillmore Election

Concept:

When retirement benefits are matured and payable at the employee spouse's election, the nonemployee spouse may choose immediate distribution of the community share even if the employee spouse elects not to retire.

Citation:

In re Marriage of Gillmore (1981) 29 Cal.3d 418.

Quote:

"He is free to continue working. However, if he does so, he must reimburse Vera for the share of the community property that she loses as a result of that decision."

"Here, Earl must divide his retirement benefits with Vera. If he does not wish to retire, he must pay her an amount equivalent to her interest."

"However, financial status is not relevant when dividing community property. The courts are statutorily required to divide community property equally."

Explanation:

Gillmore protects the nonemployee spouse from having receipt of an already matured community asset controlled entirely by the employee spouse. The court held that an employee spouse may continue working and need not retire. However, once the pension is vested and matured and the only remaining condition to payment is the employee spouse's election to retire, the employee spouse cannot use that election to postpone the nonemployee spouse's enjoyment of his or her community property. If the employee spouse continues working, the court may order payment of an amount equivalent to the nonemployee spouse's pension share.

Gillmore builds on Brown by addressing timing rather than basic characterization. Brown says the community owns the retirement benefit to the extent earned during marriage. Gillmore asks what happens when the employee spouse can start receiving the benefit but chooses not to. The Supreme Court concluded that the employee spouse controls his or her own employment decision, but not the other spouse's property right. A matured pension is an asset whose payment can begin if the employee spouse retires. If the employee spouse delays retirement, the nonemployee spouse may be deprived of present use, investment control, and security. Gillmore prevents that result by giving the nonemployee spouse an election. The nonemployee spouse may wait and share in future increases if the employee spouse later retires with a larger benefit, or may elect immediate payment based on the benefit then available. If immediate payment is elected, the employee spouse can satisfy the obligation without retiring by using separate funds or other resources. The rule is not a support remedy. It is a property division remedy, so financial need is not the governing test. The court may consider tax consequences, support consequences, and payment structure on remand, but the underlying right is the nonemployee spouse's community property share.

Examples:

Eligible but not retired: Husband is eligible to retire at age 55 and would receive $6,000 per month. The parties' community fraction is 50 percent. Wife's one-half of the community share is $1,500 per month. Husband wants to keep working. Under Gillmore, Wife may request immediate payments of $1,500 per month. Husband remains free to work, but he must compensate Wife for the community pension share he is withholding by not retiring.

Election tradeoff: Wife may prefer to wait because continued employment may produce a higher final salary and a larger pension. Gillmore allows that choice. If she elects immediate distribution instead, she receives the then-available share but ordinarily gives up later increases attributable to continued service, higher salary, or increased age.

Formula:

Gillmore payment = benefit payable at first retirement eligibility x community fraction x 1/2.

Community fraction = service during marriage before separation / total service used to calculate the benefit as of the Gillmore election date.

Example of calculation: The employee spouse is eligible to retire and receive $5,000 per month. The community fraction is 40 percent. The community portion is $5,000 x 40 percent = $2,000. The nonemployee spouse's one-half share is $1,000 per month. If the employee spouse keeps working, the court may order payments equivalent to $1,000 per month. If the nonemployee spouse chooses this immediate distribution, future increases are generally excluded from that elected share.

Further Reading:

In re Marriage of Brown (1976) 15 Cal.3d 838: See Brown Rights (pg. 68).

Family Code section 2550 (equal division presumption).

Family Code section 2610 (retirement plan division).

In re Marriage of Luciano (1980) 104 Cal.App.3d 956: Gillmore relied on Luciano for the principle that the nonemployee spouse, not the employee spouse, should control when the nonemployee spouse's share begins when the only barrier to payment is the employee spouse's retirement election.

In re Marriage of Cornejo (1996) 13 Cal.4th 381: Later California Supreme Court authority discusses the timing and procedural limits of Gillmore-type relief, especially the requirement that the nonemployee spouse seek relief rather than assume automatic payment.

28. *In re Marriage of Lehman*: Enhanced Retirement Benefits

Concept:

A nonemployee spouse's community property interest in retirement benefits includes a proportionate interest in later enhancements to those benefits when the enhancement modifies the retirement benefit already earned in part during marriage.

Citation:

In re Marriage of Lehman (1998) 18 Cal.4th 169.

Quote:

"whether a nonemployee spouse who owns a community property interest in an employee spouse's retirement benefits under such a plan owns a community property interest in the latter's retirement benefits as enhanced"

"Under that method, the community property interest in retirement benefits is the percentage representing the fraction whose numerator is the employee spouse's length of service during marriage before separation, here 17.39 years, and whose denominator is the employee spouse's length of service in total, here 32.67 years; the separate property interest is the percentage representing the remainder of 100 percent minus the community property interest percentage."

"The enhancement was a modification of the retirement benefits."

Explanation:

Lehman held that a nonemployee spouse who owns a community interest in the employee spouse's retirement benefits also owns a community interest in the benefits as enhanced. The enhancement is not necessarily all community property. Rather, once the enhancement is characterized as part of the retirement benefit, the court must apportion the enhanced benefit between the community and separate estates. The Supreme Court approved the time rule on the facts presented because the enhanced benefit was substantially related to years of service. The court also rejected adding fictitious or putative service years to the time-rule denominator or numerator when those years are merely an employer-created method of implementing the enhancement.

Lehman addresses a frequent retirement problem: a plan changes after separation or dissolution and the employee spouse receives a larger retirement benefit than the one expected at divorce. The employee spouse argued that the enhancement was post-separation compensation or a separate benefit. The Supreme Court disagreed on the facts before it. The enhancement increased retirement benefits under the existing defined benefit plan. It was a modification of the retirement asset, not a completely new asset. Because the community had earned part of the underlying retirement benefit, the community shared proportionately in the enhanced stream of payments. Lehman is important because it distinguishes characterization from apportionment. Characterization asks whether the enhancement is tied to the retirement benefit in which the community already has an interest. If yes, apportionment determines the community percentage. The case also rejects an employer-motive test. The employer may have offered the enhancement to induce early retirement, reduce payroll, or accomplish another business purpose. That motive does not control community characterization. What matters is the legal and economic nature of the payment. If the payment is an increase to retirement benefits rather than a separate severance payment, the community shares in it under the proper apportionment method.

Examples:

Voluntary retirement enhancement: Husband worked 30 total years. Twelve years occurred during marriage before separation. After dissolution, the employer offers a voluntary retirement incentive that increases the monthly pension from $6,000 to $7,500. Under Lehman, Wife's community interest applies to the $7,500 enhanced retirement benefit if the enhancement modifies the retirement benefit. Her share is not limited to the pre-enhancement amount unless a prior judgment or order lawfully fixed or cashed out her interest.

Putative service credit: An employer adds five fictitious service years to calculate a larger pension. Those years are a mechanism for increasing the plan benefit. Under Lehman, the court should not add those fictitious years to the time-rule denominator or numerator if they were not actual service supplied by either estate. The court uses actual service to apportion the enhanced benefit.

Formula:

Lehman time-rule share = enhanced retirement benefit x (actual service during marriage before separation / total actual service used for retirement) x 1/2.

Do not add fictitious years credited only to produce the enhancement unless the facts and plan terms show those years represent actual service or another legally relevant contribution. Lehman's point is that the fraction should fairly represent the relative contributions of the community and separate estates.

Example of calculation: The enhanced pension is $8,000 per month. The employee spouse worked 10 years during marriage and 25 actual years total. The community fraction is 10 / 25, or 40 percent. The community portion is $8,000 x 40 percent = $3,200. The nonemployee spouse's one-half share is $1,600 per month. If the plan used five putative service years to enhance the benefit, those fictitious years are not added to either side of the fraction under Lehman.

Further Reading:

Family Code section 2550 (equal division presumption).

Family Code section 2610 (retirement plan division).

In re Marriage of Gillmore (1981) 29 Cal.3d 418: See Gillmore Election (pg. 71).

In re Marriage of Lehman (1998) 18 Cal.4th 169: See *In re Marriage of Lehman*: Enhanced Retirement Benefits (pg. 73).

In re Marriage of Brown (1976) 15 Cal.3d 838: See Brown Rights (pg. 68).

In re Marriage of Gram (1994) 25 Cal.App.4th 859: Gram treated an early retirement enhancement as part of the retirement benefit, but Lehman disapproved Gram to the extent it required adding putative years to the denominator of the time-rule fraction.

In re Marriage of Frahm (1996) 45 Cal.App.4th 536: Frahm distinguished severance payments from retirement benefits. Lehman is useful because it focuses on whether the payment is an enhancement to an existing retirement asset or a separate post-separation benefit.

29. Hug Formula

Concept:

Employee stock options granted before separation but exercisable after separation may be partly community property and partly separate property, with apportionment based on the purpose of the options and an equitable time rule.

Citation:

In re Marriage of Hug (1984) 154 Cal.App.3d 780.

Quote:

"Thus, no single characterization can be given to employee stock options. Whether they can be characterized as compensation for future services, for past services, or for both, depends upon the circumstances involved in the grant of the employee stock option."

"Although we approve the use of the time rule fashioned by the trial court under the facts of this case, we stress that no single rule or formula is applicable to every dissolution case involving employee stock options."

"Trial courts should be vested with broad discretion to fashion approaches which will achieve the most equitable results under the facts of each case."

Explanation:

Hug held that trial courts have broad discretion to select an equitable method for apportioning stock options granted before separation and exercisable after separation. The approved formula measured the community portion by comparing the period from the start of employment to separation with the period from the start of employment to the date the option first became exercisable. The court emphasized that no single stock-option formula applies in every case. The purpose of the grant matters because options may compensate past services, encourage continued employment, reward future performance, or combine several purposes.

Hug applies Brown's deferred compensation logic to stock options. A stock option may be valuable even before it can be exercised because it is a contractual right connected to employment. If the option was granted during marriage before separation, the community may have earned part of it, even if the employee spouse must continue working after separation before exercise. The trial court must determine why the option was granted. In Hug, the evidence supported a broad time period beginning with the employee spouse's commencement of employment because the options related not only to future retention but also to recruitment, past services, and the overall employment relationship. The court therefore approved a formula that included the employee's service before the option grant. This is often called the Hug formula. The formula tends to produce a larger community share than the Nelson formula because the numerator and denominator begin at the start of employment rather than the date of grant. Hug is not rigid. It is an equitable framework. A court may use present valuation and offset if options can be valued, divide options in kind if assignable and appropriate, or reserve jurisdiction and allocate proceeds when exercised. The guiding principle is substantial justice, not mechanical uniformity.

Examples:

Options linked to recruitment and past service: Husband joins a technology company during marriage. Several years later, still during marriage, he receives options that vest after separation. Evidence shows the options were intended to reward his early service and encourage him to stay. Hug supports using a formula that begins with the start of employment because the community contributed to the employment history that produced the option grant.

Options with delayed exercisability: Wife receives 2,000 options before separation. They first become exercisable two years after separation. The options are not ignored. The court determines the community fraction and then divides the community portion equally, while the balance belongs to Wife as separate property.

Formula:

Hug formula: Community options = total options in the grant x (months from commencement of employment to date of separation / months from commencement of employment to date the options first become exercisable).

Nonemployee spouse share = 1/2 x community options, subject to valuation, tax, transferability, and plan restrictions.

Example of calculation: The employee spouse began employment 60 months before separation. A grant of 1,200 options becomes exercisable 100 months after employment began. Community options = 1,200 x 60 / 100 = 720. The nonemployee spouse's one-half share is 360 options or the cash equivalent, depending on the court's chosen division method. The remaining 480 options are the employee spouse's separate property.

Further Reading:

Family Code section 760 (community property presumption)

Family Code section 771 (separate property presumption after marriage)

In re Marriage of Hug (1984) 154 Cal.App.3d 780: See Hug Formula (pg. 75).

In re Marriage of Brown (1976) 15 Cal.3d 838: See Brown Rights (pg. 68).

In re Marriage of Nelson (1986) 177 Cal.App.3d 150: See Nelson Formula (pg. 78).

30. Nelson Formula

Concept:

When stock options are granted before separation but become exercisable after separation, a court may apportion from the date of grant to the date of separation over the date of grant to exercisability if that better reflects the purpose of the options.

Citation:

In re Marriage of Nelson (1986) 177 Cal.App.3d 150.

Quote:

"In contrast, the trial court here utilized a formula in which the numerator was the number of months from the date of grant of each block of options to the date of the couple's separation, while the denominator was the period from the time of each grant to its date of exercisability."

"Hug specifically states, "we stress that no single rule or formula is applicable to every dissolution case involving employee stock options. Trial courts should be vested with broad discretion to fashion approaches which will achieve the most equitable results under the facts of each case.""

"It was therefore appropriate to place more emphasis on the period following each grant to the date of separation, as the trial court did here, than on the employee's entire tenure with the company up to the time of separation as the Hug court did."

Explanation:

Nelson confirmed that intermediate options, meaning options granted before separation but exercisable after separation, may be partly community property. The court approved a formula using the date of each option grant rather than the start of employment because the facts showed the options were more closely tied to prospective increases in stock value and future services after each grant. Nelson also affirmed that post-separation options and a post-separation bonus were separate property where substantial evidence supported the finding that the employee spouse had not acquired any right to them before separation.

Nelson is often paired with Hug. Both cases recognize that stock options can be divisible deferred compensation. The difference is the starting point for the time rule. Hug used the beginning of employment because the options in that case were connected to recruitment, past service, and the overall employment relationship. Nelson used the date of grant because the options at issue were more closely tied to the future value of the employer's stock after the grant. This distinction is critical. A court must characterize the employment benefit by looking at the plan documents, testimony, grant history, market terms, vesting schedule, and the employer's apparent compensation purpose. If the option's value depends primarily on the employee's future service and future growth after a specific grant, the Nelson formula may be more equitable. Nelson also draws a clean line for benefits not acquired before separation. If a stock option grant or discretionary bonus is awarded after separation and the employee spouse had no enforceable right to it before separation, the court may characterize it as separate property under the post-separation earnings rule. Nelson therefore provides two practical lessons: intermediate options require apportionment, but post-separation benefits require proof that some right accrued during marriage before they can be included in the community estate.

Examples:

Grant-specific incentive options: Husband receives 3,000 options one year before separation. The options vest three years after the grant. The plan documents show the options are intended to encourage future performance and future stock growth. Nelson supports starting the fraction on the grant date, not the date Husband began employment years earlier.

Post-separation bonus: Wife receives a discretionary bonus eight months after separation. The employer decides annually whether to pay bonuses, and no contract guaranteed payment before separation. Under Nelson, the court may treat the bonus as Wife's separate property if the evidence shows only an expectancy existed during marriage.

Formula:

Nelson formula: Community options = total options in the grant x (months from date of grant to date of separation / months from date of grant to date the options first become exercisable).

Nonemployee spouse share = 1/2 x community options, subject to valuation, tax treatment, transfer restrictions, and the court's chosen method of division.

Example of calculation: The employee spouse receives 2,400 options 10 months before separation. The options first become exercisable 40 months after grant. Community options = 2,400 x 10 / 40 = 600. The nonemployee spouse's one-half share is 300 options or the equivalent value. The remaining 1,800 options are the employee spouse's separate property because they are attributed to the post-separation portion of the vesting or exercisability period.

Further Reading:

In re Marriage of Nelson (1986) 177 Cal.App.3d 150: See Nelson Formula (pg. 78).

In re Marriage of Hug (1984) 154 Cal.App.3d 780: See Hug Formula (pg. 75).

Family Code § 771: Current law states that earnings and accumulations after the date of separation are separate property. Nelson applies that principle to post-separation stock options and bonuses when no pre-separation contractual right has accrued.

31. *In re Marriage of Skaden*: Termination Benefits as Deferred Compensation

Concept:

Contractual termination benefits earned during marriage may be divisible community property even when the right is immature and payment depends on future termination and post-termination conditions.

Citation:

In re Marriage of Skaden (1977) 19 Cal.3d 679.

Quote:

"the above termination benefits, like the pension rights involved in Brown, represent a form of deferred compensation for services rendered"

"Pension benefits, we held in Brown, "represent a form of deferred compensation for services rendered.""

"the right to them, also derived from the terms of the agreement, is likewise not a mere expectancy but a chose in action -- and therefore property subject to division upon dissolution."

Explanation:

Skaden extended Brown's deferred compensation reasoning beyond traditional pensions. The employee spouse was a State Farm insurance agent whose agency agreement provided termination benefits after certain service and termination conditions. The Supreme Court held that the benefits were not a mere expectancy and should not have been awarded entirely as the employee spouse's separate property. They were contractual rights analogous to vested but immature pension rights, and they were divisible to the extent they were earned by community effort. The method of division was left to the trial court's discretion, including present valuation or reservation of jurisdiction.

Skaden is important for deferred compensation because it prevents parties from limiting Brown to conventional retirement plans. The benefit in Skaden was not labeled a pension. It was a contractual termination benefit payable under an insurance agency agreement. The court still treated it as property because the right arose from the employment or agency contract and had been earned during marriage. The fact that the agent had not yet terminated the agreement, and that future conditions could affect payment, made the right immature. It did not make the right nonexistent. Skaden therefore helps characterize severance-like, termination, retention, and contract-based benefits. The analysis asks whether the employee spouse acquired a contractual right during marriage, whether the right survived termination or other events, and whether it is deferred compensation for services rendered during marriage. If so, the community owns the appropriate share. The case also emphasizes trial court flexibility. Some termination benefits can be valued at dissolution. Others depend on future premiums, future termination, tax consequences, or post-termination covenants. When present valuation is speculative, retained jurisdiction and division of actual payments may be more equitable. Skaden is also cautious about finality. It limits retroactive disruption of final property divisions unless jurisdiction was reserved.

Examples:

Agency termination benefit: Husband enters a long-term insurance agency agreement during marriage. The contract provides a five-year stream of termination payments if the agency relationship ends after a minimum service period. The parties separate before termination. Under Skaden, the right may be a community asset to the extent earned during marriage, even though payment will not occur until termination.

Conditional deferred compensation: Wife's employment contract provides a retention or termination payment if she remains employed for a specified period and complies with post-employment restrictions. The fact that payment is conditional affects valuation. If the contractual right was earned in part during marriage, the court should determine the community share rather than treating the whole benefit as separate property.

Formula:

Skaden does not prescribe a fixed formula. The court may use present valuation and offset, or reserve jurisdiction and divide payments when made.

Reserved jurisdiction method: Nonemployee spouse share of each termination payment = actual payment received x community fraction x 1/2.

Community fraction may be measured by the period of service or contract performance during marriage before separation divided by the total period of service or contract performance that produced the termination benefit, if that measure fairly reflects the source of the benefit.

Example of calculation: A termination benefit pays $100,000 in installments. The employee spouse performed 8 years of qualifying service during marriage and 10 years total before termination. The community fraction is 8 / 10, or 80 percent. Community portion = $100,000 x 80 percent = $80,000. The nonemployee spouse's one-half share is $40,000, payable in the same installments or through an equivalent offset if the court determines present valuation is reliable.

Further Reading:

Family Code section 760 (community property presumption)

Family Code section 2550 (equal division presumption)

In re Marriage of Skaden (1977) 19 Cal.3d 679: See *In re Marriage of Skaden*: Termination Benefits as Deferred Compensation (pg. 80).

In re Marriage of Brown (1976) 15 Cal.3d 838: See Brown Rights (pg. 68).

In re Marriage of Gillmore (1981) 29 Cal.3d 418: See Gillmore Election (pg. 71).

32. Pereira Rule

Concept:

When a spouse brings a separate property business into marriage and community labor materially increases the business value or profits, the separate estate receives a reasonable return on its capital and the remaining increase is apportioned to the community.

Citation:

Pereira v. Pereira (1909) 156 Cal. 1.

Quote:

"the principal part of the large income was due to the personal character, energy, ability, and capacity of the husband."

"This share of the earnings was, of course, community property."

"But without capital he could not have carried on the business, and in the absence of circumstances showing a different result, it is to be presumed that some of the profits were justly due to the capital invested."

Explanation:

The husband owned and operated a saloon and cigar business before marriage. The trial court treated all gains received after marriage as community property. The California Supreme Court held that this was error because the husband had $15,500 of separate capital invested in the business, and that capital had to be credited with some profit or interest. At the same time, the court recognized that the principal part of the income was due to the husband's personal character, energy, ability, and capacity, making that portion community property. On modification, because no evidence showed a greater return on the separate capital, the court allowed the separate estate seven percent interest on $15,500 and classified the balance of the cash gain as community property.

Pereira is the foundational California business apportionment case. It addresses the recurring problem created when separate capital and community labor combine to produce business growth. The spouse who owned the business before marriage keeps the separate property business and receives a fair return on the capital that existed at the start of marriage. The community receives the portion of growth attributable to marital labor, skill, management, contacts, or undercompensated effort.

The approach is most useful when the business growth is driven primarily by the working spouse's personal services rather than by the inherent qualities of the separate asset. Examples include a professional practice, sales business, consulting company, small operating company, or entrepreneurial enterprise in which the owner spouse's effort is the chief reason for growth. Pereira does not transmute the business into community property. It creates an equitable allocation of the growth between separate property and community property.

The reasonable return is evidence driven. Pereira used seven percent legal interest because the record did not support a greater return. Later cases make clear that the rate can be adjusted based on the evidence, the business, risk, market conditions, and what is needed to achieve substantial justice.

Examples:

Small professional practice: Husband owns a tax practice worth $100,000 before marriage. During a ten year marriage he is the only professional, brings in nearly all clients, and the practice grows to $900,000. If the court finds that a fair return on the separate capital is $80,000, the separate property component is $180,000 and the remaining $720,000 is community property.

Founder operated business: Wife owns a small design company before marriage. Its equipment and capital are modest, but she personally develops a national client base during marriage. Even if the company remains titled in her name, the court may use Pereira because the increase is primarily attributable to her community labor.

Separate Property Business: Opening a separate property business with a value of $100,000. A fair return is $80,000. Valuation date business value is $900,000. The separate property credit is $180,000. The community component is $720,000. Under current equal division principles, each spouse's share of that community component would ordinarily be $360,000.

Formula:

Pereira separate property credit = opening separate property value + reasonable return on that value.

Pereira community component = valuation date business value less Pereira separate property credit.

Further Reading:

Beam v. Bank of America (1971) 6 Cal.3d 12: See *Beam v. Bank of America (pg. 86).*

In re Marriage of Dekker (1993) 17 Cal.App.4th 842: See *In re Marriage of Dekker (pg. 88).*

33. Van Camp Rule

Concept:

When business growth is primarily attributable to separate capital, a preexisting business structure, corporate assets, market conditions, employees, or other noncommunity factors, the community is limited to the reasonable value of the managing spouse's services, reduced by compensation and community expenses already paid.

Citation:

Van Camp v. Van Camp (1921) 53 Cal.App. 17.

Quote:

"He became the president and general manager of the corporation and received up to January, 1918, a salary of $1,000 per month. This salary was increased on January 1, 1918, to $1,500 per month and so remained at all times subsequent thereto."

"he was by the corporation paid what the evidence shows was an adequate salary"

"the balance of the profits derived from the business accredited to the use of the capital invested therein"

Explanation:

In Van Camp, the husband organized and capitalized the Van Camp Sea Food Company before marriage. During marriage he served as president and manager and received a substantial salary. The trial court treated a large portion of accumulated property as community property. The Court of

Appeal reversed the property ruling. It held that the corporation was a real entity, not a mere fiction, and that the husband's salary adequately compensated the community for his personal services. The dividends and remaining gains were attributed to the separate capital investment and the business enterprise itself. Because the salary and expense money received during marriage were community earnings and were largely consumed by family expenses, the record did not support a large community estate.

Van Camp supplies the counterpart to Pereira. It is typically used when the business is capital intensive or when the evidence shows that appreciation is mostly due to the nature of the asset rather than the spouse's individual labor. The community does not receive all appreciation simply because a spouse worked in the business during marriage. Instead, the community receives the reasonable value of the spouse's services, to the extent that value was not already paid out to the community or consumed by family expenses.

This method often favors the separate estate. It is appropriate where the business would have earned substantial returns even without the spouse's personal effort, where the spouse was paid adequate salary, or where profits are traceable to separate capital, employees, inventory, machinery, intellectual property, brand value, licenses, or external market forces.

Van Camp is especially important for corporations and larger companies. The case rejected the argument that the corporation should be ignored where the entity was duly organized and had genuine capital and shareholders. Even if a court looks through the entity for apportionment purposes, adequate compensation for the spouse's services can limit the community claim.

Examples:

Capital intensive manufacturing business: Husband owns a manufacturing company before marriage. The company owns valuable machinery, patents, and inventory, and it has a strong management team. Husband works as president during marriage and receives a market salary. The company increases in value because of market demand and capital assets. Van Camp may limit the community claim to any uncompensated value of Husband's services.

Established corporation with adequate salary: Wife owns stock in a profitable food company before marriage and manages it during marriage. She receives a salary comparable to what an outside executive would earn. Dividends and stock appreciation are primarily due to the company's capital, brand, and employees. Van Camp would generally treat the salary as the community return and preserve the remaining appreciation as separate property.

Examples:

A business owner spouse's reasonable services are valued at $300,000 for the marriage. The spouse already received $260,000 in salary that was available to the community, and $40,000 of family expenses are chargeable to community income. The net community claim is zero. The remaining appreciation stays separate property.

Formula:

Van Camp community income = reasonable value of marital services to the separate property business.

Net Van Camp community claim = Van Camp community income less salary, benefits, distributions, or other compensation already received by the community, and less family expenses chargeable against community income.

Separate property component = remaining business value and profits after the net community claim is accounted for.

Further Reading:

Beam v. Bank of America (1971) 6 Cal.3d 12: See *Beam v. Bank of America (pg. 86).*

In re Marriage of Dekker (1993) 17 Cal.App.4th 842: See *In re Marriage of Dekker (pg. 88).*

34. *Beam v. Bank of America*

Concept:

A court has discretion to select Pereira, Van Camp, or another equitable apportionment approach based on the facts, and the court must select the yardstick that best achieves substantial justice between separate capital and community labor.

Citation:

Beam v. Bank of America (1971) 6 Cal.3d 12.

Quote:

"the modest increment of Mr. Beam's estate was more probably attributable to the "character of the capital investment" than to the "personal activity, ability and capacity of the spouse.""

"Under the Van Camp test community income is determined by designating a reasonable value to the services performed by the husband in connection with his separate property."

"Under these precedents, once a court ascertains the amount of community income, through either the Pereira or the Van Camp approach, it deducts the community's living expenses from community income to determine the balance of the community property."

Explanation:

Mr. Beam inherited more than $1.6 million in cash and securities before and during the early years of marriage. He was not employed in the ordinary sense; he spent his time managing his separate estate, trading securities, and pursuing real estate projects. The trial court found that almost all property remained his separate property. The California Supreme Court affirmed. It recognized that Mr. Beam's efforts were more than minimal, so apportionment was required, but it approved the conclusion that no net community estate resulted. Under Pereira, a seven percent simple interest return would account for the estate's growth. Under Van Camp, even if a professional manager fee were imputed as community income, ordinary family expenses exceeded that amount and would consume the imputed community income.

Beam is the leading California Supreme Court case explaining how courts choose between Pereira and Van Camp. It rejects rigid formula selection. Courts are not required to use a predetermined rate of return under Pereira, and they are not required to limit the community to a salary measure under Van Camp. The selection turns on the facts: whether the character of the capital investment or the personal activity, ability, and capacity of the spouse is the chief contributing factor in producing income and appreciation.

Beam also expands the apportionment principle beyond operating businesses. Apportionment may be required when a spouse devotes more than minimal effort to managing separate investments, real estate, securities, or similar separate property assets. However, the existence of effort does not guarantee a positive community claim. The court still asks whether the effort produced a net community estate.

The family expense presumption is critical. When the court imputes community income under Pereira or Van Camp, that income is not considered in isolation. In the absence of contrary evidence, family expenses are charged against community income. If family expenses exceed imputed community income, there may be no accumulated community property to divide.

Examples:

Separate investment portfolio: Husband enters marriage with a $2 million securities portfolio and actively manages it. At dissolution the portfolio is worth $2.2 million. If a reasonable return on the opening capital would exceed

$2.2 million, Pereira may leave no community component because the increase is attributable to normal capital growth.

Investment manager valuation: Wife manages her separate real estate portfolio during marriage. A comparable outside manager would have charged $50,000 per year, but the parties' family expenses were $70,000 per year and no evidence shows a different payment practice. Under Beam, the imputed community income may be consumed by family expenses, leaving no net community estate.

Formula:

Formula selection rule: choose the method that is most appropriate and equitable under the facts.

Pereira path: community component = value or profits attributable to the business less a fair return on separate capital.

Van Camp path: community component = reasonable value of marital services less compensation and expenses chargeable to community income.

Beam expense adjustment: net community estate = community income under the selected formula less family expenses presumed paid from community income, unless the evidence supports a different treatment.

Further Reading:

Beam v. Bank of America (1971) 6 Cal.3d 12: See *Beam v. Bank of America (pg. 86).*

Estate of Neilson: Beam relies on Neilson for the rule that family expenses are presumed paid from community funds, and that if the community allocation is less than family expenses, assets traceable to the separate investment may remain separate property.

In re Marriage of Dekker (1993) 17 Cal.App.4th 842: See *In re Marriage of Dekker (pg. 88).*

Pereira v. Pereira (1909) 156 Cal. 1: See Pereira Rule (pg. 82).

Van Camp v. Van Camp (1921) 53 Cal.App. 17: See Van Camp Rule (pg. 84).

35. *In re Marriage of Dekker*

Concept:

Equitable apportionment applies when more than minimal community effort increases a separate property business, even if the business is titled to the other spouse and even if the working spouse received market salary during marriage.

Citation:

In re Marriage of Dekker (1993) 17 Cal.App.4th 842.

Quote:

"The community is entitled to the increase in profits attributable to community endeavor."

"Whether or not the community received salary, a court must determine to what extent the increased value of the separate property business is attributable to community effort."

"The Pereira approach is to allocate a fair return to the separate property investment and allocate the balance of the increased value to community property as arising from community efforts."

Explanation:

Gas Turbine Services Corporation was formed during marriage. The stock was issued solely in Barbara's name, and the trial court treated the stock as her separate property. David devoted all of his effort to building the business and was found to be primarily responsible for its success. The business was valued at $927,000. The trial court applied Pereira, credited Barbara with her original $1,000 investment plus a ten percent annual return for a total separate property credit of $1,934, and apportioned the remaining $925,066 to the community. The Court of Appeal affirmed, holding that substantial evidence supported equitable apportionment and that the trial court did not abuse its discretion in choosing Pereira.

Dekker addresses a common argument in business cases: the titled spouse argues that salary paid to the working spouse fully compensates the community. The Court of Appeal rejected that argument. A salary may compensate day to day labor, but it does not necessarily capture the increase in business value attributable to community effort. When community effort creates appreciation beyond the return fairly attributable to separate capital, the community is entitled to that appreciation.

The case also confirms that apportionment does not depend on the working spouse owning the separate property. David increased the value of Barbara's separate property business. That did not defeat the community claim because the relevant inquiry is whether community effort and separate capital combined to create increased value.

Dekker is a strong Pereira case because the capital investment was small and the growth was overwhelmingly tied to David's contacts, expertise, management, and full time effort. The separate estate received a fair return on the initial capital. The balance was community property because it represented the fruits of community labor.

Examples:

Spouse funded, other spouse operated: Wife invests $25,000 of separate property into a corporation titled solely in her name. Husband leaves his job and builds the company through his technical expertise and customer relationships. Even if Husband draws a market salary, the community may still claim the appreciation attributable to his efforts under Dekker.

Salary does not end the analysis: A business pays the working spouse $200,000 per year, but the company's value increases from $50,000 to $5 million because of that spouse's unique efforts during marriage. The titled spouse cannot defeat apportionment merely by proving that salary was fair. The court must determine whether the value increase itself was produced by community effort.

Formula:

Dekker application of Pereira: separate property credit = separate capital contribution + reasonable annual return.

Community component = business value at trial less separate property credit.

Case calculation: $1,000 initial separate investment + ten percent annual return = $1,934 separate property credit. $927,000 business value less $1,934 separate property credit = $925,066 community property component.

Practice point: Do not stop at salary. Compare the business value increase to the return fairly attributable to separate capital. If community labor produced the increase, the excess belongs to the community.

Further Reading:

In re Marriage of Dekker (1993) 17 Cal.App.4th 842: See *In re Marriage of Dekker (pg. 88).*

Pereira v. Pereira (1909) 156 Cal. 1: See Pereira Rule (pg. 82).

Beam v. Bank of America (1971) 6 Cal.3d 12: See *Beam v. Bank of America (pg. 86).*

36. *In re Marriage of Foster*: Medical Practice Goodwill

Concept:

Professional goodwill in a spouse's medical practice may be community property where it exists at dissolution. The value must be established by a legitimate valuation method that measures present value from past results and does not depend on the professional spouse's postmarital efforts.

Citation:

In re Marriage of Foster (1974) 42 Cal.App.3d 577.

Quote:

"In a divorce case it is well established that the goodwill of a husband's professional practice as a sole practitioner is taken into consideration in determining the community property award to the wife."

"Goodwill value may be measured by "any legitimate method of evaluation that measures its present value by taking into account some past result," so long as the evidence "legitimately establishes value.""'

"Community goodwill is a portion of the community value of the professional practice as a going concern on the date of the dissolution of the marriage."

Explanation:

In Foster, the husband was a general medical practitioner. His expert position was that the practice had no goodwill, while the wife's accounting expert valued goodwill at $27,000 based on past receipts and other practice factors. The Court of Appeal affirmed the valuation. It held that community goodwill is part of the value of the professional practice as a going concern. It also held that the value need not be limited to what a willing buyer would pay in an actual sale. A court may use any legitimate method that measures present value by reference to past results, so long as the method does not capitalize the practitioner's future personal labor after dissolution.

Foster is a valuation case. It confirms that goodwill is not ignored merely because it is intangible, difficult to sell, or tied to a professional practice that cannot be transferred in the same manner as an ordinary commercial business. In dissolution, the professional spouse usually keeps the practice and continues to receive the benefit of its established location, reputation, patient base, staff, and history of patronage. Those existing advantages may have community value if they were created during marriage.

The court rejected a narrow market sale test. In many professional practices, the owner may not be selling the practice at all. The relevant question is not only whether a third party would pay a stated amount for goodwill in an arm's length sale. The court may instead consider the practice as a continuing concern and determine whether the professional spouse will retain an intangible benefit that was built during marriage.

At the same time, Foster imposes an important limit. Goodwill cannot be valued by assigning value to postmarital services. The valuation must measure the goodwill that exists at the relevant valuation date, using historical information and other evidence that legitimately shows present value. Expert opinion is admissible, but it is not conclusive. The trier of fact must decide whether the evidence supports the claimed value.

In practical terms, Foster is often cited when one party argues that a professional practice has no goodwill because it depends on the owner's personal skill, or because there is no obvious third party buyer. The response under Foster is that professional dependence does not defeat goodwill as a matter of law. The court must look at the evidence and decide whether a going concern value exists apart from fixed assets and receivables.

Examples:

Medical practice with established patient flow: Husband operates a solo medical practice during a long marriage. The practice has stable patient records, a known location near a hospital, trained staff, and consistent collections. At dissolution, he will continue operating the practice. Even if no sale is planned, the court may find goodwill because Husband will keep the benefit of the practice's existing patronage and reputation.

Valuation based on past receipts: Wife's expert reviews the practice records and concludes that three months of recent collections provide a conservative measure of existing goodwill. Husband argues the number is speculative because no buyer has offered that amount. Under Foster, the absence of an actual buyer is not dispositive. The court may accept the opinion if it is based on historical practice results and other relevant facts.

No automatic goodwill finding: A professional starts a new practice shortly before separation and has no meaningful client or patient base, no stable referral stream, and no demonstrated earnings history. Foster does not require the court to assign goodwill in every case. The spouse claiming goodwill still must prove that goodwill exists and has value.

Formula:

Foster does not establish one mandatory formula. It approves a flexible evidence based approach. Two common goodwill valuation expressions consistent with Foster are:

Collections approach: Goodwill value = selected historical receipts or collections period, adjusted for the specific practice facts.

Excess earnings approach: Goodwill value = (normalized net practice income minus reasonable professional compensation) x selected capitalization factor.

Example of calculation: A medical practice has recent collections of $9,000 per month. An expert concludes that three months of collections fairly captures existing goodwill because the practice has stable patient patronage and no reliable sale market. The indicated goodwill value is $9,000 x 3 = $27,000. If the practice is community property, the nonprofessional spouse's one half share of that goodwill component is $13,500, subject to the court's complete division of all community assets and debts.

Limit on formula use: A formula must not value the professional spouse's future personal labor after separation or dissolution. It should use past results to identify the goodwill that exists at the valuation date.

Further Reading:

In re Marriage of Fortier (1973) 34 Cal.App.3d 384: Fortier is an earlier professional goodwill case involving medical practice goodwill. Foster read Fortier as allowing sale evidence to be persuasive, but not exclusive, evidence of value.

Golden v. Golden (1969) 270 Cal.App.2d 401: Golden supplied the policy rationale used in Foster. In a marital dissolution, the professional spouse continues the practice, while the nonprofessional spouse is effectively bought out of an intangible value built during marriage.

In re Marriage of Lopez (1974) 38 Cal.App.3d 93: See *In re Marriage of Lopez*: Law Practice Goodwill (pg. 93).

37. *In re Marriage of Lopez*: Law Practice Goodwill

Concept:

When the existence or value of professional goodwill is raised in a dissolution case, the court must make specific findings as to goodwill and related practice assets. The right to practice a profession is personal, but the value of the professional practice as a going concern may be community property.

Citation:

In re Marriage of Lopez (1974) 38 Cal.App.3d 93.

Quote:

"In determining the value of a law practice or interest therein, the trial court should determine the existence and value of the following: (a) fixed assets, which we deem to include cash, furniture, equipment, supplies and law library; (b) other assets, including properly aged accounts receivable, costs advanced with due regard for their collectability; work in progress partially completed but not billed as a receivable, and work completed but not billed; (c) goodwill of the practitioner in his law business as a going concern; and (d) liabilities of the practitioner related to his business."

"Finally, in light of such findings, the trial court should determine the value of the "goodwill," if any, in husband's law partnership business."

Explanation:

In Lopez, the husband was an attorney whose law practice and partnership interests grew substantially during marriage. The trial court treated certain law practice interests and proceeds as the husband's separate property and failed to value accounts receivable, goodwill, and work in progress. The Court of Appeal reversed. It held that the value of a professional practice at dissolution may be community property, and that the trial court must make specific findings on the existence and value of professional goodwill when the issue is raised. The court cautioned that expected future earnings are not the same as goodwill and should not be used as the basis for valuing postmarital efforts.

Lopez is the major analytical roadmap for professional goodwill. It distinguishes the licensed professional's personal right to practice from the economic value of an established professional business. A law license is not community property. However, the practice that the attorney built during marriage, including its receivables, work in progress, fixed assets, and goodwill, may have divisible community value.

The case emphasizes that goodwill is an economic concept, not merely an accounting label. It can exist when the professional business has expected patronage, reputation, referral relationships, or other advantages that produce value beyond identified tangible assets. But the court also warned that not every professional practice necessarily has goodwill, and that the valuation may not be precise in every case.

Lopez requires careful findings. The trial court must determine whether goodwill exists and, if it exists, what value should be assigned. The court also identified factors that may affect professional goodwill, including the practitioner's age, health, past demonstrated earning power, reputation for skill and judgment, comparative professional success, and the nature and duration of the professional business.

The case is also important for date and characterization issues. In modern practice, *Family Code section 2552* generally values assets and liabilities as near as practicable to trial unless the court selects another date for good cause. At the same time, postseparation earnings and accumulations are generally separate property under *Family Code section 771*. When valuing goodwill, the court must avoid converting future separate labor into a community asset.

Examples:

Established law practice: Husband operated a law firm during a long marriage. The firm has fixed assets, collectable receivables, unbilled work in progress, an established referral network, and a history of substantial earnings. Wife raises goodwill at trial. Under Lopez, the court should not simply award the law practice to Husband without valuation. It must make findings on the practice components, including goodwill if the evidence supports it.

Goodwill factors: A forensic accountant testifies that the attorney has a strong local reputation, long standing client relationships, and repeat referral sources. Another expert argues that the practice depends entirely on the attorney's future work. Lopez allows the court to consider both points. Reputation and demonstrated past earning power can support goodwill, but the valuation must not merely capitalize future labor.

Separate and community components: Wife opened a professional practice before marriage but expanded it substantially through community efforts during marriage. Lopez allows the court to examine whether goodwill is separate, community, or mixed. The analysis depends on when the goodwill was created, what assets existed at marriage, and what portion is attributable to community labor and accumulations.

Formula:

Lopez does not impose one goodwill formula. It does provide a practical structure for valuing a professional practice:

Professional practice net value = fixed assets + other assets + professional goodwill minus practice liabilities.

Fixed assets may include cash, furniture, equipment, supplies, and a professional library. Other assets may include properly aged accounts receivable, costs advanced, work in progress partially completed but not billed, and completed work not yet billed. Goodwill is valued separately if the evidence shows that it exists. Liabilities related to the professional business are then deducted.

Example of calculation: A law practice has $25,000 in fixed assets, $80,000 in collectable receivables, $20,000 in work in progress, $100,000 in professional goodwill, and $35,000 in practice liabilities. The net practice value is $25,000 + $80,000 + $20,000 + $100,000 minus $35,000 = $190,000. If the entire practice value is community property, each spouse's equal division share is $95,000, usually accomplished through an award of the practice to the attorney spouse and an offsetting equalization payment or asset allocation.

Limit on formula use: The formula identifies the assets to be valued. It does not answer whether goodwill exists, whether goodwill is separate or community, or which valuation date should be used. Those questions depend on evidence and on the court's findings.

Further Reading:

Todd v. Todd (1969) 272 Cal.App.2d 786: Todd supports the distinction between the personal right to practice law and the community value of the practice existing at dissolution.

Brawman v. Brawman (1962) 199 Cal.App.2d 876: Brawman framed the nonprofessional spouse as a silent partner being bought out of a going professional business.

In re Marriage of Foster (1974) 42 Cal.App.3d 577: See *In re Marriage of Foster*: Medical Practice Goodwill (pg. 90).

38. *In re Marriage of Fonstein*: Law Partnership Interest and Tax Discounting

Concept:

A professional partnership interest acquired during marriage is a community asset if it has present value. A court may use enforceable withdrawal or buyout rights to value that interest, but it should not reduce the value for speculative future taxes when no withdrawal, sale, or liquidation is required or intended.

Citation:

In re Marriage of Fonstein (1976) 17 Cal.3d 738.

Quote:

"Applying these principles to the case at bench, we first observe that the tax obligations which Harold contends should be charged against the community property of this marriage will be incurred, if at all, only after dissolution of the marriage and division of the community property."

"While the parties assumed that the partnership would be valued on the basis of a withdrawal value, the fact remains that Harold was not withdrawing and no tax liability was incurred during marriage."

"there is no indication in the record that Harold is withdrawing, must withdraw, or intends to withdraw from his firm in order to obtain the cash with which to pay Sarane her share of the community property"

Explanation:

In Fonstein, the husband became a partner in a law firm during marriage. The partnership agreement gave him an equity percentage and a contractual payment right upon voluntary withdrawal. The trial court valued the interest by calculating the present value of the withdrawal payments, but then reduced that value for estimated future income taxes that might be incurred if the husband later withdrew. The California Supreme Court reversed the tax discount. Because the husband was not withdrawing and did not have to withdraw to satisfy the property division, the tax liability was speculative and should not have been charged against the community before division.

Fonstein is not a pure goodwill formula case, but it is central to professional goodwill and professional practice valuation because the asset was a law partnership interest. The case confirms that a professional partner's contractual rights can be valued as property in dissolution, even though the partner will likely retain the interest rather than sell or liquidate it.

The partnership agreement supplied a valuation mechanism. It assigned the husband an equity percentage and specified payments if he voluntarily withdrew. The trial court used that agreement to estimate the present value of the interest. The Supreme Court did not reject the use of the partnership agreement as a valuation source. The problem was the additional reduction for hypothetical taxes.

Fonstein establishes a practical rule for tax effects. Family courts should not reduce the value of a community asset for potential taxes that may never be incurred, especially where the decision to trigger the tax will be made later by the spouse who receives the asset as separate property after division. Tax consequences may be considered when they are immediate, required, and reasonably certain. Speculative future taxes should not be used to reduce the other spouse's share.

In professional goodwill disputes, Fonstein helps prevent undervaluation of a professional interest by assuming a liquidation event that is not actually occurring. The professional spouse may receive the ongoing practice or partnership interest; the nonprofessional spouse is entitled to an equal division based on present value, not on a hypothetical future sale selected only to reduce value.

Examples:

Law partnership withdrawal right: Husband is a law partner and the partnership agreement provides a formula for payment if he withdraws. At dissolution, he will remain with the firm. The court may consider the contractual withdrawal formula as evidence of present value, but it should not automatically assume that Husband will withdraw.

Speculative tax discount: The valuation expert calculates a $500,000 present value for Husband's partnership interest, then proposes a $180,000 tax discount because a withdrawal might create taxable income someday. Under Fonstein, the discount should be rejected unless a taxable transaction is required, imminent, and sufficiently certain. The future tax decision belongs to Husband after division, and the benefit of the withdrawal payments would also belong to him.

(1) Required sale distinguished: If a court orders an immediate sale of an asset or if a transaction triggering tax is unavoidable as part of the division, tax effects may be relevant. Fonstein does not prohibit consideration of real tax liabilities. It prohibits speculative reductions based on events that may not occur.

Formula:

Fonstein involved a contractual withdrawal formula rather than a universal goodwill formula. The partnership agreement formula described in the case can be stated generally as:

Base withdrawal value = (1/2 x 3 x average annual firm earnings for the preceding three years x partner equity percentage) + partner capital account.

Present value = present value of the expected installment stream, if the agreement pays the amount over time.

Tax treatment under Fonstein: Present value should not be reduced for hypothetical future taxes unless the tax is immediate, fixed, and tied to a required transaction.

Example of calculation: A partnership agreement gives Wife a 10 percent equity percentage. The firm's average annual earnings for the prior three years are $2,000,000, and Wife's capital account is $60,000. The base withdrawal value is 1/2 x 3 x $2,000,000 x 10 percent + $60,000 = $360,000. If the agreement requires payment over several years, an expert may discount the stream to present value. If the present value is $320,000, that is the value used for division unless a real, nonspeculative tax liability must be accounted for.

Equal division effect: If the $320,000 value is entirely community property and the professional spouse retains the partnership interest, the other spouse is generally entitled to $160,000 in value through other assets, an equalization payment, or another court approved allocation.

Further Reading:

Weinberg v. Weinberg (1967) 67 Cal.2d 557: Weinberg supplied the broader rule that courts need not speculate about tax consequences that may or may not arise after the community property division.

In re Marriage of Lopez (1974) 38 Cal.App.3d 93: See *In re Marriage of Lopez*: Law Practice Goodwill (pg. 93).

In re Marriage of Fenton (1982) 134 Cal.App.3d 451: Later cases have cited Lopez and Fonstein when addressing professional goodwill and professional practice valuation methods.

39. *In re Marriage of Walrath*: *Section 2640* Tracing Through Later Community Assets

Concept:

A spouse who uses separate property to acquire community property has a statutory reimbursement right under *Family Code section 2640*, unless the spouse made a written waiver or signed a writing that has the effect of a waiver. Walrath holds that the reimbursement right can carry through to later-acquired community assets when the original separate property contribution can be traced into those assets.

Citation:

In re Marriage of Walrath (1998) 17 Cal.4th 907.

Quote:

"In the absence of a written waiver, a spouse who contributes separate property to a community property acquisition is reimbursed upon dissolution of the marriage."

"Therefore, it seems unlikely that the Legislature intended a contributing spouse would lose the right to reimbursement merely because the specific property to which the money was contributed was refinanced. Rather, the right to reimbursement should follow the assets to which the contribution can be traced."

"The community is entitled to any appreciation in these assets above the amount necessary to reimburse the parties for their separate property contributions to the Lucerne, Utah, and Nevada properties, and the joint bank account."

Explanation:

In Walrath, the husband and wife made separate property contributions to a community property residence. The residence was later refinanced, and the proceeds of that loan were used to acquire or improve other community assets, including real property and a bank account. The Court of Appeal limited the reimbursement right to the original property. The California Supreme Court reversed. It held that the phrase "the property" in *Family Code section 2640* includes community property subsequently acquired with proceeds traceable to the original contribution. The contributing spouse is limited to reimbursement of the separate property contribution itself, without interest or appreciation, and the community receives any appreciation above the amount required to reimburse traceable separate property contributions. The court also recognized that, where the property has insufficient net value to reimburse all contributing spouses fully, reimbursement should be allocated proportionately.

Walrath is one of the most important statutory reimbursement cases because it explains the scope of the *Family Code section 2640* right after the original asset has changed form. The reimbursement statute was enacted to change the preexisting Lucas rule, under which a spouse who placed separate property into a community asset or joint title asset could be treated as having made a gift absent an agreement preserving the separate contribution. *Section 2640* replaced that result with a statutory rule: the contribution is preserved unless the right is waived in writing or by a writing having the effect of waiver.

The central practical problem in Walrath was tracing. The husband did not simply contribute separate property to an asset that still existed in the same form at dissolution. Instead, the original community residence was refinanced, and the loan proceeds were moved into other community assets. The Supreme Court held that the reimbursement right was not destroyed by the refinance. If the separate property contribution can be traced into later community property, the reimbursement right follows the traceable value.

The case also imposes limits. A spouse cannot randomly seek reimbursement from any asset merely because the separate property contribution touched some part of the community estate. The claim must be traced. The reimbursement is also not a proportional ownership claim in the appreciation of the later asset. It is a dollar reimbursement for the separate property contribution, subject to the net value of the property at division.

In practice, Walrath is used when a spouse made a separate property down payment, principal paydown, or improvement contribution to a community asset, and the asset was later sold, refinanced, exchanged, or converted into other property. The case supports a carry-through claim, but only to the extent the evidence can connect the original contribution to the property being divided.

Examples:

Residence refinanced into a rental property: Husband contributes $150,000 of separate property toward a community residence. During marriage, the residence is refinanced and $100,000 of loan proceeds is used as the down payment on a community rental property. At dissolution, Husband may trace the separate property component into the rental property and seek a *Family Code section 2640* reimbursement from that asset to the extent the tracing and net value requirements are satisfied.

Multiple assets and a partial loss: Wife contributes $80,000 of separate property and Husband contributes $20,000 of separate property to a community residence. Later, loan proceeds from that residence are split between a vacant lot and a bank account. If the vacant lot has insufficient equity at division to reimburse both contributions allocated to it, the available equity should be divided proportionately between the competing reimbursement claims. The community receives appreciation only after the traceable separate property contributions are reimbursed.

No tracing into unrelated property: A spouse cannot claim reimbursement from an unrelated community brokerage account merely because the spouse once made a separate property contribution to the family residence. Walrath requires a traceable connection between the original separate property contribution and the later asset from which reimbursement is sought.

Written waiver: If the contributing spouse signs a written agreement expressly waiving *Family Code section 2640* reimbursement, the statutory claim can be defeated. A deed or title document that changes ownership may not, by itself, waive reimbursement unless it also satisfies the statutory waiver requirement.

Formula:

Basic *Family Code section 2640* reimbursement: Reimbursement = lesser of (traceable eligible separate property contributions) or (net value of the property at division).

Eligible contributions include down payments, payments for improvements, and payments that reduce principal on a loan used to finance the purchase or improvement of the property. Eligible contributions do not include interest, maintenance, insurance, or taxes. The reimbursement is dollar-for-dollar only. It does not include interest, appreciation, or inflation adjustment.

Walrath carry-through tracing formula: Traceable reimbursement in later asset = (separate property contribution to original asset / equity in original asset when proceeds were generated) x proceeds invested in the later asset.

Example of carry-through calculation: Husband contributes $120,000 of separate property to a community residence. At refinance, the residence has $200,000 of equity. Husband's contribution represents 60 percent of the equity. The refinance generates $50,000 of proceeds used to buy a community rental property. The traceable reimbursement claim in the rental property is $30,000 ($120,000 / $200,000 x $50,000). If the rental property has at least $30,000 of net value at division, Husband receives a $30,000 reimbursement before the remaining value is divided. If the rental property has only $20,000 of net value, the reimbursement is capped at $20,000 for that asset.

Multiple contribution example: Husband's separate property contribution is 70 percent of the traceable equity and Wife's separate property contribution is 20 percent. If $40,000 of refinance proceeds is invested in a later asset, Husband's traceable reimbursement is $28,000 and Wife's traceable reimbursement is $8,000. The remaining value, if any, belongs to the community and is divided under the usual community property rules.

Further Reading:

Family Code section 2640: The statute defines reimbursable contributions as down payments, payments for improvements, and payments that reduce principal on a loan used to finance the purchase or improvement of property. It excludes interest, maintenance, insurance, and taxes. Reimbursement is without interest or adjustment for changes in monetary value and cannot exceed the net value of the property at division.

In re Marriage of Fabian (1986) 41 Cal.3d 440: Fabian explains the statutory shift from the old gift presumption to a preservation of separate property reimbursement rights for qualifying contributions, subject to constitutional limits on retroactive application.

In re Marriage of Lucas (1980) 27 Cal.3d 808: See Lucas Rule (pg. 5).

40. *In re Marriage of Benson*: Strict Writing Requirements and Reimbursement Waiver Context

Concept:

A statutory reimbursement claim often turns on whether a spouse validly changed property character or validly waived the reimbursement right. Benson holds that *Family Code section 852* requires a written express declaration for a transmutation, and that oral agreements, reliance, or part performance cannot substitute for the required writing. In reimbursement practice, Benson is a gatekeeping case: before treating a reimbursement right as lost, the court must require the writing that the Family Code demands.

Citation:

In re Marriage of Benson (2005) 36 Cal.4th 1096.

Quote:

"*Family Code section 852*, subdivision (a) (*section 852 (a)*) provides that a "transmutation," or an interspousal transaction changing the character of community or separate property (id. at *§ 850*), "is not valid unless made in writing by an express declaration" approved by the adversely affected spouse."

"Even assuming Husband's transfer of the deed constituted part performance of Wife's promise to transmute the retirement accounts, *section 852 (a)* requires such agreements to be both written and express, and seeks to prevent transmutations under circumstances like those present here."

"By insisting upon a special writing expressly changing the character of the disputed property, MacDonald all but decided that *section 852 (a)* is not satisfied where no such writing exists at all."

Explanation:

In Benson, Husband claimed that he deeded his community property interest in the family residence to Wife's trust because Wife orally promised to waive her community property interest in Husband's retirement accounts. Wife never signed a writing changing the retirement accounts to Husband's separate property. The lower courts accepted Husband's part performance theory. The California Supreme Court reversed. It held that *Family Code section 852* does not operate like a general statute of frauds with an implied part performance exception. A valid transmutation requires a writing with an express declaration made, joined in, consented to, or accepted by the spouse whose interest is adversely affected. Husband's deed concerning the residence did not substitute for Wife's missing written express declaration concerning the retirement accounts.

Benson is not a *Family Code section 2640* computation case. It is included in a statutory reimbursement outline because reimbursement disputes frequently depend on the same writing principles. A party may argue that a spouse waived reimbursement, made a gift, or agreed to exchange one property right for another. Benson makes clear that a court should not enforce an oral marital property exchange when the Family Code requires a written express declaration.

The case is especially important when parties combine estate planning, title transfers, deeds, trusts, retirement accounts, and alleged oral agreements. A spouse may sign a deed affecting one asset, but that act does not prove a separate oral agreement changing the character of another asset. The writing must identify the property interest being changed and must show, on its face, that the adversely affected spouse understood and accepted the change.

For statutory reimbursement, the lesson is direct. Under *Family Code section 2640*, reimbursement generally remains available unless the statutory exception is satisfied. For contributions to community property, the exception is a written waiver or a writing having the effect of a waiver. For contributions to the other spouse's separate property estate under current *section 2640*, subdivision (c), the statute requires attention to whether there has been a valid written transmutation or a written waiver. Benson reinforces that courts should not infer those consequences from oral testimony, marital expectations, or conduct alone.

In practice, Benson supports a disciplined sequence. First, characterize the property. Second, identify any alleged transmutation or waiver. Third, test the writing. Fourth, if no valid writing changes the result, apply the relevant reimbursement statute or community property division rule. This sequencing prevents a party from defeating statutory reimbursement by describing an unwritten bargain after the fact.

Examples:

Oral waiver of reimbursement: Wife uses $90,000 of inheritance to make the down payment on a community residence. At dissolution, Husband testifies that Wife orally said she would not ask for reimbursement. There is no writing. Benson supports rejecting the oral waiver theory. If Wife traces the inheritance contribution and no valid written waiver exists, the court should analyze reimbursement under *Family Code section 2640*.

Property exchange involving different assets: Husband deeds his interest in a residence to Wife's trust. He later claims Wife orally agreed to give up her community interest in his retirement accounts in exchange. Under Benson, Husband's deed does not satisfy the written express declaration requirement for Wife's alleged waiver or transmutation of the retirement accounts.

Estate planning transfer: A spouse signs estate planning documents moving property into a trust. The documents may affect title or estate planning rights, but they should not be assumed to waive *Family Code section 2640* reimbursement unless the writing satisfies the applicable transmutation or waiver requirements.

Clear written waiver: A marital agreement states that Husband knowingly waives any *Family Code section 2640* reimbursement for his separate property contributions to a specifically identified residence, and Husband signs the agreement. Benson does not prevent enforcement of a proper writing. Its rule prevents reliance on unwritten or implied agreements.

Formula:

Benson does not create a dollar formula. It creates a writing prerequisite for property character changes that can determine whether a statutory reimbursement formula is reached.

Benson writing checklist: Identify the property affected; identify the spouse whose interest would be reduced; locate the writing; confirm that the writing contains an express declaration changing character or ownership; confirm that the adversely affected spouse made, joined in, consented to, or accepted the writing; reject oral agreements or part performance as substitutes.

If the writing fails and the claim is a contribution to community property, apply *Family Code section 2640*, subdivision (b): Reimbursement = lesser of (traceable eligible separate property contributions) or (net value of the community property at division), without interest or appreciation.

If the claim involves separate property contributions to the other spouse's separate property estate, analyze *Family Code section 2640*, subdivision (c): Reimbursement is available unless the statutory exception applies, including a valid written transmutation or written waiver. Benson is relevant because the alleged transmutation must satisfy the Family Code writing requirement.

Example of calculation after Benson analysis: Wife contributes $90,000 of traceable inheritance funds to acquire a community residence. Husband claims Wife orally waived reimbursement, but there is no writing. The oral waiver fails. If the residence has $300,000 of net value at division, Wife receives a $90,000 reimbursement first. The remaining $210,000 is divided as community property, giving each spouse $105,000. Wife's total allocation from the residence is $195,000 and Husband's allocation is $105,000.

Further Reading:

Estate of MacDonald (1990) 51 Cal.3d 262: See MacDonald Express Declaration Test (pg. 8).

Family Code section 852: *Section 852* requires a writing with an express declaration made, joined in, consented to, or accepted by the spouse whose interest is adversely affected. It is the primary statutory safeguard against informal or ambiguous marital property transmutations.

Family Code section 2640: *Section 2640* creates the reimbursement remedy. In a reimbursement dispute, Benson and *section 852* should be considered when the opposing party claims that the reimbursement right was waived, that the property was transmuted, or that conduct alone changed the legal result.

In re Marriage of Valli (2014) 58 Cal.4th 1396: See *In re Marriage of Valli (pg. 10).*

41. Brown Rights

Concept:

"Brown Rights" refers to the community property interest in a spouse's retirement benefits earned during marriage. In essence, Brown Rights ensure that both spouses have an equal claim to the portion of retirement pension benefits that accrued during the marriage, even if those benefits were not yet vested or payable at the time of divorce.

Citation:

In re Marriage of Brown (1976) 15 Cal.3d 838

Quote:

"Pension rights, whether or not vested, represent a property interest; to the extent that such rights derive from employment during coverture, they comprise a community asset subject to division in a dissolution proceeding."

"We have concluded, however, that the French court's characterization of nonvested pension rights as expectancies errs."

"Fortunately we can appropriately reflect the realistic situation by recognizing that the husband's pension rights, a contingent interest, whether vested or not vested, comprise a property interest of the community and that the wife may properly share in it."

Explanation:

This case overturned prior law and confirmed that retirement benefits (vested or not) earned during marriage are community property subject to division. Relevant statutes include *former Civil Code § 4800* (now *Family Code § 2550*), which requires equal division of community property, and *Family Code § 2610*, which governs division of retirement plan benefits in divorce.

Under Brown Rights, a spouse's pension or retirement benefits are treated as community property to the extent they were earned during the marriage. This means that both vested and unvested retirement benefits accumulated while married are viewed as a form of deferred compensation earned by the couple's joint efforts. Before Brown, non-vested pensions were seen as mere "expectancies" with no community property value. The Brown decision changed that by recognizing that even if a retirement benefit is contingent (for example, the employee must continue working or survive to a certain date), the portion attributable to years of service during the marriage is a valuable property interest of the community. In practical terms, Brown Rights prevent one spouse from walking away with the entire pension; instead, the part of the benefit earned during marriage belongs equally to both. Courts typically will divide the community portion of the retirement benefits between the spouses (often by a court order, such as a Qualified Domestic Relations Order "QDRO" for plans), so that each receives their fair share when the benefits are paid. If the benefit is not yet payable (e.g. the pension hasn't vested or the employee is not retired), the court can reserve jurisdiction and ensure that when the benefit does mature in the future, the non-employee spouse will obtain their portion. Overall, Brown Rights promote a fair division of one of the most significant assets in many marriages, the retirement pension, by acknowledging that both partners contributed to its acquisition.

Examples:

Vested Pension: Husband and Wife are married for 20 years, during which Husband works for XYZ Company and earns a pension. By the time of divorce, Husband's pension is vested and will pay $2,000 per month at retirement. Under Brown Rights, the portion of that pension earned during the 20-year marriage is community property. If Husband worked a total of 30 years before retiring, the community portion is 20/30 (two-thirds) of the pension. That means $1,333 per month is considered community property, and each spouse will ultimately receive half of that ($666 per month each). The remaining one-third of the pension is Husband's separate property (earned outside the marriage). This division reflects that the pension was in large part earned by the couple's joint efforts during marriage.

Unvested Pension: Wife works for ABC Corp for 5 years during the marriage, participating in a retirement plan that requires 10 years of service to vest. At the time of divorce, Wife's pension is not yet vested. Under the Brown Rights principle, Wife's pension rights, though unvested and not guaranteed, are still a form of property partly owned by the community. The court will acknowledge the community's interest in the pension earned during those 5 married years.

The court might not split anything immediately (since there's no current payout), but it will typically reserve jurisdiction. If Wife continues working and eventually vests in the pension (say she works a total of 10 years to vest, and perhaps 20 years total before retiring), the portion of the pension attributable to the 5 years of marriage will be divided. For instance, if she retires after 20 years total, the fraction of the pension that is community property would be 5/20 (one-quarter). The community would get one-quarter of each pension payment, and Wife and Husband would each receive half of that quarter (meaning Husband gets 12.5% of each payment as his share). If Wife never reaches 10 years and the pension never vests, then unfortunately the community interest has no payout, but the key is that the *right* was recognized at divorce. This example shows that even an unvested, uncertain pension is taken into account and, if it later matures, the spouse who helped during those working years will share in the benefit.

Formula:

Identify the marital service period: Determine the length of time the employed spouse participated in the retirement plan while married (from the date of marriage to the date of separation). This is often measured in years or months of service during the marriage.

Identify the total service period: Determine the total length of service credited toward the retirement benefit (usually from the start of employment to the date of retirement or benefit vesting). This is the total time over which the pension was earned.

Calculate the time-rule fraction: Divide the marital service period by the total service period. This gives a fraction (or percentage) representing the portion of the retirement benefit earned during the marriage. (For example, if 10 years of service were during marriage out of 30 total years of service, the fraction is 10/30 or 33.3%.)

Apply the fraction to the benefit: Multiply this fraction by the total value of the retirement benefit (e.g. the monthly pension amount or lump sum value). The result is the community property portion of the benefit. Using the above example, if the pension pays $3,000 per month, one-third of that ($1,000) is the community portion.

Divide the community portion between the spouses: Since community property is generally split 50/50, each spouse would receive half of the community portion of the benefit. In the example, each spouse would be entitled to $500 per month (half of the $1,000 community portion). The remaining portion of the benefit is the employed spouse's separate property (earned outside the marriage).

This pro-rata division is commonly known as the "time rule" or "Brown formula." It provides a fair and straightforward way to calculate each spouse's share of a pension. By basing the division on the ratio of marital service to total service, the formula ensures that only the part of the retirement benefit earned during the marriage is treated as community property. Brown Rights and the time rule work together to protect both spouses' interests: the employed spouse keeps the part of the pension earned outside the marriage, and the non-employed spouse obtains an equal share of the portion earned together during the marriage. The result is an equitable division that honors California's community property principles.

Further Reading:

In re Marriage of Judd (1977) 68 Cal.App.3d 515. This appellate decision applied the Brown principle and outlined the "time rule" to apportion a pension. The court ruled that the community interest in a retirement plan should be proportional to the amount of service time that occurred during the marriage. In Judd, the formula was explicitly stated: take the number of years (or months) the employed spouse worked during marriage, divide it by the total years worked for that employer, and that fraction of the pension benefits is community property. The trial court on remand was instructed to award the wife one-half of that community portion. Judd solidified the practice of using a pro-rata time formula to calculate each spouse's share of a pension.

In re Marriage of Stenquist (1978) 21 Cal.3d 779. Stenquist held, under California community-property principles, that a service member could not defeat the community's earned retirement interest merely by electing a disability-labeled military pension in place of ordinary longevity retirement pay; the portion equivalent to earned retirement was treated as community property, while the excess attributable to disability was treated separately. This discussion must include a federal preemption limitation. Later United States Supreme Court authority controls when federal military-retirement law applies: *Mansell v. Mansell* (1989) 490 U.S. 581 holds that state courts may not treat military retired pay waived to receive veterans' disability benefits as divisible community property, and *Howell v. Howell* (2017) 581 U.S. 214 holds that a state court may not order a veteran to indemnify a former spouse for the loss caused by the veteran's postjudgment waiver of retirement pay to receive service-connected disability benefits. Accordingly, Stenquist remains useful for the California characterization principle that a disability label is not automatically controlling, but it cannot be used to divide, restore, or indemnify federally protected military retired pay that has been waived to receive VA disability benefits.

In re Marriage of Gillmore (1981) 29 Cal.3d 418: See Gillmore Election (pg. 71).

In re Marriage of Skaden (1977) 19 Cal.3d 679: See *In re Marriage of Skaden*: Termination Benefits as Deferred Compensation (pg. 80).

In re Marriage of Lehman (1998) 18 Cal.4th 169: See *In re Marriage of Lehman*: Enhanced Retirement Benefits (pg. 73).

42. Gavron Warning

Concept:

Warning given to a spouse receiving support that they must become self-sufficient.

Citation:

In re Marriage of Gavron (1988) 203 Cal.App.3d 705.

Quote:

"Inherent in the concept that the supported spouse's failure to at least make good-faith efforts to become self-sufficient can constitute a change in circumstances which could warrant a modification in spousal support is the premise that the supported spouse be made aware of the obligation to become self-supporting."

"there should have been some reasonable advance warning"

Explanation:

A Gavron Warning is a notice given by a California family court to a spouse receiving spousal support (alimony) that they are expected to become self-supporting within a reasonable period of time. This concept originated from the case Marriage of Gavron, in which the court held that a supported spouse should be given fair warning that they are expected to seek employment or vocational training. The purpose of a Gavron Warning is to put the supported spouse on notice that spousal support is not intended to last indefinitely. It exists because California law emphasizes that each party must make good-faith efforts to become self-sufficient. In fact, *Family Code § 4320* includes the legislative goal that a supported party should become self-supporting within a reasonable period (generally, one-half the length of the marriage unless the marriage is long-term). By giving a Gavron Warning, the court makes its expectation clear: after a period of support, the recipient should prepare to meet their own financial needs. This warning significantly affects spousal support orders. If the supported spouse fails to make reasonable efforts to find work or gain skills after being warned, the court may later reduce or terminate support due to that non-compliance. On the other hand, if no Gavron Warning was given, a supported spouse can argue they had no notice that they needed to become self-sufficient, and courts may be more hesitant to cut off support abruptly. *Family Code § 4330(b)* now explicitly permits judges to give this advisory in support orders (using "may advise"), and even notes that in a marriage of long duration (generally 10+ years, per *§ 4336*) the court might decide a Gavron Warning is inadvisable. In practice, Gavron Warnings are commonly included in final divorce judgments or spousal support orders to encourage the supported spouse to work toward independence, while balancing fairness based on the marriage's circumstances (e.g. age, health, and skills of the supported spouse). The Gavron Warning thus serves as an important tool to ensure that spousal support achieves its goal of temporary assistance rather than a permanent subsidy.

Examples:

Mid-Length Marriage Example: At the conclusion of a 7-year marriage, the court orders Husband to pay Wife spousal support for a number of years. The judge issues a Gavron Warning, advising Wife that she should use the support period to obtain employment or training. Five years later, Husband files to modify support. If Wife has made little to no effort to become self-supporting (for example, not seeking a job or any education), the court can find that she ignored the Gavron Warning. As a consequence of non-compliance, the court may terminate or sharply reduce her spousal support, since she was clearly warned that support was not intended to continue indefinitely.

Long-Term Marriage Example: In a divorce after a 20-year marriage, the supported spouse is in her late 50s with limited work history. The court might decide not to give a Gavron Warning, recognizing that expecting her to become fully self-sufficient may be unrealistic. Instead, the judgment may provide for ongoing support subject to future review. By contrast, if a Gavron Warning had been issued in such a case and the spouse failed to even attempt any employment over several years, the supporting spouse could later argue for a reduction by pointing to that warning. However, because no warning was given (deemed "inadvisable" due to the long duration and the spouse's age), the supported spouse would have a stronger argument that support should continue. This example shows how courts use discretion: Gavron Warnings are typically given when the supported party is reasonably capable of becoming self-supporting, and they are withheld when circumstances make self-sufficiency an unlikely or unfair expectation.

Formula:

When to include a Gavron Warning: Judges should consider giving a Gavron Warning whenever an order for spousal support is made and the supported spouse is capable of becoming at least partially self-supporting. This is especially true in short-to-medium length marriages (e.g. under 10 years) or any case where the supported party has marketable skills, education, or the ability to acquire them. Including the warning in the divorce judgment or support order puts the expectation on record.

Tailor it to the circumstances: The decision to issue a Gavron Warning should take into account the specific facts required by *Family Code § 4320*, such as the supported spouse's age, health, job skills, work history, and the length of the marriage. For example, if the supported spouse is young, educated, or has recent work experience, a Gavron Warning is likely appropriate. If the supported spouse is older or the marriage is a "long duration" (10+ years), the court may decide that giving a Gavron Warning is inadvisable or unnecessary because immediate self-sufficiency might be unrealistic. In such cases, the warning is optional, not mandatory.

Best practice in judgments: When a Gavron Warning is deemed appropriate, it should be explicitly written into the judgment or order (or stated on the record) so that there is a clear documentation that the supported party has been advised to become self-supporting. This creates a timeline for reasonable efforts. A typical Gavron Warning clause might state: "The supported spouse is expected to make reasonable good-faith efforts to become self-supporting. Failure to do so may be considered a basis for modifying or terminating support in the future." By following this checklist, considering the marriage length, the supported spouse's capacity, and the fairness of imposing a self-sufficiency requirement, attorneys and judges can determine when a Gavron

Warning is appropriate and include it to protect the supporting party's rights while still being fair to the supported party.

Further Reading:

Family Code § 4330(b) (codifying the Gavron rule; see also *Family Code §§ 4320* & 4336).

In re Marriage of Schmir (2005) 134 Cal.App.4th 43: Fourteen years after divorce, a husband sought to terminate spousal support even though the couple's agreement had no end-date or Gavron warning. The trial court reduced support to $0, but the appellate court reversed. It held that imputing income or ending support was an abuse of discretion without giving the wife reasonable advance notice and time to become employed. In other words, the supported spouse must first be given a Gavron Warning (or equivalent notice) and an opportunity to achieve self-sufficiency before support is cut off for that reason.

In re Marriage of Shaughnessy (2006) 139 Cal.App.4th 1225: Here, the original support order assumed the wife would undergo retraining to increase her earning capacity. Three years later, she had done little to improve her employability. The court treated her failure to diligently pursue retraining as a "change in circumstances" warranting a modification of spousal support. Because there was an expectation (effectively a warning) in the initial order that she become self-supporting, her inaction justified the trial court reducing her support after those three years.

In re Marriage of Schaffer (1999) 69 Cal.App.4th 801: In this case (sometimes referred to as Schaffer II), a wife had repeatedly sought and obtained extensions of spousal support over many years. Eventually, the family court reduced support to zero at a modification hearing, essentially ending the support. The Court of Appeal upheld this decision, noting there was no abuse of discretion in considering the wife's long history of support and lack of sufficient progress toward self-sufficiency. Implicitly, over the years the wife had been given opportunities and warnings to become self-supporting, so the final termination was deemed fair.

In re Marriage of McLain (2017) 7 Cal.App.5th 262: This more recent case illustrates when a Gavron Warning may be declined. The parties divorced after a 13-year marriage, and both were already retired in their 60s. The trial court awarded the wife spousal support but specifically refused to issue a Gavron Warning, recognizing that at her age (66) and retired status, it was not reasonable to expect her to rejoin the workforce. The husband argued that she should be compelled to find work, but the court (and the Court of Appeal) disagreed, effectively ruling that a supported spouse's right to retire could outweigh the self-sufficiency goal. McLain shows that judges have discretion not to give a Gavron Warning in cases where the supported spouse's age or health makes the self-support expectation impractical.

43. Jeffries Credits

Credits given when one spouse remains in the family home post-separation.

Concept:

The Jeffries Credit is a shorthand term used in California family law for the court's process of reconciling two competing claims that often arise when one spouse remains in the family residence after the date of separation: the Epstein Credit (for paying the mortgage) and the Watts Charge (for exclusive use).

The Jeffries concept holds that the spouse who exclusively occupies the community residence and pays the associated monthly expenses (mortgage, taxes, insurance) is generally not entitled to an Epstein reimbursement unless the total monthly payments substantially exceed the reasonable rental value of the property. The payments and use claims typically "wash out."

Citation:

In re Marriage of Jeffries (1991) 228 Cal.App.3d 548.

Quote:

"Inasmuch as both spouses have an equal interest in community assets (*§ 5105*), and in light of a trial court's obligation under the Family Law Act to divide community assets equally between the parties upon a dissolution of the marriage (*§ 4800*, subd. (a)), it follows that the net effect of allocating "Epstein credits" and "Watts charges" in a division of community assets should be (1) the equal sharing of "Epstein credits" by both spouses and (2) the equal bearing of "Watts charges" by both spouses."

"Again, this is entirely consistent with the fact that these charges were reimbursed to the community estate, an estate in which Lonnie and Betty had an equal interest, from Betty's separate property award for the reasonable rental value of her exclusive use of the marital home after her separation from Lonnie."

Explanation:

The Occupying Spouse's Duty (Watts Charge): The spouse remaining in the home owes the community a Watts Charge, which is one-half of the home's fair rental value from the date of separation to the date of trial.

The Paying Spouse's Credit (Epstein Credit): The spouse who pays the mortgage, taxes, and insurance (PITI) with post-separation, separate earnings is generally entitled to an Epstein Credit for one-half of those payments.

The Jeffries Offset: If the occupying spouse is also the paying spouse, the Epstein Credit is canceled out or "offset" by the Watts Charge. This prevents the occupying spouse from receiving a net reimbursement for the payments they made to essentially cover their own use.

Court Discretion: Like Watts Charges, Jeffries Credits are discretionary. The court must find it equitable and reasonable to apply the offset given the totality of the circumstances (e.g., support orders, children in the home).

Examples:

The Wife (W) remains in the community home for 12 months post-separation. During this time, she pays the mortgage ($2,000/month) with her separate earnings. The home's Fair Rental Value is determined to be $2,000/month.

Wife's Epstein Claim (Credit for payments): W paid $24,000 total. She claims 1/2 from the Husband (H): $12,000.

Husband's Watts Claim (Charge for use): H claims 1/2 of the Fair Rental Value ($24,000 total) from W: $12,000.

Jeffries Offset: The court applies the offset. W's $12,000 claim is cancelled by H's $12,000 claim.

Apportionment: The net result is $0. Neither party owes the other, and the claims "wash out," simplifying the division.

Formula:

The Net Claim (typically applied only when one value is substantially greater):

Net Reimbursement = (Epstein Credit Claim) – (Watts Charge Claim)

Standard Result: If the Monthly Payment (PITI) roughly equals the Fair Rental Value, the claims offset and the Net Reimbursement is zero. The *Jeffries* rule encourages this practical "wash" result.

Further Reading:

The Jeffries concept is rarely cited as a standalone claim but is foundational to understanding the net effect of Epstein and Watts claims related to the family home.

In re Marriage of Epstein (1979) 24 Cal.3d 76: See Epstein Credits (pg. 50).

In re Marriage of Watts (1985) 171 Cal.App.3d 366: See Watts Charges (pg. 52).

In re Marriage of Garcia (1990) 224 Cal.App.3d 885: Established that the Epstein Credit may be denied if the payments were effectively made in lieu of spousal support, thereby also defeating the subsequent Jeffries offset.

44. Richmond Order

Concept:

A spousal support order that sets a specific future date when support will end unless the supported spouse takes action to extend it.

Citation:

In re Marriage of Richmond (1980) 105 Cal.App.3d 352.

Quote:

"a spousal support order may, in a proper case, be fashioned so as to encourage such supportive self-reliance, and to discourage delay in preparation for or in seeking, or refusal of, available employment."

"But present or future limitation, or termination, of spousal support must in all cases be reasonable; it may not be arbitrary or based upon speculation as to the supported spouse's future employment qualifications or opportunities."

"In making its decision concerning the retention of jurisdiction, the court must rely only on the evidence in the record and the reasonable inferences to be drawn therefrom."

Explanation:

In Richmond, the court upheld a spousal support order that would terminate on a specified date unless the supported spouse showed good cause to extend it before that date. This approach was important because it addressed a concern raised by the California Supreme Court in *In re Marriage of Morrison* (1978) 20 Cal.3d 437; namely, that after a lengthy marriage, it could be unfair to "cut off" spousal support at a future date unless there was evidence the supported spouse would be able to meet his or her own financial needs by that time. The Richmond Order concept provided a solution by allowing the court to set an end date for support to encourage self-sufficiency, while still retaining jurisdiction to extend support if the supported spouse had not become self-supporting as expected by that date.

In practical terms, the court orders that spousal support will automatically terminate on a given date (along with the court's jurisdiction over spousal support) unless, before that date arrives, the supported spouse files a motion to continue the support and shows good cause for the extension. This means the supported spouse is essentially put on notice that they must become self-supporting by the end date or be prepared to prove why they still need financial help at that time. A Richmond Order serves as a middle ground between an open-ended spousal support order and a hard cutoff: it encourages the supported party to strive for financial independence within a reasonable time frame, yet it also provides a safety net in case things do not go as expected (by allowing an opportunity to ask the court for more time if necessary).

In the years since Richmond, California courts have frequently used Richmond Orders in spousal support cases. For example, in *In re Marriage of Prietsch & Calhoun* (1987) 190 Cal.App.3d 645, the Court of Appeal noted that a "Richmond" style order is often an appropriate way to handle spousal support in typical divorce cases because it motivates the supported spouse to become self-supporting and places the burden on that spouse to demonstrate the need for continued support. However, courts also make it clear that any time limit placed on support must be reasonable and based on the evidence, not an arbitrary or purely hopeful date. In other words, the deadline for termination should reflect a timeframe by which the supported spouse could likely become self-sufficient, given the circumstances (education, work skills, job market, health, etc.). Richmond Orders might not be suitable in absolutely every case (for instance, they may be inappropriate in an extremely short marriage where only very brief support is needed, in an extremely long marriage where truly permanent support is justified, or if the supported spouse is physically unable to ever become self-supporting due to age or disability). But in many standard situations, courts favor Richmond Orders as a fair way to balance the goal of encouraging independence with the need to avoid unfairly cutting off support.

Examples:

Imagine a divorcing couple where the higher-earning Husband is required to pay spousal support to the Wife. Suppose the Wife is finishing a professional degree and is expected to be able to work full-time in a few years. In this situation, a judge might issue a Richmond Order specifying that the Husband will pay spousal support for five more years, after which the support will end. The order would state that spousal support is set to terminate in five years unless before that date the Wife (as the supported spouse) files a request to extend the support and shows good reason (good cause) why continued support is necessary at that time.

With such an order in place, the Wife knows she is expected to become self-supporting by the five-year mark. (Often the court will also give a "Gavron warning" (named after *In re Marriage of Gavron* (1988) 203 Cal.App.3d 705) which is a formal warning advising the supported spouse to make diligent efforts toward becoming self-sufficient by the end of the support period.) Meanwhile, the Husband can plan on the support payments stopping after five years if all goes as expected. If the Wife does nothing before the five-year deadline, the spousal support will simply end as scheduled, and the court's jurisdiction to order further support will lapse (meaning the issue of spousal support is closed at that point). However, if despite her reasonable efforts the Wife encounters unexpected difficulties — for example, if an unforeseen health problem or a poor job market prevents her from achieving self-support by that time — she can file a motion before the five years are up to ask the court to extend the support. If she can demonstrate to the judge that her need for support is still valid due to circumstances beyond what was anticipated (often referred to as showing "good cause" or sometimes "unrealized expectations"), the court can decide to continue spousal support for a longer period instead of cutting it off. In this way, a Richmond Order gives the supported spouse both an incentive to become independent and a contingency plan if legitimate hurdles delay that independence, while giving the paying spouse a light at the end of the tunnel rather than an indefinite obligation.

Caveat:

Family Code § 4330(b) codifies the current rule related to Richmond orders:

"When making an order for spousal support, the court may advise the recipient of support that the recipient should make reasonable efforts to assist in providing for their support needs, taking into account the particular circumstances considered by the court pursuant to *Section 4320*, unless, in the case of a marriage of long duration as provided for in *Section 4336*, the court decides this warning is inadvisable."

Further Reading:

In re Marriage of Khera & Sameer (2012) 206 Cal.App.4th 1467: Madhu Sameer appealed the denial of her request to modify a spousal support order that was set to terminate on June 1, 2010, unless she showed good cause to extend it. The original agreement assumed she would complete her master's degree in social work by that date and become self-supporting. Because Madhu did not show that this expectation had failed or that she was unable to support herself, the court found no basis to modify the order. The appellate court concluded the trial court did not abuse its discretion in denying her request.

In re Marriage of Shaughnessy (2006) 139 Cal.App.4th 1225: A former husband sought to reduce or terminate spousal support due to changed circumstances. The court reduced support and ordered it to end in six months unless the former wife showed a compelling reason to continue it.

The court explained that "self-supporting" does not always mean maintaining the exact marital standard of living. Over time, that standard may become less important, and courts may consider all factors under *California Family Code section 4320* when deciding whether continued support is fair and reasonable.

In re Marriage of Cheriton (2001) 92 Cal.App.4th 269: The Court of Appeal held that a trial court setting spousal support must consider and apply all relevant *Family Code § 4320* factors, and failure to do so is an abuse of discretion. The court found error because the trial court did not properly consider David's ability to pay, including his substantial assets, stock, and stock options, not just his income. The court emphasized that the marital standard of living is a reference point, not an absolute cap on support; depending on the statutory factors, support may be above, equal to, or below that standard. It also held that the trial court should determine and state the supported spouse's reasonable needs, rather than leaving them implicit. The court approved the general idea that a supported spouse's earning capacity may be considered in setting spousal support, and that the goal of becoming self-supporting may be given substantial weight.

However, the court questioned the automatic step-down provision because it could reduce support merely because Iris sold assets awarded to her in the property division, effectively penalizing her for converting separate property into cash. The court upheld the use of a contingent termination, or *Richmond*-type, order because Iris could seek an extension if she was unable to support herself by the termination date. Ultimately, the spousal support portion of the judgment was reversed and remanded so the trial court could reconsider support in light of all statutory factors, David's ability to pay, Iris's needs, the parties' hardship balance, the step-down provision, and retroactivity of temporary support.

45. Stallworth Order

Concept:

A spousal support order that has no fixed termination date.

Citation:

In re Marriage of Stallworth (1987) 192 Cal.App.3d 742.

Quote:

"A trial court should not terminate jurisdiction to extend a future support order after a lengthy marriage, unless the record clearly indicates that the supported spouse will be able to adequately meet his or her financial needs at the time selected for termination of jurisdiction."

"a spousal support order may, in a proper case, be fashioned so as to encourage supportive self-reliance, and to discourage delay in preparation for or in seeking, or refusal of, available employment."

"Appellate courts have thus upheld orders providing a tentative termination date on which the burden shifts to the payee spouse to show cause to extend the order."

Explanation:

A Stallworth Order refers to a spousal support order that has no predetermined end date, meaning support continues "until further order of the court" (or until a standard terminating event like the supported spouse's remarriage or the death of either party). In practical terms, this is an open-ended spousal support arrangement often used in long-term marriages or in situations where it's uncertain when, if ever, the supported spouse will become self-sufficient. The concept comes from *In re Marriage of Stallworth*, where the appellate court upheld a support order with no fixed termination date, ruling that it was not an abuse of discretion for the trial court to decline to set a cutoff or timeline for the supported spouse to become employed. A Stallworth Order contrasts with a Richmond Order, whereas a Richmond Order sets a future date for support to step down or end unless the supported spouse shows good cause to extend it, a Stallworth Order keeps support indefinite and places no automatic deadline on the payments. In essence, a Stallworth Order leaves the burden on the supporting spouse to later petition the court for any reduction or termination (upon a material change in circumstances), as opposed to a Richmond Order which places the onus on the supported spouse to seek an extension before support ends. This approach can complement a Richmond Order in that courts have flexibility: they may choose a Stallworth-style order in cases where an arbitrary end date would be unfair or impractical, such as very long marriages or when the supported spouse's future earning capacity is unclear, whereas a Richmond Order is used to encourage the supported party to become self-supporting by a set time.

Examples:

Long-Term Marriage Scenario: After a 25-year marriage, a 60-year-old Wife who spent most of the marriage as a homemaker is awarded spousal support. The court issues a Stallworth Order for indefinite support, recognizing the marriage's long duration and her limited recent work experience. There is no fixed end date for support. It will continue until either party's circumstances change significantly or a terminating event (death/remarriage) occurs. This gives the supported spouse security, while allowing the supporting spouse to later request a modification or termination if, for example, the supported spouse becomes self-supporting or circumstances otherwise change.

Health/Ability Consideration: In a divorce, the Husband must pay spousal support to his ex-wife who has a chronic health condition and cannot be expected to achieve full-time employment in the near future. The court orders support "until further order," a Stallworth-type arrangement, because setting a specific cutoff date wouldn't be appropriate given her condition. For instance, rather than ordering "support for two years and then terminating unless extended" (as a Richmond Order might), the court leaves the order open-ended. This means the Husband will continue paying support indefinitely, subject to future modification, acknowledging that the Wife's ability to become self-supporting is uncertain. If her condition improves or she later gains employment, the Husband can ask the court to adjust or end the support at that time.

Further Reading:

Family Code section 4336 (court retains spousal support jurisdiction indefinitely for marriages of long duration, generally 10+ years).

In re Marriage of Morrison (1978) 20 Cal.3d 437: A landmark California Supreme Court case that set the stage for Stallworth Orders. In Morrison, the Supreme Court held that in a long-duration marriage, it can be an abuse of discretion for a trial court to set a fixed termination date for spousal support without retaining the ability to extend it. The court emphasized that after a lengthy marriage, support should not automatically end on an arbitrary date unless there is evidence that the supported spouse will be self-sufficient by that time. This case established the principle that the default in long marriages is to retain jurisdiction over spousal support indefinitely, placing the burden on the party seeking to terminate support to prove why an absolute end date is justified.

In re Marriage of Richmond (1980) 105 Cal.App.3d 352: See Richmond Order (pg. 115).

In re Marriage of Stallworth (1987) 192 Cal.App.3d 742: See Stallworth Order (pg. 118).

In re Marriage of Gavron (1988) 203 Cal.App.3d 705: See Gavron Warning (pg. 109).

In re Marriage of Prietsch & Calhoun (1987) 190 Cal.App.3d 645: Another Court of Appeal case in the same era, which, while primarily about support modification, provided insight relevant to Stallworth vs. Richmond orders. In Prietsch, the court noted that a Richmond-type order places the responsibility on the supported spouse to take action to extend support because that spouse is in the best position to control the factors (like obtaining employment or education) that would justify continuing support. This observation by the court explains the rationale behind Richmond Orders and, by contrast, highlights the effect of a Stallworth Order. If a court issues a Stallworth (indefinite) support order, it implies the burden remains on the supporting spouse to show a change in circumstances to reduce or terminate support later. Prietsch & Calhoun reinforces how California courts view the "burden of proof" dynamic: a Richmond Order shifts that burden to the supported party (to prove why support should go on), whereas a Stallworth Order keeps support in place until the payor can show it should change. This case helped clarify and bolster the policy considerations judges weigh when choosing an open-ended support order versus a stepped or terminating one.

Checklist: When courts consider issuing a Stallworth Order (open-ended spousal support), they typically evaluate several key factors and conditions before deciding that an indefinite order is appropriate. Important considerations include:

Length of the Marriage: Is the marriage of long duration? Marriages lasting 10 years or more are considered "lengthy" under California law (*Fam. Code § 4336*). In long-term marriages, courts are more inclined to reserve jurisdiction indefinitely and avoid setting a fixed termination date for support, because the law presumes that ongoing support may be needed absent evidence to the contrary.

Supported Spouse's Earning Capacity and Timeframe for Self-Sufficiency: Can the supported spouse become self-supporting, and how long might that realistically take? If the supported party has been out of the workforce for many years, has limited job skills, or would require substantial education or training to re-enter the job market, the court may opt for a Stallworth Order. The less certain or more prolonged the rehabilitation period, the more sense it makes not to impose a hard end date. On the other hand, if evidence shows the supported spouse can become self-sufficient relatively soon (e.g., they have marketable skills or are already working part-time), the court might lean toward a fixed timeline or a Richmond Order instead.

Age and Health of the Supported Spouse: The court looks at whether the supported party's age or health conditions affect their ability to work. For example, an older spouse nearing retirement age, or one suffering from significant health issues or disabilities, may never become fully self-supporting. In such cases, an indefinite support order is often justified. A younger, healthy spouse might be expected to eventually rejoin the workforce, which could factor against an indefinite order (instead prompting a transitional support plan).

Contributions to the Marriage and Domestic Duties: Judges consider if the supported spouse sacrificed career opportunities to devote time to domestic responsibilities (raising children, maintaining the home, supporting the other spouse's career). If so, there is a recognition that it may be harder for that spouse to immediately gain financial independence after divorce. A Stallworth Order acknowledges this by providing sustained support, especially when the marriage was long, and the homemaker spouse's opportunities for building a career were foregone.

Child Care or Other Dependents: If the supported spouse has primary custody of young children or is caring for a child or family member with special needs, the court will consider how those responsibilities limit the spouse's ability to work. An ongoing caretaking role might warrant continuing spousal support without a set end date, since that spouse's focus is on caregiving rather than earning. (Note: child support is a separate issue, but heavy childcare duties can influence spousal support duration.)

Efforts Toward Self-Support & Warnings Given: The court will review what efforts the supported spouse has made or is expected to make to become self-supporting. Importantly, if the court anticipates potentially terminating or reducing support in the future, it should give a Gavron Warning (a formal notice to the supported spouse to make reasonable efforts to become self-sufficient). If no such warning has been given and the spouse's future prospects are unclear, the court may choose a Stallworth approach and simply reserve the right to modify support later rather than impose a deadline now. Essentially, the judge asks: Has the supported spouse been clearly told to seek employment? Are they following through? If not, it may be premature or unfair to set an end date.

Financial Resources and Needs of Each Party: As with any support decision, the court weighs the supported spouse's needs against the supporting spouse's ability to pay (see *Family Code § 4320* factors). When issuing an indefinite order, the court must be comfortable that the payor can manage the ongoing obligation and that the recipient genuinely needs support. If the supporting spouse's financial situation is strong and the supported spouse's needs remain significant, an open-ended order may be appropriate. Conversely, if the payor's ability to pay will sharply decline in the near future (for instance, imminent retirement or health issues of the payor), the court might instead structure a step-down plan.

Existence of Any Agreement or Waiver: Courts also consider whether the parties themselves agreed to any limitations on support. If, for example, the spouses signed a marital settlement agreement specifying a termination date or waiving post-judgment support, the court will follow that (absent a violation of public policy). But if there's no agreement, or if the supported spouse expressly reserved the right to seek support indefinitely (common in long marriages), the court is freer to order a Stallworth-type support arrangement.

Policy of Encouraging Self-Support vs. Avoiding Hardship: Finally, the judge balances two public policies: on one hand, spousal support is intended to be a transition toward financial independence (the law encourages every supported spouse to become self-supporting within a "reasonable period" whenever possible). On the other hand, the court must avoid undue hardship and recognize reality: some ex-spouses may never attain the prior standard of living alone, especially after a lengthy marriage. In issuing a Stallworth Order, the court leans toward preventing hardship by not cutting off support prematurely. The decision typically reflects that the supported spouse's circumstances make a time-limited support order impractical or unjust at that stage. The court retains the flexibility to modify support if conditions change (e.g., if the supported spouse later achieves independence or if the supporting spouse retires or faces financial strain, either can ask the court to adjust the order).

In summary, a Stallworth Order is all about flexibility and caution: the court keeps spousal support open-ended when the future is uncertain, especially in long marriages, rather than locking in an end date that might prove unrealistic. The above considerations guide judges in determining whether to issue such an order, ensuring they carefully weigh the fairness to both parties. This approach complements other tools (like Richmond Orders and Gavron Warnings) by protecting a dependent spouse from abrupt loss of support while still allowing for the possibility of future modifications as lives evolve after divorce.

SELECT STATUTES

1. *Family Code section 70* – Date of Separation

Explanation:

California Family Code § 70 defines the "date of separation" as the date when a marriage has fully ended, marked by both spouses: first, one spouse telling the other that they want out, and second, that spouse acting consistently with ending the marriage. In simple terms, you are legally separated when one spouse clearly communicates an intent to divorce and follows through with actions (for example, moving out or closing joint accounts). If one spouse fails to say they are ending the marriage, even if they move out, the court looks at all the facts to decide the actual separation date. *Section 70(b)* makes clear the court considers all relevant evidence in finding that date. (*Section 70* also states it was intended to overturn prior cases like *In re Marriage of Davis* and Norviel that had required spouses to live in separate homes.)

Examples:

Move-out and clear communication: Imagine a Husband tells his Wife "I want a divorce" and moves out on May 1. Under §70, their separation date is May 1. Any salary he earns or property he acquires after that date is treated as his separate property, not community property.

No clear communication, still living together: Suppose one spouse quietly moves into a spare room without telling the other they want a divorce, and they still share expenses and daily life. Under *§70*, the court may find the separation date is later; perhaps when one spouse finally speaks up. If a spouse never clearly said "I'm ending this," property acquired during that period might remain community property.

Living together during a "trial separation": It is possible for spouses to live under one roof after one has decided to end the marriage, as long as §70's requirements are met. For instance, if a Wife announces the marriage is over but they stay at home together a bit longer (to sort finances), their separation date is still the day she spoke up. All earnings or assets after that date would be separate. Conversely, if there is long overlap without any statement ending the marriage, property could continue to be community.

Further Reading:

In re Marriage of Lee & Lin (2019): The Court of Appeal affirmed a trial court's finding that the couple separated when the husband moved out and clearly intended to end the marriage. Because he expressed his intent, leased an apartment, and gave up the house keys, that date was legally considered their separation date. Everything he earned afterward was his separate property.

In re Marriage of Davis (2015) 61 Cal.4th 846: This California Supreme Court case, decided before *§70* existed, held that spouses had to live in separate residences for their earnings to become separate property. *Section 70* later abrogated this rule by removing the separate-home requirement.

In re Marriage of Norviel (2002) 102 Cal.App.4th 1152: The court ruled that because a husband and wife still lived together, they were not legally separated even though he expressed intent. *Section 70* reversed this logic by focusing on communication and conduct, not physical living situation.

In re Marriage of Hardin (1995) 38 Cal.App.4th 448: This Court of Appeal case articulated a two-part test for legal separation that aligns with current *§70* law: intent to end the marriage and conduct reflecting that intent. This precedent influenced the wording of the modern statute.

Full Text of *Family Code § 70*

(a) "Date of separation" means the date that a complete and final break in the marital relationship has occurred, as evidenced by both of the following:

(1) The spouse has expressed to the other spouse the intent to end the marriage; and

(2) The conduct of the spouse is consistent with the intent to end the marriage.

(b) In determining the date of separation, the court shall take into consideration all relevant evidence.

(c) It is the intent of the Legislature in enacting this section to abrogate the decisions in *In re Marriage of Davis* (2015) 61 Cal.4th 846 and *In re Marriage of Norviel* (2002) 102 Cal.App.4th 1152.

2. *Family Code section 92* – Family Support

Explanation:

Family Code § 92 defines "family support" as a combined support arrangement that covers both child support and spousal support in one overall sum. In simple terms, instead of specifying separate amounts for child support and for spousal support, a family support order or agreement bundles them together into a single payment. This means the paying party (often a higher-earning spouse or parent) pays one unified amount intended to meet both the children's needs and the other spouse's needs, without labeling how much of it is for the children versus the spouse.

This combined approach can be used as an alternative to having distinct child support and alimony orders. One potential benefit of family support is simplicity: it provides one consistent payment to the supported party, which can be easier to manage than two separate payments. It may also offer flexibility for the family's finances. In some cases, parties choose a family support arrangement to maximize tax or financial advantages. (Historically, when spousal support was tax-deductible to the payer and taxable to the recipient, structuring support as "family support" could allow the entire payment to be treated like alimony for tax purposes. This could benefit both sides if the payer was in a higher tax bracket and the recipient in a lower bracket. However, U.S. tax laws changed in 2019 to end the deduction for new spousal support orders, so newer family support agreements no longer carry the same federal tax benefit.)

It's important to understand that a family support order carries the characteristics of both child and spousal support. For example, because child support is always modifiable to serve a child's best interests, a family support amount (which includes child support) remains subject to court modification just like a regular child support order. The court will still use the statewide child support guidelines as a reference in approving or modifying a family support amount. Additionally, enforcement of a family support order is usually handled in the same manner as child support; for instance, the local child support agency can assist in collecting family support, and the payment can be automatically withheld from wages, etc.

One potential downside of a combined family support order is the lack of automatic adjustment when circumstances change. Because the order doesn't specify what portion is "for child" vs "for spouse," it may be unclear what should happen when the child turns 18 or graduates high school (when regular child support would ordinarily terminate). The paying parent cannot simply stop or reduce payments on their own once a child becomes an adult, since the order is a single sum, they must go back to court to modify the family support amount. In practice, courts addressing family support will look at the intent of the parties and the language of the judgment. If it's evident that the combined support was meant to include child support, the court may expect the payor to seek a modification when the child is no longer eligible, rather than just unilaterally reducing the payment. Failing to formally adjust the order can lead to misunderstandings or even legal disputes over arrears (back payments).

In summary, *Family Code § 92*'s concept of family support is a tool that divorcing or separating parents can use to streamline support obligations. It can provide a stable, single payment that covers all support duties, but it requires careful drafting and awareness of future changes. Parents considering a family support arrangement should be mindful of how it will operate over time; for example, whether it should decrease when a child grows up, and how to enforce or modify the order down the road. Because of the complexities (especially regarding tax implications and future modifications), it's often recommended to consult a family law attorney or financial advisor when deciding to use a family support order.

Examples:

Combined support with tax planning: Imagine a divorcing couple where one spouse has a much higher income. They agree that instead of paying $800 per month in child support and $700 per month in spousal support, the higher-earning spouse will pay $1,500 per month in family support. Under their agreement, the entire $1,500 is a single obligation covering both the children's expenses and spousal support for the other parent. In the past (before 2019), treating it as family support could allow the payor to deduct the whole $1,500 on their taxes as alimony (since it wasn't labeled separately as child support), and the recipient would report it as income. This could result in a net tax benefit, potentially enabling the higher earner to comfortably pay a bit more support knowing they get a tax break, which in turn gives the recipient more money overall. However, both parties would need to ensure the agreement was structured correctly (for example, the payments couldn't step down when each child turned 18, or the IRS would consider part of it disguised child support). (Note: Current law has changed federal tax treatment of alimony for new orders, so today this tax-driven scenario only applies to older agreements. But it illustrates why some couples set up unallocated family support in the first place.)

When a child turns 18, what happens to family support? Consider a court order that requires a father to pay $2,000 per month in family support to the mother, covering her support and their one child's support together. This continues for several years. When the child turns 18 and graduates high school, the father might assume he can cut the payment in half or stop the portion for the child. But because the order doesn't separate child support from spousal support, he is technically still obligated to pay the full $2,000 until the court changes the order. In one real case, a parent in this situation stopped paying the "child's share" once the child became an adult, and years later the other parent demanded tens of thousands in back payments. The dispute went to court, where the judges examined the original agreement. They found evidence that both parents had intended the support to end when the child grew up, so the court ruled that no arrears were owed for the period after the child's majority. The lesson is that if you have a family support order and a child is aging out, it's safest to return to court for a formal modification. Otherwise, you risk a misunderstanding: one party may believe the obligation automatically changed, while the other may later claim unpaid support.

Forgiving past-due support isn't so simple: Family support orders are legally enforceable just like any other support order, and California law is very strict that accrued support payments (amounts that became due in the past) cannot just be waived or forgiven by a private agreement. For example, suppose a parent falls behind on a family support obligation, owing a large sum in arrears. The parents privately agree that the supported spouse will forgive the debt if a smaller lump-sum is paid and the monthly amount is reduced going forward. They sign a deal to that effect. Later, the supported spouse gets second thoughts (or the deal falls apart) and brings the issue to court. In a scenario like this, the court is likely to invalidate the agreement to waive the arrears. California courts have held that you cannot retroactively cancel child support or family support that has already come due. In addition, if the local child support agency is involved in enforcing the support (for example, if the family received public assistance or sought help from the Department of Child Support Services), then that agency must approve any stipulated agreement to compromise or terminate support. In one case, a father's family support payments were significantly in arrears (over $200,000). He and his ex-wife signed a stipulation to permanently terminate the support and forgive the debt if he paid a smaller amount upfront. The trial court initially approved it, but later set it aside when it was revealed that the agreement hadn't been signed by the county child support agency and that the father had misrepresented his finances. The result: the large arrears balance was reinstated, and the father was still on the hook for the full past-due amount. This example shows that family support isn't easily bargained away: once support money is owed, the law treats it like a debt that the child (or supported spouse) is entitled to, and courts will enforce that debt until it's paid in full.

Further Reading:

In re Marriage of Sabine & Toshio M. (2007) 153 Cal.App.4th 1203: This decision involved a large amount of support arrears that accrued over many years. The ex-husband, who had moved overseas, owed both child support and spousal support arrearages exceeding $300,000. He later offered to pay the ex-wife about one-third of that amount as a "settlement" if she would forgive the rest. The ex-wife, desperate for funds, initially agreed and signed a settlement agreement to waive the remaining support. However, when only part of the money was paid and disputes arose, the matter ended up in California court. The Court of Appeal made it clear that past-due support cannot be waived or forgiven by agreement, unless perhaps there is a clear dispute about the amount owed. The court reaffirmed the rule that a judge has no authority to retroactively reduce or cancel accrued support obligations – those become a vested right of the payee (and, in the case of child support, a right of the child). In Sabine & Toshio M., the court invalidated the settlement that attempted to relinquish the arrears, holding that the agreement was unenforceable and that the full arrears remained due. This case is often cited for the principle that a parent cannot privately "bargain away" child support or family support that has already come due, and any attempt to do so (especially without court and agency approval) will not be upheld.

Full Text of *California Family Code § 92*

"Family support" means an agreement between the parents, or an order or judgment, that combines child support and spousal support without designating the amount to be paid for child support and the amount to be paid for spousal support.

3. *Family Code section 125* – Quasi-Community Property

Explanation:

California Family Code § 125 defines quasi-community property as property a married couple acquired while living in another state that would have been community property if they had been living in California at the time. In plain terms, if a couple moves to California and later divorces here, any assets they obtained in a non–community property state (like New York or Florida) are treated as community property in the California divorce. This prevents one spouse from gaining an unfair advantage simply because the property was acquired in a state with different marital property rules. Quasi-community property generally remains the acquiring spouse's separate property until a triggering event in California (such as a divorce proceeding) occurs, at which point it is handled the same way as community property.

Examples:

Couple relocates to California: Imagine a couple who lived and bought a home in Ohio (a separate property state) during their marriage. They later move to California and file for divorce. In the California divorce, that Ohio home is treated as quasi-community property: the court will divide it between the spouses just as if it had been acquired in California as community property.

Only one spouse moves to CA: Suppose one spouse moves to California and files for divorce while the other spouse remains in their home state (along with the couple's property). In this scenario, California's quasi-community property law generally would not apply to the out-of-state property. Both spouses need to establish California domicile for a California court to have authority to treat their out-of-state assets as quasi-community property.

Exchange of assets: Say a spouse owned a valuable asset (for example, stocks or a rental property) while living outside California, and later sold that asset and used the money to purchase a new asset after moving to California. The new asset would also be considered quasi-community property in a California divorce because it was acquired in exchange for property that would have been community property if originally acquired in California.

Further Reading:

Addison v. Addison (1965) 62 Cal.2d 558: In this landmark decision, the California Supreme Court upheld the state's quasi-community property law. The court ruled that property acquired by spouses while living in another state can be divided as quasi-community property when the couple divorces in California (after becoming California residents). This confirmed that such out-of-state assets are subject to equal division, just like regular community property, upon divorce.

In re Marriage of Roesch (1978) 83 Cal.App.3d 96: This California Court of Appeal case clarified that both spouses must establish domicile in California before quasi-community property rules can apply. In Roesch, one spouse had moved to California but the other remained in another state; the court held that a California divorce court could not treat the out-of-state property as quasi-community property because both parties were not California residents. This case underscored the requirement that the couple must both be in California for the quasi-community property provision to take effect.

Full Text of *Family Code § 125*

"Quasi-community property" means all real or personal property, wherever situated, acquired before or after the operative date of this code in any of the following ways:

(a) By either spouse while domiciled elsewhere which would have been community property if the spouse who acquired the property had been domiciled in this state at the time of its acquisition.

(b) In exchange for real or personal property, wherever situated, which would have been community property if the spouse who acquired the property so exchanged had been domiciled in this state at the time of its acquisition.

4. *Family Code section 308* – California Recognizes All Valid Marriages

Explanation:

Family Code § 308 is a rule that tells us when California will recognize marriages that happen outside of California. In simple terms, if you get married in another state or another country, and that marriage is legal and valid in that place, then California will also consider you legally married. This applies to all kinds of valid marriages from elsewhere, whether it's a traditional ceremony in another country or even a common-law marriage in a state that allows couples to be married without a ceremony. Essentially, California honors the marriage laws of the place where the wedding took place, so long as the marriage was valid under those laws.

There are some important caveats. California will not recognize an out-of-state marriage if it violates a strong public policy here. For example, a marriage involving bigamy (one person already has a spouse) or an incestuous marriage (close relatives) won't be recognized in California, even if it was allowed somewhere else. But aside from such exceptions, the general rule is that a marriage valid where it was celebrated will be treated as a valid marriage in California. This principle ensures that couples don't lose their marital status or rights just because they cross into California.

It's also worth noting that California's approach has evolved over time for certain types of marriages. For instance, at one point California law (*former Family Code § 308.5*) refused to recognize same-sex marriages from other jurisdictions, but that is no longer the case. Today, California fully recognizes same-sex marriages performed out-of-state just as it would any other marriage, thanks to changes in state law and court decisions. In summary, *Family Code § 308* makes California a "marriage-friendly" state for lawful marriages established elsewhere, guaranteeing that those marriages carry the same legal weight as California marriages.

Examples:

Destination Wedding: Jack and Jill live in California but decide to get married in Hawaii. Their Hawaiian marriage follows all the legal requirements in Hawaii, so it's completely valid there. When they come back home to California, *Family Code § 308* means their marriage is automatically recognized here as well. They don't need to "re-marry" in California: California treats them as a legally married couple because their Hawaii wedding was valid under Hawaiian law.

Common-Law Marriage from Another State: Maria and Tom lived together in Texas for many years and presented themselves as spouses, which is enough to form a common-law marriage under Texas law. Even though California itself doesn't allow common-law marriages to start here, California will acknowledge Maria and Tom as married because their informal marriage is considered valid in Texas. If they move to California, they have all the same rights and obligations as any married couple (and would need to go through a normal divorce in California if they split up) thanks to *§ 308*.

Marriage with a Public Policy Violation: John is already married to Alice in California, but he goes to another country and goes through a marriage ceremony with another partner, Jane, where polygamy is legal. Even if John's second marriage to Jane is considered valid in that other country, California will not recognize it. Because California law forbids having more than one spouse at a time (bigamy), the second marriage is void here. Family Code § 308 does not force California to recognize marriages that violate fundamental California laws, so Jane would not be considered John's Wife in California.

Further Reading:

Colbert v. Colbert (1946) 28 Cal.2d 276: In this California Supreme Court case, the court dealt with a couple who had entered into a common-law marriage in

Texas (which at the time recognized common-law marriages). The wife, Mrs. Colbert, claimed she was married in Texas without a formal ceremony, and she sought a divorce and support in California. The husband argued they weren't really married because California doesn't allow common-law marriage. The Supreme Court sided with the wife, explaining that under the predecessor of *§ 308*, a marriage valid in the state where it was formed (Texas) must be recognized as valid in California. In plain language, even though California wouldn't itself create a marriage without a ceremony, it honored the Texas common-law marriage: meaning the Colberts were considered legally married in California and had to go through a formal divorce to end the relationship.

In re Marriage of Smyklo (1986) 180 Cal.App.3d 1095: This case from the California Court of Appeal also involved a common-law marriage, but the couple's informal marriage was formed in Alabama. Alabama recognized their relationship as a valid marriage (even without a license or ceremony), so when the couple later found themselves in California's courts (in a divorce proceeding), the question was whether California would treat them as married. The court applied *Family Code § 308*'s principle and concluded that yes, it would. The Smyklo decision confirmed that California must acknowledge a marriage that was legally established in another jurisdiction. In short, the couple's Alabama common-law marriage was deemed valid in California, so they had to go through the California divorce process to legally end their marriage.

Rosales v. Battle (2003) 113 Cal.App.4th 1178: In this Court of Appeal case, the issue was whether a woman could sue for wrongful death as the "surviving spouse" of a man she lived with in Mexico. The couple had lived together and even had children, and a Mexican court had acknowledged her as the man's "concubine" (a status somewhat similar to an unmarried partner). However, they never had a civil marriage ceremony, which is required to be legally married under Mexican law. The California court turned to Family Code § 308 and reasoned that it must look at Mexican law to see if the two were legally married in Mexico. Because they did not fulfill Mexico's legal requirements for marriage, their union wasn't a valid marriage in Mexico: it was just a non-marital cohabitation. Therefore, California did not recognize them as a married couple. The court concluded that Ms. Rosales was not a "surviving spouse" under California law, illustrating that § 308 will recognize foreign marriages only if the couple actually complied with the marriage laws of that foreign jurisdiction.

Full Text of *California Family Code § 308*

A marriage contracted outside this state that would be valid by the laws of the jurisdiction in which the marriage was contracted is valid in California.

5. *Family Code section 309* – Spouse Denies Validity of Marriage

If one spouse denies the existence of a marriage or refuses to cooperate in officially acknowledging it, *California Family Code § 309* allows the other spouse to ask a court to formally recognize the marriage.

Explanation:

California Family Code § 309 deals with situations where one party to a marriage denies the marriage or refuses to join in a declaration of the marriage. The statute does not itself create an informal marriage; it allows the other party to proceed by an action under *Health and Safety Code §103450* to have the validity of the marriage determined and declared. In practice, the court determines whether the legal requirements for a valid marriage were satisfied and, if so, may declare the marriage valid despite the other spouse's denial or refusal to cooperate. *Section 309* is therefore a recognition-and-declaration remedy, not a substitute for the licensing and solemnization requirements for creating a California marriage.

Examples:

Officiant Error, Spouse Denies Marriage: Imagine a couple has a wedding ceremony and obtains a marriage license, but due to a mistake (for example, the officiant fails to file the license with the county), the marriage was never officially recorded. Later, the Husband tries to argue they aren't legally married (perhaps to avoid obligations like spousal support). The Wife can use Family Code § 309 to file an action in court to have the marriage legally recognized. The court would review evidence of the ceremony and license. If the only issue was a paperwork error, the court can declare the marriage valid despite the Husband's denial.

No License at Wedding: In another scenario, a couple participates in a marriage ceremony but never actually obtained a marriage license at all. They live as a married couple, but the Husband refuses to file any official marriage declaration. The Wife eventually seeks legal status as a spouse. Under § 309, she can initiate a court proceeding to determine the validity of the marriage. However, because they skipped the essential step of getting a marriage license, the court may find that no valid marriage was created. In California, a license and proper solemnization are required for a lawful marriage, so § 309 cannot be used to create a marriage where the fundamental legal requirements were not met in the first place. The outcome would likely be that the court informs the parties they must go through the proper licensing process to be legally married.

Further Reading:

In re Marriage of Cantarella (2011) 191 Cal.App.4th 916: The Court of Appeal held that a marriage was still valid even though the marriage license was never registered with the county. In this case, the parties had a proper ceremony and obtained a marriage license, but the completed license was returned to them for a minor error and they never re-filed it. Years later, the husband claimed the 1991 marriage was not valid (to shorten the duration of the marriage for a spousal support dispute), since the license wasn't on file. The court disagreed and ruled the marriage valid. The reasoning was that the couple had fulfilled the core requirements (obtaining a license, consenting, and having a ceremony). The failure to register the license was a clerical issue by the officiant or a party, which § 306 of the Family Code excuses if done by a non-party. The Cantarella court extended this protection even if the parties themselves failed to re-submit the license. In short, a mere failure to file the marriage certificate did not void the marriage.

Estate of DePasse (2002) 97 Cal.App.4th 92: The Court of Appeal reached a different result where the parties never obtained any marriage license at the time of the ceremony. In DePasse, a couple participated in an urgent bedside marriage ceremony because one person was terminally ill, but they intentionally did not get a license due to the circumstances. After the death, the surviving partner attempted to establish that a valid marriage existed (to inherit as a spouse) by petitioning under *Health & Safety Code § 103450* (the procedure referenced in *Family Code § 309*). The court ruled that the marriage was not valid because a marriage license is a mandatory requirement in California. Simply having a ceremony without a license meant no legal marriage was created. Moreover, the post-ceremony court order (through H&S *§ 103450*) to record the marriage did not retroactively make the marriage valid — it only created a record of the ceremony. The court also noted that the surviving partner could not be considered a "putative spouse" (someone who wrongly but in good faith believes they are married) because he knew no license was obtained. Thus, under *§ 309* and related laws, one cannot circumvent the licensing requirement; a court can declare a marriage valid only if the basic legal steps for marriage were initially satisfied.

Full Text of *California Family Code § 309*

If either party to a marriage denies the marriage, or refuses to join in a declaration of the marriage, the other party may proceed, by action pursuant to *Section 103450* of the Health and Safety Code, to have the validity of the marriage determined and declared.

6. *Family Code section 721* – Fiduciary Duty Between Spouses

Explanation:

Family Code § 721 says that spouses must deal with each other with the highest good faith and fair dealing. In transactions between themselves, neither spouse may take unfair advantage of the other. The statute aligns spousal duties with those of business partners—requiring open access to transaction records, full information about community-property dealings, and accounting for benefits gained without the other spouse's consent. When one spouse gains an advantage in an interspousal transaction (for example, a title transfer), courts often apply a presumption of undue influence that the advantaged spouse must rebut by showing the deal was voluntary, informed, and understood.

Examples:

Title transfer advantage: Spouse A signs a deed that advantages Spouse B (e.g., moving a home from community to B's separate property). Courts may presume undue influence under *§ 721*. Spouse B must prove the transfer was freely and knowingly made, with a full understanding of its effect.

Hidden transactions: One spouse takes out a loan or cash advance without disclosure. *§ 721*'s fiduciary baseline supports remedies—often pursued under *Family Code § 1101* (including fee-shifting and percentage awards depending on the misconduct).

Reconciliation/post-marital agreements: Agreements made during reconciliation may be enforced when both parties are represented and obtain mutual advantages, which can rebut an undue-influence presumption.

Access to records: A spouse refusing to share account statements or "books" related to community transactions may be violating *§ 721* duties requiring access and full information.

Dissolution disclosure misconduct: While detailed disclosure rules live in *§ 2100* et seq., courts regularly invoke *§ 721*'s fiduciary duties when imposing sanctions for nondisclosure during divorce cases.

Further Reading:

In re Marriage of Haines (1995) 33 Cal.App.4th 277: See Haines Presumption of Undue Influence (pg. 17).

In re Marriage of Delaney (2003) 111 Cal.App.4th 991: Applies and refines the Haines rule in a transmutation to joint tenancy; the advantaged spouse must rebut undue influence by proving a voluntary act done with full knowledge of the facts and a complete understanding of its effect.

In re Marriage of Feldman (2007) 153 Cal.App.4th 1470: See *In re Marriage of Feldman*: Disclosure Duties and Monetary Sanctions (pg. 58).

In re Marriage of Fossum (2011) 192 Cal.App.4th 336: See *In re Marriage of Fossum*: Undue Influence and Mandatory *Section 1101(g)* Fees (pg. 66).

In re Marriage of Burkle (2006) 139 Cal.App.4th 712: Enforces a reconciliation-stage post-marital agreement where both parties had counsel and obtained mutual advantages; explains when the undue-influence presumption does not control and when certain dissolution disclosure statutes do not apply.

Full Text of *California Family Code § 721*

(a) Subject to subdivision (b), either spouse may enter into any transaction with the other, or with any other person, respecting property, which either might if unmarried.

(b) Except as provided in *Sections 143, 144, 146, 16040, 16047, and 21385* of the Probate Code, in transactions between themselves, spouses are subject to the general rules governing fiduciary relationships that control the actions of persons occupying confidential relations with each other. This confidential relationship imposes a duty of the highest good faith and fair dealing on each spouse, and neither shall take any unfair advantage of the other.

This confidential relationship is a fiduciary relationship subject to the same rights and duties of nonmarital business partners, as provided in *Sections 16403, 16404, and 16503* of the Corporations Code, including, but not limited to, the following:

(1) Providing each spouse access at all times to any books kept regarding a transaction for the purposes of inspection and copying.

(2) Rendering upon request, true and full information of all things affecting any transaction that concerns the community property. Nothing in this section is intended to impose a duty for either spouse to keep detailed books and records of community property transactions.

(3) Accounting to the spouse, and holding as a trustee, any benefit or profit derived from any transaction by one spouse without the consent of the other spouse that concerns the community property.

7. *Family Code section 752* – Management and Control of Separate Property

Explanation:

California Family Code Section 752 states that, unless a law specifically says otherwise, each spouse has no ownership interest in the other spouse's separate property. In simple terms, this means any property that is classified as one spouse's separate property (for example, assets owned before the marriage or acquired by gift or inheritance to one spouse alone) belongs solely to that spouse. The other spouse has no automatic claim to or control over such separate property just because they are married. *Section 752* essentially draws a clear line: community property (generally property acquired during the marriage by either spouse) is co-owned by both spouses, but separate property of one spouse remains entirely that spouse's and is not co-owned or controlled by the other.

This law protects each spouse's separate assets. For instance, if one spouse owned a business or a home before getting married, the other spouse doesn't gain an ownership share in that business or home merely by virtue of the marriage. Likewise, if during the marriage one spouse receives a personal gift or inheritance (which by law is separate property), *Section 752* ensures the other spouse has no inherent rights to that gift or inheritance. The only time this would change is if some other statute or legal action (like a valid written agreement between the spouses, known as a transmutation, or a statutory exception) provides otherwise. In summary, *§ 752* means "what's mine is mine and what's yours is yours" when it comes to separate property, unless both spouses or the law explicitly decide to convert it into shared property.

Examples:

Inherited Money: During their marriage, Alice inherits $50,000 from her grandmother and keeps it in a bank account in her name only. Under § 752, that inheritance is Alice's separate property. Her Husband Bob has no legal interest in or claim to that $50,000. If Bob wanted to use some of Alice's inheritance, he would need Alice's permission, since the money belongs solely to her.

Property Owned Before Marriage: Before marrying, John owns a house by himself. After the wedding, John's house remains his separate property (absent any agreement to share or change it). His Wife, Mary, doesn't automatically gain ownership or control of the house under § 752. Mary couldn't mortgage or sell John's house because she has no ownership interest in it. If they divorce, the house would not be treated as community property to be divided. It would remain John's property (unless there was a written agreement during the marriage to make it community property).

No Interest in Separate Business: Suppose during the marriage, Maria starts a business using only funds she had before marriage, and she keeps the business entirely in her name. That business is Maria's separate property. Her spouse, Kevin, doesn't own any portion of the company under *§ 752*. Kevin can't make decisions for the company or claim its profits as his, because the law recognizes that the business is Maria's separate asset. (However, if Kevin contributed labor or community funds to the business, the community might have a right to some reimbursement or a share of increased value, but Kevin still wouldn't own the business itself. He would only have a claim for compensation under other legal principles, not an ownership interest.)

Keeping Separate Funds Separate: Erin has a savings account from before marriage with $10,000 (her separate property). She never mixes these funds with any joint accounts. Under § 752, her Husband Liam has no interest in that account. She doesn't need Liam's consent to spend or manage that $10,000 because it's legally not part of the community property. If Erin passes away or the couple divorces, that account remains Erin's property alone, and Liam would generally have no claim to it as community property.

Further Reading:

In re Marriage of Walker (2006) 138 Cal.App.4th 1408: This appellate case involved a wife managing a retirement account that was originally the husband's separate property. The court noted that under *§ 752*, one spouse normally has no interest in the other's separate property. However, in this situation the account had become so mixed with community funds that it lost its separate property status. The court found the retirement account was community property (because the separate and community contributions were commingled and couldn't be traced apart), which meant the wife had a fiduciary duty in managing it. The wife was held accountable for depleting the account without the husband's knowledge. Walker illustrates that while *§ 752* protects separate property, if separate funds get commingled indistinguishably with community property, the entire asset may be treated as community property, and then both spouses have equal rights and responsibilities in it.

In re Marriage of Ciprari (2019) 32 Cal.App.5th 83: In this case, a husband had large investment accounts containing both separate and community funds. The wife argued a substantial portion of those accounts should be treated as community property. The husband, however, used detailed tracing to show which portions of the investments were purchased with his separate property funds. The Court of Appeal upheld the trial court's decision accepting the husband's tracing analysis. The ruling emphasized that, under *§ 752*, a spouse's separate property remains their own unless there's clear proof otherwise. Because the husband could trace and identify the separate property contributions, those investments stayed his separate property, and the wife had no ownership interest in them. Ciprari demonstrates how courts apply *§ 752*: if an asset acquired during marriage can be traced to one spouse's separate funds, the other spouse has no interest in that asset.

In re Marriage of Benson (2005) 36 Cal.4th 1096: See *In re Marriage of Benson* *(pg. 12)*.

Full Text of *California Family Code § 752*

Except as otherwise provided by statute, neither spouse has any interest in the separate property of the other.

8. *Family Code section 754* – Freeze on Separate Property Transfers

Explanation:

California Family Code § 754 is a law that temporarily prevents one spouse from unilaterally selling or mortgaging certain property when a divorce or legal separation is underway. In plain terms, here's what it means:

Once a notice of a pending divorce or separation (called a lis pendens) is officially recorded on a piece of real estate owned solely by the other spouse (i.e., the property is that spouse's separate property), that property is effectively "frozen" from being transferred.

For three months after the notice is recorded, the property cannot be sold, refinanced, or otherwise transferred by either spouse unless both spouses agree (by signing the papers) or a court gives permission. In other words, both spouses must join in approving any transfer, or a judge must order it, during this period.

This rule applies to both voluntary actions (like a sale or a new mortgage initiated by the owner spouse) and involuntary actions (like a foreclosure or forced sale by a creditor). The law places a temporary hold on the property's title so that it can't be disposed of without oversight right after divorce proceedings begin.

The purpose of *§ 754* is to prevent rash or unfair disposals of property at the start of a divorce. It protects the non-owner spouse's potential rights and living situation. For example, stopping an owner from quickly selling a home that the other spouse is living in or might have a financial interest in until the matter can be reviewed by the court.

Examples:

Family Home Protection: Alice owns a house that she purchased before the marriage (her separate property), and her Husband, Ben, has been living there with her. When their marriage falters, Ben files for divorce and records a notice of the pending divorce (lis pendens) on Alice's property with the county. Under *Family Code § 754*, Alice cannot sell or refinance that house for the next three months unless Ben agrees to the transaction or the court permits it. This gives Ben assurance that the home won't be sold out from under him in the early stages of the divorce.

Attempted Sale of an Investment Property: John owns a rental duplex in his name only, making it his separate property. After John's Wife files for legal separation, she records a lis pendens (a notice of the pending proceeding) on the property. A few weeks later, John finds a buyer and tries to quickly sell the duplex. Because of the § 754 freeze, the sale cannot go through without his Wife's written consent or a court order as long as it's within the three-month period after the notice was recorded.

Stopping a New Loan: Maria is going through an annulment with her spouse. Maria's beach cottage is her separate property, so her spouse records a notice of the pending annulment on that property. Shortly after, Maria attempts to take out a home equity loan on the cottage. The bank discovers the lis pendens and informs her that, due to *Family Code § 754*, it cannot proceed with the loan unless Maria's spouse also signs off or the court allows the lien. The law prevents Maria from unilaterally encumbering the property with new debt during the freeze period.

Further Reading:

Family Code § 754 is rarely cited in appellate decisions. In the only published opinion, *L.G. v. M.B.* (2018) 25 Cal.App.5th 211, the court did not interpret *§ 754* or apply it to the parties' property. Instead, the court explained that dissolution actions routinely involve many types of relief beyond changing marital status, including temporary orders about custody/support, property restraint/disposition, and protection of the parties. To make that point, the Court listed multiple Family Code provisions authorizing such interim relief, including *Family Code §754*, along with *§§ 2045*, 2047, 3022, 3060, and 3600.

Full Text of *California Family Code § 754*

If notice of the pendency of a proceeding for dissolution of the marriage, for nullity of the marriage, or for legal separation of the parties is recorded in any county in which either spouse resides on real property that is the separate property of the other, the real property shall not for a period of three months thereafter be transferred, encumbered, or otherwise disposed of voluntarily or involuntarily without the joinder of both spouses, unless the court otherwise orders.

9. *Family Code section 760* – Community Property

Explanation:

California Family Code § 760 establishes California's fundamental community-property presumption for property. The statute provides that, except as otherwise provided by statute, all property, real or personal, wherever situated, acquired by a married person during the marriage while domiciled in California is community property. *Section 760* does not itself define, characterize, or allocate marital debts. Debts and liabilities are addressed in other provisions, including *Family Code sections 2620 through 2628*; for example, debts incurred by either spouse after the date of marriage and before the date of separation are generally divided under *Family Code section 2622*, subject to the statutory exceptions and equitable rules in the debt-division statutes. For property acquired during marriage, *§ 760* supplies the default characterization rule; at dissolution, the community estate is then divided under the applicable division statutes, including *Family Code sections 2550 through 2552*, unless a statute, valid agreement, or tracing rule produces a different result.

Examples:

Marital Earnings Used to Buy Property: John and Jane are married and live in California. During the marriage, Jane saves money from her salary and buys a car, putting only her name on the title. Under *Family Code § 760*, that car is still presumed to be community property of both John and Jane because it was purchased with marital earnings during the marriage. In a divorce, a court would treat the car as belonging equally to both spouses, regardless of whose name is on it or who paid for it, unless there is proof that the money used was Jane's separate property.

Inheritance During Marriage: While married, Maria inherits $50,000 from her late father. Even though she received this money in the middle of her marriage, it is not subject to the community property presumption of *§ 760* because another law (*Family Code § 770*) says that property acquired by gift or inheritance is separate property. In this example, the $50,000 inheritance remains Maria's separate property and would not be split with her spouse in a divorce. *Family Code § 760* doesn't override specific statutes that label certain property (like inheritances) as separate.

Title in One Spouse's Name Only: Alex and Sam buy a house during their marriage, and the deed is recorded only in Alex's name. Despite the title being in one name, a court applying *Family Code § 760* would presume the house is community property because it was acquired during the marriage. The fact that only Alex's name is on the deed does not by itself make it separate property. Unless there was a written agreement or other legal proof to show

Sam gave up any interest, the law will treat the house as owned equally by both spouses under the community property presumption.

Further Reading:

In re Marriage of Valli (2014) 58 Cal.4th 1396: See *In re Marriage of Valli (pg. 10).*

Speier v. Brace (2020) 9 Cal.5th 677: The California Supreme Court reaffirmed that the *Family Code § 760* presumption can prevail over contrary title in disputes involving third parties. In this case, a married couple had purchased real estate during their marriage with community (marital) funds but took title as joint tenants. Later, in a bankruptcy context, the question was whether the property should be treated as community property (belonging entirely to the couple's community) or as separate property due to the joint tenancy title. The Supreme Court held that when spouses acquire property during marriage with community funds, it is presumed to be community property under *§ 760*, even if the deed names them as joint tenants. The form of title (joint tenancy) did not by itself transmute the property into separate property, especially for property acquired after 1985, since California law requires a clear written agreement to change community property into separate property. Thus, the community property presumption stood, meaning the entire property was considered part of the community.

Estate of Murphy (1976) 15 Cal.3d 907– In this landmark case, the California Supreme Court applied the community property presumption to assets acquired during a marriage when determining a widow's share of her husband's estate. The husband's heirs claimed that certain assets (purchased during the marriage) were the husband's separate property because they were bought with money from his separate-property bank account. However, the court found there was no clear tracing of the funds to a separate source. As a result, the assets were presumed to be community property under the predecessor of *§ 760* (and the husband's estate failed to rebut that presumption). The widow was therefore entitled to half of those assets. *Estate of Murphy* illustrates that if a spouse (or their estate) asserts an item acquired during marriage is separate property, they bear the burden of proving it with evidence; otherwise, it will be treated as community property.

In re Marriage of Deluca (2020) 45 Cal.App.5th 184: This Court of Appeal case shows how *§ 760* works when a spouse acquires property through an inheritance-related transaction during marriage. In Deluca, a husband received title to an apartment building from his sister as part of a family trust settlement after their father's death. The trial court initially treated the property as the husband's separate property (assuming it was like an inheritance). The Court of Appeal disagreed and held that the apartment building was community property because the transfer to the husband occurred during the marriage in exchange for payments (it was essentially a purchase of the sister's share, not a gift or bequest directly from the father). *Family Code § 760*'s community property presumption applied, meaning the property had to be split as community property. The husband was entitled only to reimbursement for any separate funds he contributed to acquiring that property (under *Family Code § 2640*). This case highlights that only assets directly inherited or gifted are separate by statute; if a spouse buys out someone's interest during the marriage (even in an estate settlement), that acquired interest is presumptively community property.

Full Text of *California Family Code § 760*

Except as otherwise provided by statute, all property, real or personal, wherever situated, acquired by a married person during the marriage while domiciled in this state is community property.

10. *Family Code section 761* – Property Held in Trust

Explanation:

California Family Code § 761 addresses what happens when a married couple places community property into a trust (especially a revocable living trust). In simple terms, this law ensures that putting community property into a revocable trust doesn't change its status as community property, unless the trust document clearly says otherwise. Here are the key points in plain language:

Community property stays community when the statutory conditions are met. Unless the trust instrument or transfer instrument expressly provides otherwise, community property transferred to a trust remains community property during marriage, regardless of the trustee's identity, if the trust is revocable as to that property during marriage and any power to modify the trust as to the rights and interests in that property during marriage may be exercised only with the joinder or consent of both spouses.

Either spouse can revoke (unless stated otherwise): Unless the trust document explicitly forbids it, either spouse acting alone can revoke or pull back community property from the trust. If community property (and any earnings or growth from it) is taken out of the trust (whether by revocation, withdrawal, etc.), it remains community property unless at the time it's taken out both spouses agreed in writing to change it to separate property (a valid "transmutation").

Trustee's management power: The trustee of the trust can manage, sell, or control the trust property per the trust's terms without needing both spouses to sign off on every decision, unless the trust document itself says the trustee needs one or both spouses' consent for certain actions. In other words, by default the trustee has the power to handle the assets, but the trust can require spousal approval if that's what the spouses wanted when they set it up.

Applies to past and future transfers: These rules apply to property put into a trust before, on, or after July 1, 1987. (This date is when a law change took effect, but the statute makes the rule retroactive and forward-looking. Even older trust transfers are covered so long as they meet the conditions.)

Transfers outside *§ 761* are not automatically recharacterized by this section. Subdivision (e) preserves the community character of property transferred before, on, or after July 1, 1987, in a manner or to a trust other than the trust described in *§ 761*; characterization then depends on the transfer instrument, trust terms, transmutation rules, and other applicable Family Code and Probate Code rules.

Examples:

Joint Property into Trust: Maria and John, a married couple, transfer their jointly owned home (community property) into a revocable living trust. John is named as the sole trustee. Under *Family Code § 761*, the home is still considered community property during the marriage, even though it's now held in a trust with John as trustee. The fact that the property is in a trust (and who the trustee is) doesn't change their equal ownership. If they later divorce, the house will be treated as community property because placing it into the trust didn't alter its character.

Trust Transfer Without Consent: Assume the same trust as above, and it allows either spouse to revoke the trust. John decides to revoke the trust as to the home and transfers the house back into their names alone, without Maria's explicit consent at that moment. Because the trust didn't require both spouses to agree to a revocation, John is permitted under *§ 761(b)* to revoke the trust on his own. Once the house is removed from the trust, it is still community property (because there was no agreement or document changing it to separate property). John cannot claim the house as his separate asset simply because he took it out of the trust. It remains a jointly owned marital asset.

Unauthorized Trust Revocation: Now consider a trust where the document says both spouses must agree in writing to any revocation or removal of property. If John alone attempts to revoke that trust and withdraw the home, that action would violate the terms of the trust (since the trust explicitly required both spouses' consent). In this scenario, *§ 761* would not override the trust's requirement. John's unilateral revocation would be invalid because the trust "expressly provides otherwise" (requiring both spouses to act together). The law defers to the spouses' own agreement in the trust instrument.

Irrevocable or different trust arrangement: Lisa and Mark transfer community funds to a trust that does not meet *§ 761*'s revocable-trust conditions. *Section 761(a)*'s specific revocable-trust rule may not control the transfer, but that does not mean the community character is automatically lost. The court would examine the trust instrument, transfer documents, any valid transmutation, and other applicable law to decide whether the property remains community property or has been legally changed.

Further Reading:

Estate of Powell (2000) 83 Cal.App.4th 1434: In this case, a husband revoked a joint revocable trust after his wife's death and claimed the entire trust property. The Court of Appeal discussed *Family Code § 761(b)* and *Probate Code § 15401*. It confirmed that, during both spouses' lifetimes, either spouse may revoke a community property trust and that such revocation would ordinarily cover all the community property in the trust (not just the revoking spouse's half), unless the trust document says otherwise. However, the court also noted that when one spouse dies, the community property in the trust effectively splits into separate property halves (each spouse's half interest becomes their separate property at death). In Powell, because the wife had died (transmuting the community property into a half-interest for each as separate property by operation of law), the husband's post-death revocation could only reclaim his half of the trust assets. The other half had to go according to the wife's will. This case illustrates both the broad power to revoke under *§ 761* and the limitation that death imposes on community property status.

Masry v. Masry (2008) 166 Cal.App.4th 738: This published appellate decision involved a married couple (Edward and Joette Masry) who created a joint revocable trust. Shortly before Edward's death, he unilaterally revoked the trust (without telling Joette) and moved his share of assets into a new trust benefiting his children from a prior marriage. Joette challenged this move, arguing it was invalid since she didn't receive notice during Edward's lifetime. The Court of Appeal upheld Edward's unilateral revocation. It reasoned that because the trust did not explicitly make its own revocation method exclusive, Edward could use the default method allowed by law. *Family Code § 761(b)* and *Probate Code § 15401(b)* together allow one settlor of community property to revoke the trust as to that community property, unless the trust expressly says otherwise. In Masry, delivering the revocation to himself as trustee was deemed sufficient. The case underscores that absent a clear trust provision requiring both spouses' consent or some other exclusive procedure, either spouse may revoke a community property trust on their own under *§ 761*.

Full Text of *California Family Code § 761*

(a) Unless the trust instrument or the instrument of transfer expressly provides otherwise, community property that is transferred in trust remains community property during the marriage, regardless of the identity of the trustee, if the trust, originally or as amended before or after the transfer, provides that the trust is revocable as to that property during the marriage and the power, if any, to modify the trust as to the rights and interests in that property during the marriage may be exercised only with the joinder or consent of both spouses.

(b) Unless the trust instrument expressly provides otherwise, a power to revoke as to community property may be exercised by either spouse acting alone. Community property, including any income or appreciation, that is distributed or withdrawn from a trust by revocation, power of withdrawal, or otherwise, remains community property unless there is a valid transmutation of the property at the time of distribution or withdrawal.

(c) The trustee may convey and otherwise manage and control the trust property in accordance with the provisions of the trust without the joinder or consent of either spouse unless the trust expressly requires the joinder or consent of one or both spouses.

(d) This section applies to a transfer made before, on, or after July 1, 1987.

(e) Nothing in this section affects the community character of property that is transferred before, on, or after July 1, 1987, in any manner or to a trust other than described in this section.

11. *Family Code section 770* – Separate Property

Explanation:

California's *Family Code § 770* defines what counts as a married person's separate property. In simple terms, separate property is anything one spouse owns individually, rather than together with the other spouse. Under *§ 770*, separate property includes:

Any property the spouse owned before they got married.

Any property the spouse acquires during the marriage by gift, inheritance (bequest or devise), or descent.

The rent, income, or other profits generated by any of the above separate property.

All other property acquired during the marriage is presumed community property (jointly owned), unless it falls into one of these separate-property categories. In practical terms, marriage alone does not convert a person's separate assets into community assets. For example, if a person owned a house before marriage, that house remains their separate property even after they marry. Likewise, if a spouse inherits money from a parent while married, that inheritance is that spouse's separate property, not community property. (Note that separate property can generally be sold or transferred by the owning spouse without the other spouse's consent, per subsection (b) of *§ 770.*)

Examples:

Pre-marriage asset: Jane owns a condominium before her wedding. The condominium and any income from it (rent, sale proceeds, etc.) are separate property under *§ 770(a)(1).*

Gift during marriage: During the marriage, Bob's aunt gives him a car as a gift. The car is Bob's separate property under *§ 770(a)(2)* because it was acquired by gift.

Inheritance: Carol inherits her parents' ranch while she is married. The ranch is Carol's separate property under *§ 770(a)(2).* Any rents or crops (profits) from the ranch are also separate under *§ 770(a)(3).*

Separate earnings (after separation): Although not in *§ 770* itself, *Family Code § 771* makes earnings a spouse receives while living apart (after separation) their separate property. For instance, if during a legal separation one spouse works and earns wages, those earnings are separate property under the law.

Further Reading:

Kircher v. Kircher (2010) 189 Cal.App.4th 1105: In this published decision, the court explained that under *Family Code § 770*, property owned by a person before marriage or acquired by gift or inheritance is separate property. The case involved property held by spouses as joint tenants. The court held that even though title was joint, the character of the property (community or separate) must be determined by when and how it was acquired. Here the husband had transmuted separate property into joint tenancy with his wife, so the property was treated as community property for purposes of the surviving spouse's liability.

In re Marriage of Deluca (2020) 45 Cal.App.5th 184*: In this divorce case, the wife appealed the trial court's ruling about a piece of real estate (the "Florida Street property"). The Court of Appeal noted that § 770(a)(2) makes inheritances separate property, but held that here the husband had bought the property from his sister after a trust settlement. Because he did not receive it as a direct inheritance or devise, it did not qualify as separate property under § 770. Instead, the statutory presumption of community property applied to the property acquisition.*

In re Marriage of Green (2013) 56 Cal.4th 1130: The California Supreme Court reiterated that the character of property is fixed at the time of acquisition. It explained that under *§ 770(a)(1)* "property owned by [a] person before marriage" remains that person's separate property. Thus, if a spouse owned an asset outright before the marriage, it is separate property even after marriage and divorce. (In Green, the court was dividing retirement benefits but emphasized that pre-marriage service credits remained separate property.)

Full Text of *California Family Code § 770*

(a) Separate property of a married person includes all of the following: (1) All property owned by the person before marriage. (2) All property acquired by the person after marriage by gift, bequest, devise, or descent. (3) The rents, issues, and profits of the property described in this section. (b) A married person may, without the consent of the person's spouse, convey the person's separate property.

12. *Family Code section 771* – Earnings After Separation

Explanation:

California Family Code § 771 provides that once spouses are separated, each spouse's earnings and accumulations are generally considered that spouse's own separate property. In plain language, this means that money earned or assets acquired by one spouse after the spouses have separated will belong only to that spouse, not to both spouses as community property. The idea is to draw a clear line at the date of separation: after that point, the "community" ceases to accumulate new property from either spouse's labor. An important exception in this law is that if a minor child earns money under certain types of contracts (for example, some entertainment or sports contracts defined in another law), those earnings belong solely to the child, not to either parent.

Explanation:

Family Code § 771 embodies a key concept in California community property law: after spouses have separated (meaning they have a complete, final break in the marriage), the earnings or income of each belong only to that person. During a marriage (before separation), most income either spouse earns is community property, owned equally by both. *Section 771* creates an endpoint to that sharing by saying essentially "when you're truly separated, new earnings aren't shared." This protects spouses from having to split money they earn after the marital relationship has ended in substance.

For *Section 771* to apply, there must be a true date of separation. California law (*Family Code § 70*) defines "date of separation" as the date when there is a complete and final break in the marital relationship, proved by two factors: (1) one spouse has expressed to the other an intent to end the marriage, and (2) that spouse's conduct is consistent with ending the marriage. Both intent and conduct are considered; often called a subjective intent and objective conduct test. Before 2017, the law required spouses to be "living separate and apart," which courts interpreted to generally require living in separate households. In fact, in a 2015 California Supreme Court case, the court ruled that living in separate residences was a threshold requirement to be "separated" (meaning spouses who still lived under one roof could not be considered separated even if they acted like it). This was the Marriage of Davis case discussed below. In response, the Legislature changed the law. Now, after the 2017 amendment, the focus is on the date of separation as defined by the two-part test above, and physical separation into different homes is not strictly required (though it is often strong evidence of separation).

In practical terms, *Family Code § 771* generally separates post-separation earnings and accumulations from each spouse's labor from the community estate once the statutory date of separation has occurred. It does not automatically convert existing community property, or income and value attributable to existing community property, into one spouse's separate property. When an asset is mixed-character or was partly acquired with community contributions before separation, the court must first identify the character of the asset and the source of any post-separation payments or earnings, then apply the appropriate apportionment, reimbursement, valuation, or use-and-occupancy rule.

Valuation caveat: *Family Code § 771* is a characterization statute, not the general valuation-date statute. In a Moore/Marsden real-property case, post-separation separate earnings used by the owner spouse to reduce principal do not increase the community's pro tanto ownership percentage. Mohler holds that the Moore/Marsden percentage stops increasing once community funds stop building equity, often at separation; *In re Marriage of Freeman* (2025) 110 Cal.App.5th 406 confirms that the community's pro tanto percentage interest is calculated as of separation, while the property's value is generally determined as near as practicable to the time of trial under *Family Code § 2552*, absent a proper alternate valuation date for good cause.

Subdivision (b) of *§ 771* is a narrower provision. It was added to clarify that if a minor child (not yet emancipated) earns income from certain contracts, for example, contracts in entertainment or sports that minors can enter with court approval (as described in *Family Code § 6750*), those earnings remain the child's separate legal property, even if the child is living with one parent. Normally, the wages of minor children could be considered to belong to their family unit, but this subdivision ensures that child actors/performers or similar retain their earnings for themselves.

Examples:

Post-Separation Salary Increase: Imagine a couple separates on June 1. The Wife gets a new job or a big promotion on July 1. Under § 771, the increased salary she earns after June 1 is her separate property. In a divorce, the Husband would not be entitled to half of the Wife's post-separation paycheck. Only the earnings up to June 1 (while they were together) would be considered community property to be split.

Bonuses or Commissions Straddling Separation: Sometimes a spouse receives a bonus or commission after the date of separation, but it was partly earned by work done before separation. For example, a Husband separates from his spouse in March, and in April he receives a quarterly bonus for work performed in January through March. In that case, a portion of the bonus (for January and February work when the spouses were together) would be community property, and the portion attributable to March (after separation on, say, March 1) would be the Husband's separate property. In practice, courts might prorate such earnings to determine the community vs. separate portions.

Lottery Winnings After Separation: If spouses have separated and one spouse then wins the lottery or receives a large payout, that windfall would be that spouse's alone. For example, if a couple separated in 2024 and the Wife happens to win a lottery in 2025, the winnings are her separate property under § 771. (Had they still been married with no separation, lottery winnings would be community property to split.)

Accumulations from Separate Business: Suppose a Husband and Wife separate, and afterward the Husband starts a new business or continues an existing one on his own. The profits he accumulates in that business after the separation date belong solely to him as separate property. However, if the business existed before separation and increased in value due in part to efforts or funds during marriage, there may be some community claim for the before-separation portion of growth, but anything purely earned after the cutoff date is separate by virtue of § 771.

Child Performer's Earnings: As an example of subdivision (b), imagine a 16-year-old child stars in a movie and earns income under a contract approved by the court. Even though that child lives with one parent, the money the child earned from the movie is the child's own property, not the parent's community or separate property. *Section 771(b)* ensures the minor's earnings from certain contracts remain with the minor.

Formula:

Family Code § 771 itself is a definition statute rather than a mathematical formula, but its application can involve some calculations in divorce proceedings. Key examples include:

Proration of Earnings or Bonuses: If a spouse receives income that spans the separation date, courts may calculate what portion of that income is community vs. separate. A simple method is pro-rating based on time. For instance, if a yearly bonus of $10,000 covers January–December and the couple separated on April 1 (i.e., 3 out of 12 months of that year they were together), about 25% of the bonus might be deemed community property and 75% separate property. Similarly, salary earned before the date of separation is community, and salary after is separate, so if a paycheck period straddles the separation, it can be divided by days to allocate the community share.

Epstein credits: Because post-separation earnings are generally separate property under *§ 771*, a spouse who uses those separate funds after separation to pay a preexisting community obligation may request an Epstein credit. The payment is first identified as a qualifying reimbursement claim in the community accounting; after equal division, the practical net effect between spouses often equals one-half of the qualifying amount, subject to the Epstein exceptions, support treatment, agreement, and equitable offsets such as Watts charges.

Watts charges: If one spouse has exclusive post-separation use of a community asset, the community may be credited for the reasonable value of that use. For a wholly community home with a $2,000 monthly rental value used exclusively for six months, the starting gross Watts value is $12,000 to the community; the non-occupying spouse's practical net benefit is generally one-half, or $6,000, subject to offsets and the court's equitable discretion.

Asset valuation: *Section 771* characterizes post-separation earnings and accumulations; it is not the general valuation-date statute. Existing community assets are generally valued under *Family Code § 2552* as near as practicable to trial unless the court selects another valuation date for good cause. Post-separation changes in value may still require apportionment, tracing, reimbursement, or separate-effort analysis depending on the asset and governing authority.

Overall, the common theme in calculations derived from *§ 771* is dividing or reimbursing money according to the timeline: before separation (community) vs. after separation (separate). Many of the financial adjustments in a divorce (like the credits and charges above) aim to fairly allocate expenses and benefits that occur around the separation date.

Further Reading:

In re Marriage of Baragry (1977) 73 Cal.App.3d 444: This early case involved a husband who had moved out of the family home and was living with a girlfriend, yet he continued to come back home frequently (dinner with the family, attending events with his wife, even doing laundry at the marital home). He argued that he was "living separate and apart" from his wife, starting when he moved out, so his substantial earnings after that date should be his separate property. The Court of Appeal disagreed under those facts. It held that despite living in a different residence, the couple had not truly effected a "complete and final break" in the relationship because the husband kept one foot in the door (maintaining the semblance of marriage for social and family purposes). The court noted it would be unfair to let the husband benefit by claiming separation while still enjoying marital benefits. Thus, the court set the date of separation later (when he filed for divorce), making the earnings in that interim period community property. Baragry established that physical separation alone wasn't enough. The spouses' conduct must clearly show a final break.

In re Marriage of Norviel (2002) 102 Cal.App.4th 1152: This case took a stricter view. The husband and wife in Norviel were still living in the same house even though the wife claimed they had emotionally and practically separated. The Court of Appeal (Sixth District) ruled that living in the same residence is fundamentally incompatible with "living separate and apart." The court held that to qualify as separated under *§ 771*, the spouses must be living in different residences. It called physical separation an "indispensable threshold requirement." In other words, after Norviel, if you were still under the same roof, you legally could not be considered separated for purposes of ending community property. This decision created a bright-line rule but was controversial because it could force spouses to maintain two households to establish separation, which is not always financially feasible.

In re Marriage of Davis (2015) 61 Cal.4th 846: This is a California Supreme Court decision that addressed the very issue raised by Norviel. In Davis, the Supreme Court agreed with Norviel's interpretation of the then-current law: it ruled that spouses must be living in separate residences to be considered "living separate and apart" under the wording of *§ 771(a)* as it existed at that time. In the Davis case, the couple had a complete breakdown of their marriage and were living largely separate lives (separate bedrooms, separate finances, etc.) but under one roof for a period of time. The Supreme Court, interpreting the phrase "living separate and apart," concluded that the statute's language required a physical separation into different homes. As a result, the wife's earnings during the period they lived together (even though they considered themselves separated) were deemed community property. The Davis ruling provoked the Legislature to change the law. Soon after, SB 1255 was passed, which amended *§ 771* (and enacted *Family Code § 70*) to eliminate the strict separate-residence requirement. Effective January 1, 2017, the statute now uses "after the date of separation" and *§ 70* defines that term, allowing courts to find a separation date based on intent and conduct without absolute necessity of separate households.

In re Marriage of Lee & Lin (2019) 41 Cal.App.5th 698: The court applied the new definition of "date of separation" from *Family Code § 70* to a pre-2017 situation. The court affirmed that the couple's date of separation was when the husband moved out, and they showed no intent to reconcile. The decision also commented that the new statutory definition in *§ 70* is consistent with the older case law interpreting *§ 771*. This shows that under current law, courts take a full view of spouses' intent and behavior to fix the separation date, rather than simply asking if they live at different addresses.

Full Text of *California Family Code § 771*

(a) The earnings and accumulations of a spouse and the minor children living with, or in the custody of, the spouse, after the date of separation of the spouses, are the separate property of the spouse.

(b) Notwithstanding subdivision (a), the earnings and accumulations of an unemancipated minor child related to a contract of a type described in *Section 6750* shall remain the sole legal property of the minor child.

13. *Family Code section 780* – Personal Injury Damages

Explanation:

California Family Code § 780 provides that if a married person receives money or property due to a personal injury (for example, through a lawsuit judgment or settlement) and the underlying injury happened during the marriage, that compensation is considered community property. In other words, personal injury damages obtained while the spouses are married belong to both spouses jointly. The law treats these funds like any other asset acquired during marriage.

This rule is not absolute. The statute begins with "Except as provided in *Section 781*," which means there are important exceptions. *Family Code § 781* (not detailed here) says that if the cause of action (the event giving rise to the injury claim) arose after the marriage ended (such as after a divorce judgment or while the spouses were living separate and apart), then the recovery is the separate property of the injured spouse. Likewise, if one spouse injured the other (e.g., domestic violence or an intentional tort against the spouse), any damages paid to the injured spouse are treated as that spouse's separate property. These exceptions prevent an unfair result where the non-injured spouse would otherwise share in a recovery that accrued after separation or from harming their own partner.

Family Code § 780 also mentions that its rule is "subject to the rules of allocation set forth in *Section 2603*." *Section 2603* comes into play during a divorce to decide how to divide "community estate personal injury damages." In a divorce, even though personal injury awards from during the marriage are labeled community property under *§ 780*, the law recognizes that the injured spouse has a special claim to that money. Under *Section 2603*, community personal injury damages are usually assigned to the injured spouse rather than split equally. A family court can deviate and give a portion to the other spouse only if the interests of justice strongly warrant it, considering factors like each party's financial needs and how much time has passed since the injury or recovery. Even then, the injured spouse must receive at least 50% of those damages. In practical terms, this means that while an injury settlement from during marriage is jointly owned, the injured spouse will typically keep most or all of it if the marriage ends, unless a court finds a good reason to award some to the other spouse.

Examples:

Car Accident During Marriage: John and Mary are married when John is injured in a car accident caused by a negligent driver. John later receives a $100,000 settlement for his injuries. Because the cause of action (the accident) arose while John and Mary were married, *Family Code § 780* says that the $100,000 is community property. If John and Mary divorce, that settlement is part of the community estate. However, under the special rules for personal injury awards, a court would likely award most or all of that $100,000 to John as the injured spouse (ensuring, at a minimum, John gets 50% or more of it), rather than splitting it 50/50. This reflects the law's recognition that the compensation is intended primarily to make the injured person whole.

Injury After Separation: Suppose John and Mary separate on January 1, and later that year (while the divorce is still pending) Mary is injured at work and wins a judgment for her injuries. Even though they are still legally married until the divorce is finalized, the cause of action arose while they were living separately and the marriage had effectively ended. Under the exception in *Section 781*, Mary's injury award would be her separate property, not community property. John would have no ownership interest in that recovery, and it would not be subject to division in the divorce.

Spousal Wrongdoing: In another scenario, imagine during the marriage one spouse physically injures the other (a domestic violence incident) and the injured spouse sues and obtains damages from the wrongdoing spouse. Even though this occurred during marriage, California law (*Section 781(c)*) classifies the compensation for this inter-spousal injury as the injured spouse's separate property. It would be unjust for the perpetrator to benefit from the damages paid for harming their spouse, so the law ensures those damages belong solely to the victim spouse.

Further Reading:

In re Marriage of Devlin (1982) 138 Cal.App.3d 804: Although decided before the Family Code was enacted (under previous Civil Code provisions), this case illustrates the principle carried into *§ 780*. The husband had received a large personal injury settlement during marriage and used it to purchase various assets. Upon divorce, the trial court awarded the bulk of those assets to the husband (the injured party) instead of splitting them equally. The Court of Appeal upheld this, explaining that personal injury recoveries are community property during marriage but are to be assigned to the injured spouse upon divorce (absent special circumstances). This early case confirmed that it is equitable for the injured spouse to retain most of the injury compensation, foreshadowing the rules now in *Family Code §§ 780 and 2603*.

Meighan v. Shore (1995) 34 Cal.App.4th 1025: In this case, the Court of Appeal noted that *Family Code § 780* simply continues the prior law (formerly *Civil Code § 4800*) classifying personal injury claims arising during marriage as community property. The case involved a legal malpractice situation where an attorney failed to inform a wife of her right to file a loss of consortium claim. While the core issue was the attorney's duty, the court's discussion recognized that any loss of consortium damages (a spouse's claim for their own suffering due to the other spouse's injury) would fall under *§ 780* if the underlying injury occurred during marriage. In short, Meighan reaffirms that personal injury causes of action arising in the marital period are community assets under California law.

In re Marriage of Klug (2005) 130 Cal.App.4th 1389*:* This case applied Family Code § 780 and the related sections to a unique scenario. Here, a wife had received a $346,000 legal malpractice settlement, and the issue was whether that settlement was community property (because the events leading to it began during marriage) or her separate property (because the harm was realized after separation). The Court of Appeal determined that the malpractice cause of action accrued after the spouses' separation, meaning the settlement was the wife's separate property and not subject to division as a community asset. Klug underscores how courts determine the character of injury-related recoveries by looking at when the underlying cause of action arose. If it arose during the marriage, § 780 makes it community property; if it arose after separation, it belongs to the injured spouse alone. This decision also highlights that even for community personal injury claims, the injured spouse's interests are strongly protected. The husband in Klug was not entitled to share in a recovery that was deemed to have arisen after the marital community ended.

Full Text of *California Family Code § 780*

Except as provided in *Section 781* and subject to the rules of allocation set forth in *Section 2603*, money and other property received or to be received by a married person in satisfaction of a judgment for damages for personal injuries, or pursuant to an agreement for the settlement or compromise of a claim for such damages, is community property if the cause of action for the damages arose during the marriage.

14. *Family Code section 781* – Personal Injury Awards as Separate Property

Explanation:

California Family Code § 781 sets out when money from personal injury settlements or court judgments is treated as the separate property of the injured spouse rather than community property. In general, if the injury happened during the marriage, the default rule (under *Section 780*) is that any resulting damages are community property to be split in a divorce. *Section 781* creates exceptions to that rule: it protects certain personal injury awards so that they belong solely to the injured spouse.

In plain terms, *Section 781(a)* says that if an injury occurs after the marriage is effectively over or while spouses are living apart, any compensation received belongs only to the injured person. This includes injuries that happen after a divorce or legal separation is finalized, or when the spouses are living separate and apart (even if not yet divorced). Additionally, *Section 781(c)* ensures that if one spouse has a legal claim against the other (for example, one spouse injures the other), any damages paid to the injured spouse are that spouse's separate property. Finally, *Section 781(b)* provides that if the non-injured spouse paid for injury-related expenses (like medical bills) out of community funds or their own funds, they have the right to be reimbursed from the injury award. In summary, *§ 781* aims to fairly allocate personal injury awards by recognizing when those funds should be treated as the individual property of the injured spouse and by reimbursing a spouse who contributed to the costs of the injury.

Examples:

Accident After Separation: Alice and Bob separate, and a month later Alice is in a car accident. She eventually receives a settlement for her injuries. Under *§ 781(a)(2)*, because the cause of action (the accident) arose while Alice and Bob were living separate from each other, the settlement is Alice's separate property. Bob would not be entitled to any share of that money in the divorce. If Bob had paid any of Alice's medical bills from his own savings or from a joint account, he could claim reimbursement of those costs from the settlement under *§ 781(b)*.

Injury After Divorce Finalized: Tom and Maria's marriage is dissolved by a final divorce judgment in January. In March, Tom is injured at work and wins a personal injury lawsuit. Because the injury occurred after the divorce was final (*§ 781(a)(1)*), the entire award is Tom's separate property. Maria has no claim to any portion of that money, since they were no longer married when the cause of action arose.

One Spouse Injures the Other: During their marriage, John accidentally causes serious injury to Jane through negligent driving. Jane sues John for personal injury. Even though this happened while they were married, *§ 781(c)* specifies that any damages John pays (or his insurer pays on his behalf) to Jane for her injuries are Jane's separate property. In other words, money paid from one spouse to the other for a marital tort is not treated as community property. It belongs entirely to the injured spouse (Jane). John also would not have any claim to that money, and it wouldn't be split in the property division.

Using Community Funds for Injury Expenses: While still married, Linda is injured in an accident, and the couple uses $10,000 from their joint savings to cover her medical bills. Later, after they separate, Linda's lawsuit results in a $50,000 settlement. Because the injury happened during marriage, normally that settlement could be community property, but here the cause of action actually arose while they were living apart (assume they were separated when the injury occurred), so *§ 781(a)* makes it Linda's separate property. However, under *§ 781(b)*, Linda must reimburse the community for the $10,000 spent on her treatment. In practice, this means $10,000 from her settlement would be paid back or accounted for so that her ex-husband is compensated for the community funds that went toward her injury expenses. The remainder of the settlement is Linda's separate property.

Further Reading:

In re Marriage of Mason (1979) 93 Cal.App.3d 215: One of the earliest cases applying these principles. Here, the husband received a large personal injury award during the marriage. The Court of Appeal upheld a division of property on divorce that gave the injured husband the bulk of the assets traceable to his injury compensation. This case recognized that personal injury damages (though community property when received during marriage) are subject to special handling at divorce, often allocated predominantly to the injured spouse (similar to what is now codified in *§ 781* and related provisions).

In re Marriage of Devlin (1982) 138 Cal.App.3d 804: In this case, the husband had been seriously injured during the marriage and received personal injury damages. Upon divorce, the trial court awarded most of the couple's community property (which was derived from that injury settlement) to the husband. The wife appealed, but the Court of Appeal affirmed the decision. The ruling explained that, under the law (then *Civil Code § 4800(c)*, the precursor to *Family Code §§ 780–781*), personal injury recoveries are "community property" during marriage but are to be assigned to the injured spouse at divorce except in unusual circumstances. Devlin confirmed that a court may award more than half (in fact, all, in this instance) of the injury-related assets to the injured spouse, without requiring an equal division, as long as the injured spouse gets at least 50%. This case illustrates the policy later embodied in *§ 781* — treating injury awards like the injured party's separate property upon dissolution.

In re Marriage of Morris (1983) 139 Cal.App.3d 823: This appellate decision involved a wife who had received about $42,000 from a personal injury settlement during the marriage. In the divorce, the trial court awarded the entire settlement amount to the wife and divided the rest of the community property equally. The husband argued that the court should have offset that award by giving him more of the other property (to equalize the division). The Court of Appeal disagreed and upheld the award entirely to the wife. The opinion made clear that the law (*former Civil Code § 4800(c)*, now reflected in *§ 781* and *§ 2603*) allows personal injury damages to be treated essentially as the injured spouse's separate property at divorce. The equal division rule does not apply to those damages. The injured spouse can receive 100% of the settlement without any "offset" to the other spouse, so long as the statutory minimum of one-half to the injured party is met. Morris confirmed that giving the injured spouse the entire recovery is permissible and consistent with legislative intent.

In re Marriage of Klug (2005) 130 Cal.App.4th 1389: This more recent case dealt directly with the timing aspect codified in *§ 781(a)*. In Klug, the wife had filed a legal malpractice lawsuit (considered a personal injury/tort claim) against an attorney after the spouses had separated. She settled that lawsuit and received money after the marriage had ended. The husband claimed that settlement was a community asset. The Court of Appeal held that the malpractice cause of action "arose" after separation, meaning the settlement was the wife's separate property under the exception now found in *§ 781(a)(2)* (injury cause of action arising while living separate from spouse). The court emphasized that whether a tort recovery is separate or community property depends on when the underlying cause of action arose. Because the wrongful acts and resulting harm happened when the parties were no longer together, the recovery did not belong to the community. Klug illustrates how courts apply *§ 781* to characterize post-separation injury claims as the separate property of the injured spouse.

Full Text of *California Family Code § 781*

(a) Money or other property received or to be received by a married person in satisfaction of a judgment for damages for personal injuries, or pursuant to an agreement for the settlement or compromise of a claim for those damages, is the separate property of the injured person if the cause of action for the damages arose as follows:

(1) After the entry of a judgment of dissolution of a marriage or legal separation of the parties.

(2) While the injured spouse is living separate from the other spouse.

(b) Notwithstanding subdivision (a), if the spouse of the injured person has paid expenses by reason of the personal injuries from separate property or from the community property, the spouse is entitled to reimbursement of the separate property or the community property for those expenses from the separate property received by the injured person under subdivision (a).

(c) Notwithstanding subdivision (a), if one spouse has a cause of action against the other spouse that arose during the marriage of the parties, money or property paid or to be paid by or on behalf of a party to the party's spouse of that marriage in satisfaction of a judgment for damages for personal injuries to that spouse, or pursuant to an agreement for the settlement or compromise of a claim for the damages, is the separate property of the injured spouse.

15. *Family Code section 782* – Community Property in Interspousal Tort Cases

Explanation:

California Family Code § 782 addresses what happens when one spouse causes injury to the other spouse, creating a legal liability (for example, a personal injury claim or court judgment between spouses). This law ensures that the spouse who was harmed (the "injured spouse") is not forced to use their share of community property to pay for the damages caused by the other spouse. In simpler terms, if your spouse harms you and owes you damages, they must first use their own separate money or assets to pay what they owe, before any shared marital assets are used.

Specifically, *§ 782* provides that community property (the assets acquired during marriage that belong equally to both spouses) cannot be used to satisfy the wrongdoer spouse's liability to the injured spouse until the wrongdoer's separate property is exhausted. This prevents the wrongdoer from depleting assets that belong in part to the victim spouse in order to pay for their own wrongdoing. It effectively protects the innocent spouse's half of the community property from being taken to cover the other spouse's tort liability.

There are a couple of important exceptions built into the law. First, the injured spouse can consent in writing, after the incident, to allow community property to be used to satisfy the liability. For example, spouses might agree as part of a settlement or divorce that some community funds will go toward the injury damages. This written consent is the only way community assets can be used to pay the debt before the wrongdoer's separate property is exhausted. Second, *§ 782* makes clear that it does not affect insurance or indemnity agreements. If an insurance policy (such as auto insurance or homeowner's insurance) covers the injury, the insurer can pay the claim as normal, even if the insurance was paid for with community funds. In other words, insurance payouts are not restricted by this law. The injured spouse can still benefit from insurance coverage without first exhausting the wrongdoer's separate property.

Examples:

Domestic Violence Scenario: A Wife intentionally injures her Husband during an incident of domestic violence, and the Husband later sues her for his medical costs and pain and suffering. Under Family Code § 782, any judgment the Husband obtains must be paid out of the Wife's separate property first (for example, her own savings, inheritance, or other separate assets). The couple's community property, such as joint bank accounts or the family home, which are owned 50/50, cannot be used to pay the Husband's damage award until the Wife's separate assets are completely used up. This rule ensures the Husband does not effectively have to pay himself with assets that are partly his; it protects his half of the community property from being taken to satisfy the Wife's debt for injuring him.

Negligent injury with insurance: Imagine Husband accidentally backs the car into Wife, causing injury. If Husband is liable to Wife, *§ 782* generally prevents community property from being used to discharge Husband's interspousal tort liability until Husband's nonexempt separate property is exhausted. Wife may also give written consent after the injury to use community property sooner. If an auto insurance policy covers the accident, the insurer may pay the claim under the policy; *§ 782* does not impair the right to contractual indemnity even if community property paid the premiums.

Further Reading:

There are relatively few published appellate cases interpreting *Family Code § 782* directly, likely because the statute's mandate is clear and often applied straightforwardly in divorce property divisions or settlements. However, California courts have long recognized the principle that an innocent spouse should not have to bear the financial burden of the other spouse's wrongful acts. Prior to the Family Code (which took effect in 1994), similar rules existed under the Civil Code. Some notable cases illustrate how courts handle these situations:

In re Marriage of Stitt (1983) 147 Cal.App.3d 579: In this pre-*§ 782* case (decided under former Civil Code provisions), a wife had incurred legal debts and restitution obligations due to embezzlement (a crime she committed which did not benefit the community). The Court of Appeal upheld the trial court's decision to assign those debts entirely to the wife rather than treating them as community obligations. In effect, the wife's separate property and her share of community property were responsible for the debt, and the innocent husband's 50% share of the community was not used to pay for the wife's wrongdoing. This case exemplifies the policy later codified in *§ 782*: an innocent spouse's portion of community assets shouldn't be diminished because of the other spouse's intentional wrongdoing.

In re Marriage of McNeill (1984) 160 Cal.App.3d 548: Here, the wife defrauded the husband during the marriage (convincing him to sign over assets through deceit). The husband obtained a civil judgment against the wife for fraud, including compensatory and punitive damages, and that civil case was consolidated with their divorce. The Court of Appeal approved an outcome where the husband's damages award was satisfied from the wife's assets, specifically by charging it against the wife's share of the community property (after her separate property was exhausted), rather than reducing the husband's share. This ensured the husband received the full benefit of his damages award and didn't essentially pay himself with property he owned. McNeill, though decided before *§ 782* existed, reflects the same equitable principle: a spouse who is victimized by the other can be made whole out of the offending spouse's share of assets, without raiding the victim's half.

If an interspousal injury occurs today, courts handling a divorce or civil lawsuit will apply *Family Code § 782* to reach a fair result along the lines of the above cases. Notably, since *§ 782*'s enactment, no published appellate decision has had to overturn or clarify it. The rule is straightforward, and spouses or their insurers typically settle these matters in line with the statute's requirements.

Full Text of *California Family Code § 782*

(a) Where an injury to a married person is caused in whole or in part by the negligent or wrongful act or omission of the person's spouse, the community property may not be used to discharge the liability of the tortfeasor spouse to the injured spouse or the liability to make contribution to a joint tortfeasor until the separate property of the tortfeasor spouse, not exempt from enforcement of a money judgment, is exhausted.

(b) This section does not prevent the use of community property to discharge a liability referred to in subdivision (a) if the injured spouse gives written consent thereto after the occurrence of the injury.

(c) This section does not affect the right to indemnity provided by an insurance or other contract to discharge the tortfeasor spouse's liability, whether or not the consideration given for the contract consisted of community property.

16. *Family Code section 850* – Transmutation of Property

Explanation:

California Family Code § 850 allows married persons (spouses) to change the ownership classification of their property between them, a process known as a "transmutation." In simple terms, spouses can agree to convert community property into one spouse's separate property, convert one spouse's separate property into community property, or even convert one spouse's separate property into the separate property of the other spouse. These changes can be made with or without consideration, meaning no money or compensation is required: one spouse can essentially make a gift of property to the other or to the marital community.

Transmutations are subject to important safeguards and requirements. First, California law (specifically, *Family Code § 852*) requires that any transmutation be made in writing with an "express declaration" of the change, signed or accepted by the spouse whose interest is adversely affected. In other words, a verbal agreement or casual conversation is not enough. The spouses must put the agreement in a clear written document (such as an interspousal transfer deed or postnuptial agreement) explicitly stating the intent to change the property's status. (There is a narrow exception for gifts between spouses of personal items, like clothing or jewelry, that are used solely by the recipient spouse and are not substantial in value given the couple's circumstances. Such small gifts can be valid without a formal writing.) Additionally, *Family Code § 851* provides that transmutations are subject to laws against fraud, meaning a spouse cannot transmute property in a way that defrauds creditors or others. Furthermore, because spouses owe each other a duty of honest and fair dealing (a fiduciary duty), any transaction where one spouse gains an advantage (for example, a transmutation that greatly benefits one spouse) may be closely scrutinized by courts for undue influence. In practice, as long as the proper formalities are observed, clear written documentation and voluntary, informed consent, a transmutation is a legally effective way for spouses to rearrange the ownership of their assets between them.

Examples:

Converting Separate Property to Community Property: Jane owned a house by herself before marriage (it was her separate property). After marrying John, she decides she wants the house to be owned by both of them as a couple. Jane and John sign a written agreement (and record a deed) stating that the house is now community property. This is a transmutation under *Section 850*: Jane's separate property home has been converted into a community asset that both spouses own equally.

Converting Community Property to Separate Property (Gift to Spouse): Mike and Anna, while married, jointly own a car as community property. Mike wants to gift the car entirely to Anna for her birthday so that it will be her sole property. To do this, Mike signs a simple written statement (an interspousal transfer form) declaring that he is transferring his interest in the car to Anna as her separate property. Once properly executed, the car becomes Anna's separate property. (If Mike had simply told Anna "the car is yours now" without a written document, the law would not recognize that as a valid transmutation.)

Transferring One Spouse's Separate Property to the Other Spouse: Laura inherited investment stocks from her parents, which are her separate property. She decides to transfer half of these stocks to her Husband, David, to be his separate property as a gift. Laura executes a written agreement clearly stating that a specified number of shares are transferred to David as his separate property, and David accepts it. This transaction transmutes that portion of Laura's separate property into David's separate property. Without such a clear written agreement, if Laura had just put the stocks in an account under David's name, it might not be considered a valid transmutation.

Further Reading:

Estate of MacDonald (1990) 51 Cal.3d 262: See MacDonald Express Declaration Test (pg. 8).

In re Marriage of Benson (2005) 36 Cal.4th 1096: See *In re Marriage of Benson (pg. 12).*

In re Marriage of Valli (2014) 58 Cal.4th 1396: See *In re Marriage of Valli (pg. 10).*

In re Marriage of Begian (2018) 31 Cal.App.5th 506: A California Court of Appeal case illustrating the importance of clear language in transmutation documents. In Begian, a husband and wife (along with a third party) signed a "Trust Transfer Deed" to transfer real estate, and the deed stated it was "for no consideration" and was a gift. The wife claimed this deed transmuted the husband's interest to her as her separate property. However, the Court found the deed's language ambiguous: it wasn't clear whether the husband intended to give up his ownership or merely place the property in trust. Because the deed did not contain an express, unequivocal declaration that the husband's share was being transferred to the wife's separate property, it failed to meet the requirements of *Family Code § 852* and was not a valid transmutation.

In re Marriage of Kushesh & Kushesh-Kaviani (2018) 27 Cal.App.5th 449: Another Court of Appeal case, but with a different outcome from Begian. In Kushesh, during a brief marriage the spouses purchased a home, and the title was taken in the wife's name "as her sole and separate property." The husband also signed a grant deed explicitly acknowledging that the property was the wife's separate property. The court held that this deed met the "express declaration" requirement: the language clearly stated the character of the property as the wife's separate property, and it was signed by the spouse whose interest was affected (the husband). Therefore, this was a valid transmutation of the property to the wife's separate property. This case contrasts with Begian and shows that when the written language is clear and unambiguous (for example, using the phrase "sole and separate property" and having the transferor spouse sign it), the transmutation will be upheld by the courts.

Full Text of *California Family Code § 850*

Subject to *Sections 851 to 853*, inclusive, married persons may by agreement or transfer, with or without consideration, do any of the following:

(a) Transmute community property to separate property of either spouse.

(b) Transmute separate property of either spouse to community property.

(c) Transmute separate property of one spouse to separate property of the other spouse.

17. *Family Code section 851* – Transmutations Cannot Defraud Creditors

Explanation:

California Family Code § 851 is a safeguard against spouses abusing "transmutation" agreements to cheat creditors or others. A transmutation is a legal agreement between spouses changing property from community property (owned by both) to separate property (owned by one spouse), or vice versa. In general, California law (see *Family Code § 850*) permits spouses to transmute property during marriage. However, *§ 851* makes clear that any such change in property ownership is still subject to the state's fraudulent transfer laws. In simple terms, spouses cannot re-title or transfer assets between themselves if the purpose is to hinder, delay, or defraud someone else's legitimate rights to those assets (such as creditors or people owed support). If a husband and wife attempt to shuffle property between them to put it out of reach of creditors, a court can undo that transfer under the Uniform Voidable Transactions Act (formerly known as the Uniform Fraudulent Transfer Act). The law is designed to prevent couples from exploiting marital property agreements to dodge debts, judgments, or support obligations. In summary, you can't avoid your liabilities or cheat someone out of their claim by simply transferring your money or property to your spouse. *Family Code § 851* ensures that those kinds of spousal transfers can be treated as fraudulent and reversed.

Examples:

Dodging a Tax Debt: Imagine a Husband owes substantial back taxes. Upon learning the state plans to garnish his wages, he and his Wife sign an agreement transmuting all of their community property and future earnings into the Wife's separate property. Shortly thereafter, the Wife starts earning a high salary. Family Code § 851 allows the tax authorities to challenge that transmutation. In a real case, a California court agreed that the couple's post-nuptial agreement making the Wife's future salary her separate property was a fraudulent transfer intended to evade the Husband's tax debt. The court invalidated the agreement, and the Wife's wages could still be garnished to pay what was owed.

Evading Child Support: In another case, a Husband going through a divorce transferred his entire interest in the family home to his Wife as part of their marital settlement, leaving himself with no assets. It turned out he did this just as he faced a claim for child support from an extramarital relationship. The child's mother challenged the property transfer as fraudulent. The California Supreme Court held that even though the transfer was part of a divorce agreement, it could be undone if it was meant to defraud a creditor. In this case, the child entitled to support. In the end, the courts allowed the mother to pursue reversing the home transfer so that the property could be available to satisfy the support obligations.

Shielding Assets from Lawsuit Creditors: Consider a scenario where one spouse is about to lose a big lawsuit (for example, from a business debt or injury claim). In anticipation, the couple might agree to transmute a valuable asset, say a house or a bank account, from community property into the other spouse's separate property, hoping it will be off-limits to the lawsuit judgment.

Family Code § 851 prevents this tactic. Such a transfer can be deemed a fraudulent conveyance and set aside by the court. In practice, if a judge finds that the primary reason for the transmutation was to keep the asset away from the suing creditor, the transfer will not be honored, and the asset can still be used to satisfy the judgment.

Further Reading:

State Bd. of Equalization v. Woo (2000) 82 Cal.App.4th 481: A California appellate court upheld the tax authority's claim that a marital agreement transmuting community property into separate property was void as a fraudulent transfer. In this case, a couple had entered a post-marital contract to make the wife's future earnings her separate property after the husband incurred a $35,000 tax debt. The court found the husband had a present community-property interest in his wife's future earnings, and that converting those earnings to the wife's separate property (right after learning of an impending wage garnishment) was done to hinder creditors. Relying on *§ 851*, the court ruled that the transmutation intended to avoid the tax debt was unlawful and the wife's income remained reachable by the creditor.

Mejia v. Reed (2003) 31 Cal.4th 657: The California Supreme Court confirmed that *Family Code § 851* and fraudulent transfer laws apply even to property divisions in a divorce. In this case, a divorcing husband transferred all his interest in the family's real estate to his wife in their marital settlement agreement. An outside creditor, the mother of the husband's child from another relationship, argued this transfer left the husband insolvent and unable to pay future child support. The Supreme Court agreed that creditors (including someone owed child support) can invoke fraudulent transfer laws against transfers in an MSA (marital settlement agreement). The Court emphasized California's strong policy of protecting creditors from spousal transactions intended to defeat legitimate claims. However, the Court also noted that for constructive fraud analysis, future child support obligations shouldn't be counted as a "debt" against current assets. This nuance meant that while the case was sent back for further proceedings, the core holding was that spouses cannot use a divorce agreement as a one-time chance to defraud creditors by shifting assets to one spouse.

Sturm v. Moyer (2019) 32 Cal.App.5th 299: This recent Court of Appeal decision extended the reach of *§ 851* to premarital agreements. In Sturm, a man with a $600,000 judgment against him got married after executing a prenuptial agreement that designated each spouse's earnings and acquisitions during marriage as their separate property. The creditor from before the marriage argued the prenup was effectively a transfer designed to thwart collection of the debt once the couple married. The court agreed that even though the agreement was made before marriage, it took effect upon marriage and immediately transmuted what would have been community property (the debtor-spouse's share in community earnings) into the other spouse's separate property. Citing *Family Code § 851*, the court held that such a premarital arrangement is subject to fraudulent transfer law just like any post-marital transmutation. In short, if a prenup or postnup is used with actual intent to hinder or defraud creditors, it can be invalidated. The Sturm case was a matter of first impression and confirmed that creditors are protected from fraudulent asset shielding in the context of marriage, whether the agreement is made before or during the marriage.

Full Text of *California Family Code § 851*

A transmutation is subject to the laws governing fraudulent transfers.

18. *Family Code section 852* – Transmutation of Property Between Spouses

Explanation:

California Family Code § 852 governs how married spouses can change the status or ownership of property between them: a process known as a "transmutation." This law ensures that if spouses want to alter property from one form to another (for example, turning one spouse's separate property into community property, or vice versa), they do so in a clear and deliberate way. In essence, it requires a formal approach to prevent accidental or fraudulent changes in property ownership during marriage.

Written agreement required: Under *Section 852*, any transmutation of real or personal property is only valid if made in writing with an explicit declaration of the change. In other words, an informal oral agreement or casual conversation isn't enough to alter property rights. The writing must clearly state that the character (ownership status) of the property is being changed, and it must be signed or otherwise expressly agreed to by the spouse who is giving up or adversely affecting their interest. This means, for example, a document might say something like, "I hereby transfer my interest in [Asset] to my spouse as his/her separate property." Without such a clear written statement, the law will not recognize the change.

No unwritten or implied transmutations: The strict writing rule (effective since 1985) was designed to prevent disputes and misunderstandings. Before this rule, spouses could allegedly transmute property through oral agreements or ambiguous actions, which led to messy legal fights. Now, courts will not consider outside evidence (like verbal promises or partial performance) to prove a transmutation. The intent to change ownership must be evident from the written document itself. This protects both parties by ensuring there's a concrete record of any significant change in property rights.

Real estate must be recorded: If the transmutation involves real property (land or a home), *Section 852(b)* adds another requirement for the protection of third parties. The change is not effective against third parties (such as future buyers or creditors who rely on public title records) unless the written agreement or deed is properly recorded with the county. This means if spouses sign a transmutation agreement for a house but never record it, someone who later deals with that property (not knowing about the unrecorded agreement) might not be bound by the change. Recording gives public notice of the new ownership status.

Personal gifts exception: *Section 852(c)* provides an important exception for certain gifts between spouses. Small gifts of personal nature, for example, clothing, jewelry, or other tangible items intended for the use of the receiving spouse, do not require a written transmutation agreement, as long as these gifts aren't "substantial in value" considering the couple's overall circumstances. This exception exists so that spouses can continue to give each other ordinary personal gifts (like birthday or anniversary presents) without needing a formal contract each time. However, if a gift between spouses is of significant economic value (relative to their finances), it may not fall under this exception and would still require a written agreement to be a valid transmutation.

Commingled property not covered: *Section 852(d)* clarifies that the statute doesn't apply to situations where separate and community property have been mixed together (commingled) in such a way that tracing is required to determine their character. In those cases, other principles and presumptions (like tracing rules or community property presumptions) govern how the property is characterized, rather than the strict writing requirement. In short, if funds or assets are blended during the marriage (for example, separate money deposited into a joint account), the characterization of that commingled property is decided by different laws and not by *Section 852.*

Applies only after 1984: *Section 852(e)* specifies that these rules apply to transmutations made on or after January 1, 1985. Any property agreements or changes made between spouses before that date are evaluated under the law that existed at the time (which was more permissive of oral or implied transmutations). The law change in 1985 was a deliberate reform to make property exchanges between spouses more transparent. So, older transactions aren't invalidated by this newer requirement but rather are "grandfathered" under the prior legal standards.

Family Code § 852 is intended to promote certainty and fairness in marriage property arrangements. By requiring a clear written declaration (and recording for real estate), it reduces the chance of later disputes about "he-said, she-said" intentions, and it protects spouses from unintentionally losing rights to property without knowingly signing off. Spouses should approach any change in property ownership with formality and caution, often with the help of a lawyer, to ensure it meets the requirements of the law and truly reflects both parties' wishes.

Examples:

Verbal agreement versus written deed: Jack owns a house as his separate property, and he tells his Wife, Jill, "I want this to be our joint property now." They never put anything in writing. Later, during a divorce, Jill claims the house became community property. Because of Section 852's requirements, Jack's verbal statement alone is not enough. Without a written document expressly transmuting the house to community property, the court would still view it as Jack's separate property. By contrast, if Jack had signed a written agreement or deed saying "I grant this house to myself and my Wife as community property" and gave it to Jill (and ideally recorded it), that would be a valid transmutation making the house community property.

Interspousal grant deed: During their marriage, Maria owns a rental condo in her name alone. She decides to add her Husband, Luis, as an equal owner. They execute an Interspousal Transfer Grant Deed in which Maria expressly grants a one-half interest in the condo to Luis as community property, and they record this deed with the county. This written, signed, and recorded deed clearly shows the intent to change the character of the property, satisfying Section 852. Later, if a creditor checks the record or either spouse claims the condo, it will be recognized as a community property asset because the formalities were followed.

Gift of jewelry: Assume John gives his Wife, Alice, a diamond necklace on their anniversary. It's an expensive piece, but relative to their wealthy lifestyle it's not considered "substantial in value." John did not write a formal contract saying "this is now your separate property," but under Section 852(c) he doesn't have to. The gift exception covers ordinary gifts between spouses like jewelry. Alice can keep the necklace as her own property (in fact, in California it's presumptively her separate property as a gift). However, if John were to gift Alice something far more valuable (say, a house or a very costly asset), that likely wouldn't fall under the personal gift exception, and a written transmutation would be required to solidify Alice's sole ownership of that item.

Commingling scenario: During marriage, suppose Emma had $10,000 of savings from before the marriage (her separate property) which she then deposits into a joint bank account with her Husband, Ryan, where both spouses also deposit earnings (community property). Over time, the separate funds become mixed with community funds. Later, a question arises about the character of the money in that account. Section 852's writing requirement doesn't directly apply here because no one is claiming there was an agreement to transmute; instead, the issue is commingling. The characterization will be determined by tracing and community property presumptions, not by a written transmutation document (Section 852(d) makes it clear that the statute doesn't govern this kind of situation).

Further Reading:

Estate of MacDonald (1990) 51 Cal.3d 262: See MacDonald Express Declaration Test (pg. 8).

In re Marriage of Benson (2005) 36 Cal.4th 1096: See *In re Marriage of Benson (pg. 12).*

In re Marriage of Valli (2014) 58 Cal.4th 1396: See *In re Marriage of Valli (pg. 10).*

In re Marriage of Begian & Sarajian (2018) 31 Cal.App.5th 506: This Court of Appeal case dealt with a "Trust Transfer Deed" that a husband signed, granting real estate to his wife. The question was whether that deed met the *Section 852* requirement of an express written declaration. The deed was somewhat unclear: it transferred title but did not explicitly state that the husband's interest was being given to the wife as her separate property (and its title "Trust Transfer Deed" created confusion about intent). The court found the language ambiguous regarding the change in ownership character. Because of this ambiguity, the deed was held not to be an effective transmutation. Begian illustrates that even a signed writing can fail to qualify if it isn't unambiguous about altering the property's character. The writing must clearly state the donor spouse's intent to divest their interest in the property.

In re Marriage of Kushesh & Kushesh-Kaviani (2018) 27 Cal.App.5th 449: In this Court of Appeal case, the spouses bought a home during marriage and took title in the wife's name "as her sole and separate property." The husband also signed an Interspousal Transfer Grant Deed confirming that the property was granted to the wife as her separate property. The trial court had initially found the deed lacked "magic words" of transmutation, but the Court of Appeal disagreed and reversed. It held that the deed's language, including phrases like "a married woman as her sole and separate property" and the word "grant," clearly demonstrated an express intent to change the marital property character of the condo. Therefore, it satisfied *Section 852*'s requirements. Kushesh is a practical example that certain well-drafted interspousal deeds do meet the statutory standard (especially when they explicitly state the separate property status), and it highlights how courts will interpret clear language as sufficient to transmute.

Full Text of *California Family Code § 852*

(a) A transmutation of real or personal property is not valid unless made in writing by an express declaration that is made, joined in, consented to, or accepted by the spouse whose interest in the property is adversely affected.

(b) A transmutation of real property is not effective as to third parties without notice thereof unless recorded.

(c) This section does not apply to a gift between the spouses of clothing, wearing apparel, jewelry, or other tangible articles of a personal nature that is used solely or principally by the spouse to whom the gift is made and that is not substantial in value taking into account the circumstances of the marriage.

(d) Nothing in this section affects the law governing characterization of property in which separate property and community property are commingled or otherwise combined.

(e) This section does not apply to or affect a transmutation of property made before January 1, 1985, and the law that would otherwise be applicable to that transmutation shall continue to apply.

19. *Family Code section 910* – Community Property Liability for Debts of Either Spouse

Explanation:

California Family Code § 910 establishes that all community property (the assets and income a married couple acquires together during marriage) can be used to satisfy a debt incurred by either spouse. In other words, if one spouse has a debt — whether it was incurred before the marriage or during the marriage — creditors can generally reach the couple's community property to collect on that debt.

This rule applies regardless of which spouse incurred the obligation and regardless of whose name is on the debt or judgment. Even if only one spouse signed for a loan or credit card, that debt is considered a community debt as long as it was incurred during the marriage (up until the point of separation). The non-debtor spouse's separate property (property that belongs only to that spouse, such as assets acquired before marriage or after separation) is not liable for the other spouse's personal debts. However, the couple's joint assets and earnings (community assets) are at stake for debts either spouse owes.

Importantly, California law now clarifies that "during marriage" does not include the period after the spouses have separated. If spouses separate (with the intent to end the marriage), new debts one spouse incurs after that separation date will generally not be chargeable to the community. In 2016, the Legislature defined "date of separation" (*Family Code § 70*) to mean the point when a complete and final break in the marital relationship has occurred. Thus, a debt incurred by one spouse after the date of separation and before a divorce is finalized is treated as that spouse's own separate debt: the community property won't be automatically liable for it under *Section 910.*

Examples:

Pre-Marriage Debt: Alice has a $10,000 credit card debt from before her marriage to Bob. After they marry, Alice's creditor can go after Alice and Bob's community property (for example, a joint savings account or other assets acquired during the marriage) to satisfy that debt. Even though Bob didn't incur the debt, their community property is on the hook because the debt existed before or during the marriage.

During Marriage Debt in One Spouse's Name: During the marriage, Bob takes out a loan solely in his name to buy new furniture. He later defaults on the loan. Under *§ 910*, the lender can seek repayment from Bob and Alice's community assets — it doesn't matter that Alice never signed the loan agreement. The debt was incurred during the marriage, so both spouses' community property interests are liable for it. (However, the creditor cannot touch Alice's own separate property for this debt.)

Post-Separation Debt: Now assume Alice and Bob separate on January 1, 2025, with the intention of ending the marriage. If Alice opens a new credit card account in February 2025 (after the separation date) and accumulates debt, that obligation is considered Alice's separate debt. Because it was incurred after the date of separation and before divorce, Bob will not be responsible for it under *Family Code § 910.* The credit card company could pursue Alice's separate property and any assets she acquires going forward, but not the community property that existed before separation or Bob's separate assets.

Further Reading:

Oyakawa v. Gillett (1992) 8 Cal.App.4th 628: A judgment creditor obtained a judgment against a husband alone and later tried to add the wife to the judgment to reach community assets (after the couple moved out of state). The Court of Appeal rejected this, holding that even though community property is liable for either spouse's debt, a spouse who was not named in the lawsuit cannot be added to a judgment after-the-fact without having had an opportunity to defend herself. In short, creditors cannot simply tack on an uninvolved spouse to an existing judgment to access community property.

11601 Wilshire Associates v. Grebow (1998) 64 Cal.App.4th 453: A landlord sued a husband for a lease guarantee and also named the wife (who had no involvement in the lease) as a defendant solely to make it easier to reach the couple's community property. The Court of Appeal ruled that the wife could not be held personally liable just because she was married to the debtor.

Family Code § 910 makes community assets available to satisfy the husband's obligation, but it does not create a separate cause of action against the non-debtor spouse. In this case, the court affirmed that a creditor cannot sue or obtain a judgment against a spouse who did not incur the debt, purely as a "community representative." The proper course for the creditor is to enforce the judgment against the community property of the debtor spouse, without dragging the other spouse into the litigation.

Sturm v. Moyer (2019) 32 Cal.App.5th 299: This case dealt with a premarital agreement and its effect on creditors' rights. The husband had a large unpaid judgment against him prior to marriage. He and his fiancée signed a prenuptial agreement stating that after marriage, each of their earnings and property would remain separate (preventing any community property from accumulating). The creditor later argued this agreement was a fraudulent attempt to evade debt under the Uniform Voidable Transactions Act, since normally the husband's earnings during marriage would be community property reachable by creditors under *§ 910*. The Court of Appeal agreed that the UVTA can apply to a premarital agreement in this way. It held that a premarital agreement characterizing all post-marriage income as separate property could be voided as to the creditor because it was executed with the intent to hinder or avoid the creditor's ability to reach assets that would have become community property. In essence, you cannot use a private agreement to circumvent *Family Code § 910*'s principle that community earnings are liable for premarital debts.

Full Text of *California Family Code § 910*

(a) Except as otherwise expressly provided by statute, the community estate is liable for a debt incurred by either spouse before or during marriage, regardless of which spouse has the management and control of the property and regardless of whether one or both spouses are parties to the debt or to a judgment for the debt.

(b) "During marriage" for purposes of this section does not include the period after the date of separation, as defined in *Family Code § 70*, and before a judgment of dissolution of marriage or legal separation of the parties.

20. *Family Code section 911* – Pre-Marriage Debt Protection

Explanation:

Under California's community property rules, most debts of a married person can usually be paid out of the couple's shared (community) property. *Family Code § 911* creates a narrow exception to that rule. In simple terms, if one spouse earned wages or other income during the marriage, that income cannot be used to pay off a debt the other spouse incurred before the marriage, but only if certain conditions are met. Specifically, after you receive your paycheck or other earnings, you must deposit that money into a separate bank account in which your spouse has no withdrawal rights and must keep it separate from any joint or community funds. As long as the funds stay in that separate account and are not commingled with community property (aside from negligible amounts), they are protected from creditors trying to reach a spouse's pre-marriage debts.

In practical terms, "earnings" under *§ 911* means the pay, salary, or other compensation you receive for services as an employee or self-employed person. The code refers to a "deposit account" by cross-reference to commercial law (essentially an ordinary bank or savings account). *Section 911*'s protection only applies to debts incurred before marriage by the other spouse; it does not shield earnings from debts incurred by either spouse during the marriage. Also, if the protected spouse uses those earnings to buy a home, car, or other community assets, that purchased property generally can be reached by creditors, because once the money is spent on community property it loses the special protection of *§ 911*.

Put another way: imagine a wife had a large student loan from before marriage. After marrying, she works and earns a salary. If she deposits her paychecks into a bank account held only in her name (with no right of withdrawal by her husband), her salary income is not liable for her husband's old student loan debt. But if her husband had signature power on the account or if she mixed that money with joint funds (for example, transferring it into a joint checking account), the protection is lost and creditors could reach that money.

Examples:

Separate Paycheck Account: A married person opens a personal savings account in only their name and deposits each paycheck there. The other spouse has no access to that account (cannot withdraw money). Under *§ 911*, those deposited earnings cannot be used to pay the other spouse's pre-marriage debt. This means if the non-debtor spouse later cashes those funds out (and as long as they were never commingled), creditors have no claim to that money for a debt the other spouse had before marriage.

Joint Account Beware: Suppose instead that the paychecks were deposited into a joint bank account. Even if that account was intended to be separate, co-ownership or withdrawal rights by the other spouse would cause *§ 911*'s protection to fail. In that case, the earnings become part of community property and could be reached by the creditor of the pre-marriage debt.

Buying a House with Earnings: A spouse keeps wages in a protected account under *§ 911*, but later uses those earnings to buy a house held as community property. At that point, the new house can be used to satisfy the other spouse's old debt because the protected earnings have been converted into a community asset. So *§ 911* only protects the funds while they are still in the separate account.

Debt After Marriage vs. Before: Consider a spouse who was later sued for an incident during the marriage (e.g., a car accident). That debt is treated as incurred during marriage (see *Fam. Code § 903(b)*), so *§ 911* does not apply. In that scenario, community property (including earnings in the community) would normally be liable for the debt under the general rule.

Income vs. Other Property: *Section 911* only mentions "earnings" (pay or wages). Other types of income (like rental income, passive investment earnings, or gifts) are not covered by this shield. For example, inheritance or gift money is usually already considered separate property by other rules, but passive investment income (interest, dividends) would not automatically be protected by *§ 911* and could be reachable for a spouse's prior debt.

Tax Debts: If one spouse had tax bills from before marriage, § 911 can help protect the other spouse's wages. For example, if the Husband had old taxes and the Wife keeps her salary in her own separate account, the IRS (or other creditor) cannot levy her separate wages for his old tax debt. But again, if she used that money on joint property or let him access the account, the protection would end.

Further Reading:

Sturm v. Moyer (2019) 32 Cal.App.5th 299: In this case, the Court of Appeal explained the scope of *§ 911*. The court noted that normally community earnings are liable for either spouse's premarital debts under *Fam. Code § 910*, but *§ 911* carves out an exception for the non-debtor spouse's wages if kept separate. The opinion quotes *§ 911(a)* verbatim, emphasizing that the non-debtor spouse's "earnings and income" are "shielded from liability for [the debtor-spouse's] premarital debt to the extent that those earnings and income are held in an account to which the debtor-spouse does not have access and are not commingled". Sturm ultimately addressed a related issue (fraudulent transfers in a premarital agreement), but it reaffirmed that *§ 911* requires the earnings to be kept in a separate deposit account in which the other spouse has no withdrawal rights.

Full Text of *California Family Code § 911*

(a) The earnings of a married person during marriage are not liable for a debt incurred by the person's spouse before marriage. After the earnings of the married person are paid, they remain not liable so long as they are held in a deposit account in which the person's spouse has no right of withdrawal and are uncommingled with other property in the community estate, except property insignificant in amount.

(b) As used in this section:

(1) "Deposit account" has the meaning prescribed in paragraph (29) of subdivision (a) of *Section 9102* of the Commercial Code.

(2) "Earnings" means compensation for personal services performed, whether as an employee or otherwise.

21. *Family Code section 913* – Liability of Separate Property for Debts

Explanation:

Family Code §913 means that each spouse is responsible for their own debts. In other words, one spouse's separate property (such as an inheritance or premarital savings) is liable only for debts they incurred. A spouse's separate assets generally cannot be used to pay the other spouse's bills. In practice, courts note that creditors usually cannot garnish the non-debtor spouse's wages or property: they must look to the debtor spouse's own assets.

There are important exceptions. For example, under *§914*, if one spouse uses the other's separate property to pay for basic living expenses (necessaries of life), then that debt may be paid from the payer's separate funds (with a right to be reimbursed). Similarly, merely co-signing a mortgage or loan on community property does not put your separate assets at risk. *Section 913(b)(2)* makes clear your separate property is still protected unless you yourself took on the debt.

Examples:

Inheritance vs. Spousal Debt: If one spouse brings a large inheritance or premarital savings into the marriage (their separate property) and the other spouse owes money, the inheritance generally cannot be taken to pay the other spouse's debt. Only the debtor spouse's own assets would satisfy that debt.

Necessaries Exception: If a spouse uses their separate funds to pay for household necessities (rent, groceries, utilities) that benefit the family, *§914* allows that debt to be repaid from the payer's separate property. For example, if one spouse uses an inheritance to cover the mortgage, that payment may be treated as a loan from their separate property (with the community owing them reimbursement).

Co-signing a Loan: Even if a spouse consents to encumber community property (e.g. signs a mortgage on the family home), *§913(b)(2)* protects the spouse's separate assets. The spouse's separate property will not be liable for the loan unless that spouse was personally obligated on it.

Further Reading:

In re Ciprari (2019) 32 Cal.App.5th 83: The court affirmed that property acquired before marriage or by gift is separate property, underscoring that such separate assets are not reachable for the other spouse's debts under *§913*.

Full Text of *California Family Code § 913*

(a) The separate property of a married person is liable for a debt incurred by the person before or during marriage.

(b) Except as otherwise provided by statute:

(1) The separate property of a married person is not liable for a debt incurred by the person's spouse before or during marriage.

(2) The joinder or consent of a married person to an encumbrance of community estate property to secure payment of a debt incurred by the person's spouse does not subject the person's separate property to liability for the debt unless the person also incurred the debt.

22. *Family Code section 914* – Spousal Liability for Necessaries of Life Debts

Explanation:

Under *California Family Code § 914*, each spouse is personally responsible for certain debts the other incurs during marriage if those debts are for the "necessaries of life." In practice, this means if one spouse buys food, pays for housing, medical care, or other basic needs for the family, the other spouse can be held liable for that debt as well. The statute distinguishes between debts incurred before the couple separates and those incurred after separation. A debt is covered if it was for necessaries of life before the date of separation; or, if after separation, it must be for "common necessaries of life" (i.e. mutually needed expenses). Notably, a spouse's separate property (assets owned individually) can be used to pay these debts, but the paying spouse has a right to reimbursement if community property or the other spouse's assets were available to pay instead. In a nutshell: the law makes spouses each responsible for the other's basic-life expenses incurred during marriage, but it also provides ways (through agreements or divorce orders) for the parties to limit that liability. For example, after divorce any unpaid necessaries debt will generally only remain the former spouse's responsibility if the divorce decree specifically assigned that debt to them.

Examples:

Medical Expenses: Imagine a Husband is hospitalized while the couple is still married. Under § 914, the Wife could be held liable for his hospital bill because medical care is a necessity of life. If she uses her own separate savings to pay it, she can later seek reimbursement from the community property if available.

Housing or Utilities: Suppose the couple lives together and the Husband falls ill. The Wife takes out a loan to pay for home mortgage or utilities during his illness. Those payments may be considered necessaries of life, so the Husband could be jointly liable for that debt under § 914.

Post-Separation Necessities: After the spouses separate, certain costs can still bind the non-debtor spouse if they are "common necessaries." For example, if after separation the Husband must buy extra medicine for both spouses' benefit, the Wife might still be responsible for her share. (By contrast, if she had already received her divorce decree, she could avoid liability if the decree didn't assign the debt to her.)

Further Reading:

Collection Bureau of San Jose v. Rumsey (2000) 24 Cal.4th 301: The Court confirmed that *Family Code § 914* makes a spouse "personally liable" for debts incurred by the other spouse for necessaries of life. It also emphasized that if the non-debtor spouse uses separate property to pay such debts, that spouse has a right to reimbursement from any available community or spouse's assets.

CMRE Financial Services, Inc. v. Parton (2010) 184 Cal.App.4th 263: California Court of Appeal, Fourth District. In this case the court explained that after a divorce (*§ 916*), a former spouse is only liable for the other's debts if the divorce judgment assigns that debt to them. Even though *§ 914* ordinarily would make a wife liable for her husband's hospital bills, the court held that the dissolution judgment relieved her of liability because those debts weren't assigned to her.

Robertson v. Willis (1978) 77 Cal.App.3d 358: California Court of Appeal, Second District. The court held that even though the husband's business debt could be paid from community property, the wife was not personally liable for it under the facts. In other words, the mere fact that community assets might cover a husband's debt did not, by itself, create personal liability for his wife.

Full Text of *California Family Code § 914*

(a) Notwithstanding *Section 913*, a married person is personally liable for the following debts incurred by the person's spouse during marriage:

(1) A debt incurred for necessaries of life of the person's spouse before the date of separation of the spouses.

(2) Except as provided in *Section 4302*, a debt incurred for common necessaries of life of the person's spouse after the date of separation of the spouses.

(b) The separate property of a married person may be applied to the satisfaction of a debt for which the person is personally liable pursuant to this section. If separate property is so applied at a time when nonexempt property in the community estate or separate property of the person's spouse is available but is not applied to the satisfaction of the debt, the married person is entitled to reimbursement to the extent such property was available.

(c)

(1) Except as provided in paragraph (2), the statute of limitations set forth in *Section 366.2* of the Code of Civil Procedure shall apply if the spouse for whom the married person is personally liable dies.

(2) If the surviving spouse had actual knowledge of the debt prior to expiration of the period set forth in *Section 366.2* of the Code of Civil Procedure and the personal representative of the deceased spouse's estate failed to provide the creditor asserting the claim under this section with a timely written notice of the probate administration of the estate in the manner provided for pursuant to *Section 9050* of the Probate Code, the statute of limitations set forth in *Section 337* or 339 of the Code of Civil Procedure, as applicable, shall apply.

(d) For purposes of this section, "date of separation" has the same meaning as set forth in *Section 70*.

23. *Family Code section 915* – Support From Prior Relationships

Explanation:

California Family Code §915 applies when one spouse has a child or spousal support duty that arose outside the current marriage (for example, an obligation to an ex-spouse or to children from another relationship). The law says any such outside support obligation is treated as if it were a debt incurred before the marriage. In practical terms, this means that if community (marital) assets are used to pay that prior support obligation, the community may be able to get reimbursed under certain conditions.

Specifically, *§915(b)* provides that if community property was used to satisfy the support obligation while the spouse had separate income available but did not use it, then the community estate is entitled to reimbursement from the spouse's separate income (up to the amount of community property applied). In other words, the spouse who paid the support must reimburse the community to the extent their own income could have paid it. Finally, *§915(c)* clarifies that this reimbursement rule does not prevent a court from considering any relevant factors (such as each spouse's earnings) when determining support amounts.

Examples:

Prior child support obligation: Imagine a Husband has children from a previous marriage and pays child support during his current marriage. If he uses joint savings or income to make those payments, and he had separate income available that he didn't use, then his Wife may claim reimbursement for those community funds under §915. In essence, the support debt to the ex-spouse is treated as premarital debt, and the community can recover the amount that should have been covered by the Husband's own income.

Prior spousal support obligation: Similarly, if a Wife owes alimony to a former Husband and ends up using the couple's joint accounts to pay it while she had personal income available, the community estate may seek reimbursement. Section 915 would treat the past alimony obligation as premarital, and the Wife would have to repay the community for the support payments up to the amount of her unused separate income.

No reimbursement if no separate funds were available: If a spouse truly had no separate (non-marital) income available to pay the old support obligation, then *§915*'s reimbursement rule does not apply. In that situation, even though the debt is treated as premarital, the community cannot demand repayment because the condition (having unused separate income) wasn't met.

Further Reading:

Weinberg v. Weinberg (1967) 67 Cal.2d 557: A landmark California Supreme Court case that set the stage for the reimbursement rule. Weinberg held that when community funds pay a spouse's premarital support obligations, the community is entitled to reimbursement proportional to the spouse's separate earnings. This case inspired the statutory rule now found in *§915*.

In re Marriage of Smaltz (1978) 82 Cal.App.3d 568: A Court of Appeal case decided before *§915* was enacted. The court held that the community could not be reimbursed for spousal support payments to an ex-wife when the husband had no separate funds available. This illustrates that reimbursement is only allowed if separate income was available to pay the debt.

In re Marriage of Sherman (2005) 133 Cal.App.4th 795: The key case directly applying *§915*. The court agreed that each support payment to a prior relationship is a separate obligation. It held that to recover community funds, the spouse must show he or she had separate income available at the time each payment was made. This case emphasized that reimbursement under *§915* requires proof of available separate income for each payment.

Full Text of *California Family Code § 915*

(a) For the purpose of this part, a child or spousal support obligation of a married person that does not arise out of the marriage shall be treated as a debt incurred before marriage, regardless of whether a court order for support is made or modified before or during marriage and regardless of whether any installment payment on the obligation accrues before or during marriage.

(b) If property in the community estate is applied to the satisfaction of a child or spousal support obligation of a married person that does not arise out of the marriage, at a time when nonexempt separate income of the person is available but is not applied to the satisfaction of the obligation, the community estate is entitled to reimbursement from the person in the amount of the separate income, not exceeding the property in the community estate so applied.

(c) Nothing in this section limits the matters a court may take into consideration in determining or modifying the amount of a support order, including, but not limited to, the earnings of the spouses of the parties.

24. *Family Code section 916* – Liability of Spouses for Debts After Property Division

Explanation:

After a divorce or legal separation, each person generally remains responsible for the debts they incurred. *Family Code § 916(a)(1)* confirms that a spouse's separate property (and the share they received in the divorce) is liable for debts that person incurred before or during the marriage. By contrast, *§ 916(a)(2)* makes clear that one spouse's assets are not responsible for the other spouse's debts unless those debts were specifically assigned to them in the divorce settlement. In practical terms, if a debt is not assigned to you by the divorce decree, creditors generally cannot touch your property or income to pay that debt.

If, however, the divorce agreement does assign a debt to you (for example, your ex agreed you would pay a joint credit card), then you must honor that assignment. *Section 916(a)(3)* reflects that rule: the spouse who took responsibility for the debt remains personally liable for it. Additionally, *§*

916(b) protects the paying spouse: if you pay a debt that your ex was supposed to pay, you can recover the amount you paid (with legal interest and attorney fees) from your ex.

Examples:

Suppose John and Jane divorce. John had a car loan he took out during the marriage, and Jane's name was never on that loan. The divorce decree assigns John's car to John and does not assign any of John's debts to Jane. Later, John stops paying the loan. Under *§916(a)(2)*, Jane's house or savings (her separate property) cannot be seized to pay John's loan, because the debt was not assigned to her.

In another divorce, the decree specifies that Jane will pay John's $20,000 student loan. If Jane ends up paying that loan out of her own funds after the divorce, *§916(b)* allows her to seek reimbursement from John for that payment (with interest). In other words, Jane can make John repay her for the money she spent on his behalf.

Further Reading:

Bijan Boutiques, LLC v. Isong (2024) 104 Cal.App.5th 132: In this recent case, the Fourth District Court of Appeal held that after a contested property division, neither spouse nor the property awarded to them can be held liable for debts of the other spouse. The court explained that "[b]ecause we conclude that *Family Code section 916* precludes [the creditor] from seeking to satisfy its judgment … out of the property awarded to [the wife] in the marital dissolution action," the creditor could not enforce a judgment against the wife's house (the divorce had assigned the debt to the husband).

C.M.R.E. Financial Services, Inc. v. Parton (2010) 184 Cal.App.4th 263: In this case involving post-separation medical bills, the Court of Appeal reversed a judgment that had held the wife liable for her husband's hospital debt. The court noted that the divorce judgment made the husband solely responsible for those bills, and under *§916(a)(2)* the wife could not be forced to pay them. In short, *§916(a)(2)* "relieves [the] non-debtor spouse of liability for [the] other spouse's debt not assigned to him or her in the divorce judgment".

Full Text of *California Family Code § 916*

(a) Notwithstanding any other provision of this chapter, after division of community and quasi-community property pursuant to Division 7 (commencing with *Section 2500*):

> (1) The separate property owned by a married person at the time of the division and the property received by the person in the division is liable for a debt incurred by the person before or during marriage and the

person is personally liable for the debt, whether or not the debt was assigned for payment by the person's spouse in the division.

(2) The separate property owned by a married person at the time of the division and the property received by the person in the division is not liable for a debt incurred by the person's spouse before or during marriage, and the person is not personally liable for the debt, unless the debt was assigned for payment by the person in the division of the property. Nothing in this paragraph affects the liability of property for the satisfaction of a lien on the property.

(3) The separate property owned by a married person at the time of the division and the property received by the person in the division is liable for a debt incurred by the person's spouse before or during marriage, and the person is personally liable for the debt, if the debt was assigned for payment by the person in the division of the property. If a money judgment for the debt is entered after the division, the property is not subject to enforcement of the judgment and the judgment may not be enforced against the married person, unless the person is made a party to the judgment for the purpose of this paragraph.

(b) If property of a married person is applied to the satisfaction of a money judgment pursuant to subdivision (a) for a debt incurred by the person that is assigned for payment by the person's spouse, the person has a right of reimbursement from the person's spouse to the extent of the property applied, with interest at the legal rate, and may recover reasonable attorney's fees incurred in enforcing the right of reimbursement.

25. *Family Code section 920* – Right of Reimbursement

Explanation:

Family Code section 920 is a California law that creates a right of reimbursement when marital (community) property pays for one spouse's separate debts. This means if community funds or property are used to satisfy a debt belonging to one spouse (for example, a debt incurred before marriage or an obligation from another relationship), the other spouse or the community can demand repayment. *Section 920* makes clear that the right to reimbursement arises no matter which spouse applied the property or whether the payment was voluntary. For instance, if Husband uses community money to pay off Wife's premarital credit card debt, Husband can claim half of those payments back.

Section 920 also sets how much is repaid and strict deadlines for asserting the claim. It provides that reimbursement is based on the property's value when the right arises, and it must be pursued promptly. Specifically, a spouse must exercise the reimbursement right within three years of learning about the payment, or during divorce or separation proceedings. If the spouse does not act within these deadlines, the right is lost. Courts enforce this strictly. For example, in *In re Marriage of Kristie J.* (2009) 175 Cal.App.4th 323, the Court of Appeal held a wife's reimbursement claim was barred because she filed more than three years after the payments were made. And the California Supreme Court has interpreted *section 920(c)* to mean that when a spouse dies, the claim must be asserted in the death proceedings (generally within one year of death).

Examples:

Credit card debt: If one spouse has pre-marital credit card bills and the community pays them off, the paying spouse can claim half of those payments back.

Child support: If the marital community pays one spouse's pre-marital child support obligations, the other spouse can recover half of the support paid.

Separate-to-community payment: If a spouse uses separate funds (e.g. an inheritance) to pay down a community debt (such as a mortgage), the contributing spouse may claim reimbursement from the community for that contribution.

Community-to-separate payment: If community property is used to pay a debt on a spouse's separate property (for example, a premarital tax liability on one spouse's home), the spouse who used community funds can seek reimbursement under *§920.*

Further Reading:

In re Marriage of Sherman (2005) 133 Cal.App.4th 795: The court held that a husband's reimbursement claim was time-barred under *§920.* It noted the trial court correctly rejected the claim because "more than three years had elapsed" since he learned community funds paid his spouse's separate debts.

In re Marriage of Kristie J. (2009) 175 Cal.App.4th 323: The court affirmed the judgment dividing the community property but observed that the wife's claim for reimbursement was defeated by *§920*'s three-year limit. In other words, because she filed more than three years after the payments were made, the claim failed.

In re Marriage of Mullonkal & Kodiyamplakkil (2020) 51 Cal.App.5th 604: The court held that *§920* applies to community payments on a spouse's non-education debts (such as family loans). It reversed a trial court's refusal to reimburse one spouse for paying the other's family loans, emphasizing that *section 920* "does not include a mechanism for the court to deny reimbursement" once its requirements are satisfied.

Full Text of *California Family Code § 920*

A right of reimbursement provided by this part is subject to the following provisions:

(a) The right arises regardless of which spouse applies the property to the satisfaction of the debt, regardless of whether the property is applied to the satisfaction of the debt voluntarily or involuntarily, and regardless of whether the debt to which the property is applied is satisfied in whole or in part. The right is subject to an express written waiver of the right by the spouse in whose favor the right arises.

(b) The measure of reimbursement is the value of the property or interest in property at the time the right arises.

26. *Family Code section 1000* – Liability of Married Persons for Spouse's Actions

Explanation:

Family Code § 1000 says that marriage itself does not make one spouse automatically responsible for the other's accidents or wrongs. In general, a married person is not liable for injury or damage caused by the other spouse, except in situations where the person would have been liable if they were not married. In other words, spouses are usually not on the hook for each other's torts unless the law independently imposes liability.

If liability does exist, *§ 1000* specifies how to pay it: if the offending spouse was acting for the benefit of the family (for example, on a work errand), any judgment is paid first from community property, then from the spouse's separate property. If the act was personal (not for the family's benefit), then the spouse's separate property pays first, then any remaining liability may fall on community property. Insurance proceeds pay first. Also, any right to reimbursement from community property must be asserted within seven years after the community property was used to satisfy the debt.

Examples:

Car Accident (Personal Errand): A Husband runs a stop sign while driving to do grocery shopping and injures a pedestrian. Because he was not acting for a community purpose, only his own separate assets (and then community assets if needed) would pay any damages. The Wife's share of community property would not automatically cover the injury.

Car Accident (Work Errand): A Wife, acting as an employee of the family business, causes a crash while driving to a court hearing for the company. Here the act was for the community's benefit, so community property would satisfy the damages first (and only if exhausted would her separate assets pay).

Intentional Crime: A spouse deliberately embezzles funds (like in a divorce case). Because this criminal act does not benefit the family, *§1000* prevents the innocent spouse or community from having to pay for it. The guilty spouse's own property alone (or his or her separate share of community property) must cover fines or restitution.

Further Reading:

In re Marriage of Stitt (1983) 147 Cal.App.3d 579: Wife had embezzled money, and the court held she alone must repay it. Because her acts brought no benefit to the marriage, the community estate was not responsible for the debts. The innocent husband was not required to share in losses from his wife's criminal misconduct.

In re Marriage of Hirsch (1989) 211 Cal.App.3d 104: Husband was sued for losses stemming from his service on a bank board. The court found his board service (and salary) benefited the community. It reversed the trial court and ruled that the community must share the liability for settling his claims, because his acts were for the community's benefit under *§1000.*

In re Marriage of Bell (1996) 49 Cal.App.4th 300: Wife embezzled $150,000 from her employer. The appellate court held that the community estate was responsible for repaying that amount (since all the stolen money had gone into joint accounts and thus benefited the family). However, the court also held that the wife alone had to pay her legal defense fees and penalties for the crime, reasoning her husband (and their community property) should not bear the cost of her intentional wrongdoing.

In re Marriage of Whitman (2023) 98 Cal.App.5th 456: In a divorce involving a husband convicted of insider trading, the court applied *§1000* to several liabilities. It found the husband's criminal defense fees and fines (including a $250,000 criminal fine and a $935,306 SEC penalty) were his separate debts (community property was not liable). However, $290,000 of related legal fees (incurred in defending an SEC enforcement action that involved the marital business) were paid from community funds, since that expense benefited the community enterprise.

Full Text of *California Family Code § 1000*

(a) A married person is not liable for any injury or damage caused by the other spouse except in cases where the married person would be liable therefor if the marriage did not exist.

(b) The liability of a married person for death or injury to person or property shall be satisfied as follows:

(1) If the liability of the married person is based upon an act or omission which occurred while the married person was performing an activity for

the benefit of the community, the liability shall first be satisfied from the community estate and second from the separate property of the married person.

(2) If the liability of the married person is not based upon an act or omission which occurred while the married person was performing an activity for the benefit of the community, the liability shall first be satisfied from the separate property of the married person and second from the community estate.

(c) This section does not apply to the extent the liability is satisfied out of proceeds of insurance for the liability, whether the proceeds are from property in the community estate or from separate property. Notwithstanding *Section 920*, no right of reimbursement under this section shall be exercised more than seven years after the spouse in whose favor the right arises has actual knowledge of the application of the property to the satisfaction of the debt.

27. *Family Code section 1100* – Management and Control of Community Personal Property

Explanation:

California Family Code § 1100 outlines the rules that govern how spouses can manage and control community personal property. Each spouse generally has equal rights to manage community property, including bank accounts, vehicles, household furnishings, and other jointly owned assets. However, there are limits to this control—especially when one spouse tries to give away or sell community property without the other's knowledge or consent.

The section includes rules meant to protect both spouses, prevent unfair transfers of shared property, and ensure transparency and accountability during marriage and divorce proceedings. Special protections apply to gifts and transfers made without the other spouse's consent.

Examples:

Unauthorized gift of money: If one spouse donates a large sum of money to a friend or relative from a joint bank account without the other spouse's knowledge or consent, the transaction may be voided under *§ 1100(b)*.

Selling shared assets without agreement: A spouse who tries to sell a jointly owned car or valuable artwork without informing the other may be liable for breach of fiduciary duty and required to reimburse the community.

Misuse during divorce: During a pending divorce, if a spouse withdraws large amounts of money or transfers community property for personal use, the court may view that act as a violation of this statute.

Further Reading:

In re Marriage of Feldman (2007) 153 Cal.App.4th 1470: See *In re Marriage of Feldman*: Disclosure Duties and Monetary Sanctions (pg. 58).

In re Marriage of Kamgar (2017) 18 Cal.App.5th 136: Husband made extensive options trades with community funds beyond the risk level authorized by wife and then concealed the losses, violating the mutual fiduciary duty. The Court of Appeal held he breached his duty under *Fam. Code §1100(e)* to disclose material financial dealings and upheld the award of wife's half of the community losses (with interest) as compensation for the breach.

In re Marriage of DeSouza (2020) 54 Cal.App.5th 25: While divorce was pending, husband used community funds to buy bitcoin through intermediaries and failed to tell wife, causing a loss when the exchange later went bankrupt. The First District held this nondisclosure breached the duty of disclosure in *Fam. Code §1100(e)* and impaired the community interest, ordering husband to transfer wife's 50% share of the cryptocurrency (or its value) to her.

In re Marriage of Ciprari (2019) 32 Cal.App.5th 83: The court there reviewed whether husband's use of community funds to benefit their children violated the statutory fiduciary rules. It noted that *Fam. Code §1100(b)* forbids a spouse from gifting community property without the other's consent, but observed that this prohibition "does not apply to gifts mutually given by both spouses." In Ciprari the trial court found, based on the record, that the husband's payments were part of a joint estate plan (gifts made by both spouses), so *§1100(b)* did not apply. On appeal the court affirmed that holding, saying that substantial evidence supported treating the transfers as mutual gifts (thus not a breach of the *§1100(b)* duty).

Kirwan v. Kirwan (2017) 15 Cal.App.5th 473: The appellate court there emphasized that *Fam. Code §1100(e)* imposes "the highest good faith and fair dealing" duty and full-disclosure obligations on spouses managing community property. In Kirwan, the husband (a financial professional) spent all of the community funds from employer loans without reserving anything for the couple's tax liabilities. The court held this conduct grossly negligent in light of the fiduciary duty of *§1100(e)*. As a result, it found he breached his duty to his wife by failing to set aside funds for taxes, and that he alone must bear the tax burden because his reckless spending had impaired the community estate.

In re Marriage of Wiese (2024) 102 Cal.App.5th 917: The Fourth District in Wiese clarified that the rules in *Family Code §§1100–1103* apply only to community property. It held section 1100 "contains specific rules governing a spouse's management of 'community personal property'" and that these provisions do not reach separate property. In that case the court declined to extend the statute-of-limitations exception for fiduciary breaches to misconduct involving separate property, confirming that §1100's fiduciary rules (and the remedies in §1101) are limited to breaches affecting the community estate. (Thus, Wiese reinforces that §1100 is geared exclusively to protecting the other spouse's interest in community assets.)

Full Text of *California Family Code § 1100*

(a) Except as provided in subdivisions (b), (c), and (d) and *Sections 761 and 1103*, either spouse has the management and control of the community personal property, whether acquired prior to or on or after January 1, 1975, with like absolute power of disposition, other than testamentary, as the spouse has of the separate estate of the spouse.

(b) A spouse may not make a gift of community personal property, or dispose of community personal property for less than fair and reasonable value, without the written consent of the other spouse. This subdivision does not apply to gifts mutually given by both spouses to third parties and to gifts given by one spouse to the other spouse.

(c) A spouse may not sell, convey, or encumber community personal property used as the family dwelling, or the furniture, furnishings, or fittings of the home, or the clothing or wearing apparel of the other spouse or minor children, which is community personal property, without the written consent of the other spouse.

(d) Except as provided in subdivisions (b) and (c), and in *Section 1102*, a spouse who is operating or managing a business or an interest in a business that is all or substantially all community personal property has the primary management and control of the business or interest. Primary management and control means that the managing spouse may act alone in all transactions but shall give prior written notice to the other spouse of any sale, lease, exchange, encumbrance, or other disposition of all or substantially all of the personal property used in the operation of the business (including personal property used for agricultural purposes), whether or not title to that property is held in the name of only one spouse. Written notice is not, however, required when prohibited by the law otherwise applicable to the transaction.

Remedies for the failure by a managing spouse to give prior written notice as required by this subdivision are only as specified in *Section 1101*. A failure to give prior written notice shall not adversely affect the validity of a transaction nor of any interest transferred.

(e) Each spouse shall act with respect to the other spouse in the management and control of the community assets and liabilities in accordance with the general rules governing fiduciary relationships which control the actions of persons having relationships of personal confidence as specified in *Section 721*, until such time as the assets and liabilities have been divided by the parties or by a court. This duty includes the obligation to make full disclosure to the other spouse of all material facts and information regarding the existence, characterization, and valuation of all assets in which the community has or may have an interest and debts for which the community is or may be liable, and to provide equal access to all information, records, and books that pertain to the value and character of those assets and debts, upon request.

28. *Family Code section 1101* – Breach of Fiduciary Duty Between Spouses

Explanation:

Family Code § 1101 allows one spouse to sue the other for violating fiduciary duties involving community property. These duties include full disclosure, honesty, and fair dealing. If a spouse hides, misuses, or improperly transfers community property without consent, the other can seek legal remedies — including monetary awards, reallocation of assets, or full ownership of the wrongfully handled property. *Section 1101* applies during marriage, separation, and even after a spouse's death. The law protects each spouse's equal interest in marital property and ensures that neither takes unfair advantage of the other.

Examples:

Hidden assets: A spouse wins a lottery but does not disclose it during divorce. The court can award 100% of the hidden asset to the innocent spouse, as a penalty for breach of fiduciary duty.

Unauthorized transfers: One spouse deeds a jointly owned house to a third party without consent. The harmed spouse may bring a *§ 1101* claim to unwind the transaction and recover their interest.

Wasting community assets: A spouse spends large amounts of community funds on gambling or an extramarital affair. The court can reimburse the other spouse for their share of the loss.

Nondisclosure in divorce: A spouse fails to list a business account in the divorce disclosures. The court may reopen the case and award a monetary remedy under *§ 1101(g)* or (h).

Claims after death: Even if a spouse dies, the surviving spouse may bring a *§ 1101* claim against the decedent's estate for breaches that impaired their share of the community property.

Further Reading:

In re Marriage of Rossi (2001) 90 Cal.App.4th 34: See Rossi 100 Percent Remedy (pg. 61).

Yeh v. Tai (2017) 18 Cal.App.5th 953: The court clarified that *§ 1101(d)*'s three-year limitations period, not the one-year probate statute, governs claims for breach of fiduciary duty brought after a spouse's death.

In re Marriage of Brewer & Federici (2001) 93 Cal.App.4th 1334: See *In re Marriage of Brewer & Federici*: Incomplete Disclosure and Judgment Set Aside (pg. 63).

In re Marriage of Schleich (2017) 8 Cal.App.5th 267: Court ruled that *§ 1101* does not apply to separate property or pre-separation actions that did not affect the community estate, narrowing the scope of the statute's remedies.

In re Marriage of DeBenedetti & Ensberg (2025) 110 Cal.App.5th 1035: A monetary award under § 1101(g) was treated as a property right enforceable by QDRO against a retirement plan, confirming the enforceability of fiduciary-duty remedies in property division.

Full Text of *California Family Code § 1101*

(a) A spouse has a claim against the other spouse for any breach of the fiduciary duty that results in impairment to the claimant spouse's present undivided one-half interest in the community estate, including, but not limited to, a single transaction or a pattern or series of transactions, which transaction or transactions have caused or will cause a detrimental impact to the claimant spouse's undivided one-half interest in the community estate.

(b) A court may order an accounting of the property and obligations of the parties to a marriage and may determine the rights of ownership in, the beneficial enjoyment of, or access to, community property, and the classification of all property of the parties to a marriage.

(c) A court may order that the name of a spouse shall be added to community property held in the name of the other spouse alone or that the title of community property held in some other title form shall be reformed to reflect its community character, except with respect to any of the following:

(1) A partnership interest held by the other spouse as a general partner.

(2) An interest in a professional corporation or professional association.

(3) An asset of an unincorporated business if the other spouse is the only spouse involved in operating and managing the business.

(4) Any other property, if the revision would adversely affect the rights of a third person.

(d)

(1) Except as provided in paragraph (2), any action under subdivision (a) shall be commenced within three years of the date a petitioning spouse had actual knowledge that the transaction or event for which the remedy is being sought occurred.

(2) An action may be commenced under this section upon the death of a spouse or in conjunction with an action for legal separation, dissolution of marriage, or nullity without regard to the time limitations set forth in paragraph (1).

(3) The defense of laches may be raised in any action brought under this section.

(4) Except as to actions authorized by paragraph (2), remedies under subdivision (a) apply only to transactions or events occurring on or after July 1, 1987.

(e) In any transaction affecting community property in which the consent of both spouses is required, the court may, upon the motion of a spouse, dispense with the requirement of the other spouse's consent if both of the following requirements are met:

(1) The proposed transaction is in the best interest of the community.

(2) Consent has been arbitrarily refused or cannot be obtained due to the physical incapacity, mental incapacity, or prolonged absence of the nonconsenting spouse.

(f) Any action may be brought under this section without filing an action for dissolution of marriage, legal separation, or nullity, or may be brought in conjunction with the action or upon the death of a spouse.

(g) Remedies for breach of the fiduciary duty by one spouse, including those set out in *Sections 721 and 1100*, shall include, but not be limited to, an award to the other spouse of 50 percent, or an amount equal to 50 percent, of any asset undisclosed or transferred in breach of the fiduciary duty plus attorney's fees and court costs. The value of the asset shall be determined to be its highest value at the date of the breach of the fiduciary duty, the date of the sale or disposition of the asset, or the date of the award by the court.

(h) Remedies for the breach of the fiduciary duty by one spouse, as set forth in *Sections 721 and 1100*, when the breach falls within the ambit of *Section 3294* of the Civil Code shall include, but not be limited to, an award to the other spouse of 100 percent, or an amount equal to 100 percent, of any asset undisclosed or transferred in breach of the fiduciary duty.

29. *Family Code section 1500* – Alteration of Spouses' Property Rights by Agreement

Explanation:

Under California law, married people normally follow set rules about who owns property (for example, income earned during marriage is usually owned jointly by both spouses). *Family Code §1500* says those default rules can be changed if the spouses agree. In plain English, this means a husband and wife can use a written agreement, before marriage (a prenuptial agreement) or during marriage (such as a postnup or marital settlement agreement), to decide their own property arrangement. For example, a couple might agree that each person's earnings and assets during the marriage will remain separate property of that spouse, rather than community property shared 50/50. *Section 1500* makes clear that such agreements are valid to override the usual statutory property rights, as long as the agreement is valid and voluntarily made. In short, spouses can contract to set their own property rules instead of relying on the default legal rules.

Examples:

Premarital Agreement: Alice and Bob plan to marry. They sign a prenuptial agreement stating that Alice's family home and Bob's business will be kept as each person's separate property. Under *§1500*, this agreement is recognized by law, so those assets will not be treated as community property in the future.

Postnuptial Property Agreement: After marriage, Carla and Dan execute a postnuptial agreement specifying that Carla's inheritance and Dan's pension contributions will remain separate property. Although community-property rules would normally apply, *§1500* allows them to change that outcome by mutual agreement.

Divorce Settlement Agreement: Emily and Frank are divorcing and enter into a marital settlement agreement dividing assets differently than the default law. For instance, the agreement gives Emily the entire equity in the family home (instead of splitting it) and gives Frank a larger share of the savings account. *Section 1500* means the court will enforce that agreed division of property because the spouses have altered the statutory property rights by contract.

Case Law

Sturm v. Moyer (2019) 32 Cal.App.5th 299: The Court of Appeal upheld a premarital agreement that made each spouse's earnings and property during marriage their separate property. The court noted that *Family Code §1500* "authorizes the use of a premarital agreement" to change the default community property presumption. In Sturm, the husband's prenup removed his wife's income from the community estate. The court confirmed that this alteration of statutory property rights was valid under *§1500* (though the agreement's effect was later examined for fraud under other laws).

In re Marriage of Bonds (2000) 24 Cal.4th 1: The California Supreme Court enforced a prenuptial agreement in which the spouses waived any rights in each other's earnings and assets. The Court emphasized that spouses have the power to contractually set their property rights. Although Bonds focused on spousal support, the Court discussed *§1500* to explain that premarital contracts altering property ownership are generally enforceable. The ruling confirms that a valid premarital agreement can override the usual marital property rules, so long as the contract meets legal requirements (such as voluntary execution with disclosure).

Full Text of *California Family Code § 1500*

California Family Code § 1500. The property rights of spouses prescribed by statute may be altered by a premarital agreement or other marital property agreement.

30. *Family Code section 1610* – Definition of Premarital Agreement

Explanation:

California Family Code Section 1610 defines the basic terms used in the state's Uniform Premarital Agreement Act. Specifically, it explains what a "premarital agreement" is and what qualifies as "property" for the purposes of such agreements.

A premarital agreement is a written contract made between two people who are planning to marry. It only becomes effective once they are legally married.

Property is defined broadly. It includes any legal or equitable interest, whether present or future, vested or contingent, in both real (land, buildings) and personal (money, belongings) property. This includes income and earnings.

Examples:

Written Agreement: John and Maria create a written agreement before marriage stating that any income earned during marriage will remain the separate property of the person who earned it. Under *§ 1610*, this agreement is a valid premarital agreement and the income is considered "property."

Home Owned Before Marriage: Lisa owns a home before marriage. Her premarital agreement with Tim states that the house remains hers after marriage. Because the house is a present interest in real property, it is clearly covered by the definition of "property" under *§ 1610.*

Agreed Inheritance: A couple agrees that any future inheritance either person receives will remain their separate property. Even though the inheritance is not yet received, *§ 1610* allows it to be included in the agreement as a future contingent interest.

Further Reading:

Last v. Superior Court (2023) 94 Cal.App.5th 30: The California Court of Appeal (4th Dist.) dealt with a premarital agreement that waived spousal support. The court explained that such waivers are not automatically enforced unless the agreement satisfies specific requirements (found in *§ 1615(c)*), which include certain written findings of voluntariness. In Last, the trial court had not made the required findings under *§ 1615(c)* that the prenup was entered into voluntarily, so the court treated the waiver as unenforceable for purposes of awarding temporary support. This case shows how a premarital agreement (as defined by *§ 1610*) can still be invalidated if procedures (from *§ 1615*) aren't followed.

In re Marriage of Bonds (2000) 24 Cal.4th 1: Another California Supreme Court case about a premarital agreement. Here the issue was whether one spouse's lack of independent legal counsel at signing made the agreement invalid. The Court held that an agreement (as defined by *§ 1610*) isn't automatically void just because one spouse had no independent lawyer. Instead, the enforceability is determined by *§ 1615* factors. The court said subjecting the agreement to special "strict scrutiny" was inconsistent with the Act, which generally enforces voluntarily made agreements. This case shows that the simple fact of no counsel does not change the definition of a premarital agreement under *§ 1610*, and such agreements are judged by the usual statutory rules.

In re Marriage of Pendleton & Fireman (2000) 24 Cal.4th 39: In this California Supreme Court case, spouses had signed a premarital agreement waiving spousal support. The court discussed *§ 1610*'s definition, noting that a premarital agreement is "an agreement between prospective spouses made in contemplation of marriage". The court also summarized *§ 1612*, which lets couples contract about "the rights and obligations of each of the parties in any of the property of either or both of them whenever and wherever acquired". This shows that *§ 1610*'s definitions form the foundation: once an agreement falls under this definition, courts will enforce it under the rules of the Act. (Pendleton & Fireman ultimately held that a waiver of spousal support wasn't per se unenforceable, meaning the spouses could validly include it in their premarital agreement.)

Sturm v. Moyer (2019) 32 Cal.App.5th 299: In this Court of Appeal case, a judgment creditor challenged a premarital agreement that left each spouse's future earnings as separate property. The court explicitly cited *§ 1610(a)*'s definition, stating that at the time the agreement was signed (before marriage), neither spouse had any rights in community property. The court then reasoned that on the date of marriage, each spouse immediately acquires community property rights, which then "immediately transfer" back to separate property under the agreement. In other words, the agreement, defined by *§ 1610*, restructures property ownership once marriage occurs. The court's analysis illustrates how *§ 1610*'s timing ("effective upon marriage") affects when and how property is deemed transferred under a premarital agreement.

Full Text of *Family Code § 1610*

(a) "Premarital agreement" means an agreement between prospective spouses made in contemplation of marriage and to be effective upon marriage.

(b) "Property" means an interest, present or future, legal or equitable, vested or contingent, in real or personal property, including income and earnings.

31. *Family Code section 1612* – Matters that Can be Addressed in a Premarital Agreement

Explanation:

Section 1612 of the California Family Code lists what prospective spouses can include in a premarital agreement. In plain language, it lets couples decide in advance how to handle their property and financial matters. They can define ownership of any property (present or future), how it's managed, and how it will be distributed if they separate, divorce, or one spouse dies. *Section 1612* also explicitly allows couples to make arrangements about wills, trusts, and even life insurance proceeds. For example, spouses may agree which assets stay separate, or how community property is divided (subparts (1)–(3) of *§1612(a)*). They can also choose the governing law for the agreement (subpart (6)).

The law protects certain rights as well. *Section 1612(b)* says a child's right to support cannot be affected by the prenup. Subsection (c) adds rules on spousal support waivers. It says any clause waiving spousal support is unenforceable if the spouse against whom support would be enforced did not have independent legal counsel or if enforcing the waiver would be unfair (unconscionable). In other words, a prenup can include a support waiver only if the other spouse was fully informed and the waiver is fair when it's time to enforce it.

Examples:

Managing property rights: Alice and Bob sign a prenup stating that each of them retains full rights over the property they bring into the marriage, and any future property they acquire on their own. They also agree that any business Bob starts during marriage remains his separate property. These terms are allowed under *§1612(a)(1)* and (2), which permit contracting about the parties' property rights and how they control it.

Planning for future events: Carla and Dan's agreement says that if they divorce or one spouse dies, Carla will receive certain savings and Dan will keep his family home. They also include provisions for wills and trust distributions to carry out the agreement (covered by *§1612(a)(4)*). Additionally, they specify that California law will govern their contract (*§1612(a)(6)*). All of these subjects, disposition at divorce or death, and choice of law, are expressly permitted by *§1612*.

Insurance and support: Eva and Frank agree that the life insurance policies they hold will benefit the other spouse equally (*§1612(a)(5)*). They also agree in writing that neither will claim spousal support if they divorce. Knowing *§1612(c)*, they make sure Eva has her own attorney review the agreement. Because Eva was advised by independent counsel and the waiver is not unfair at enforcement, the waiver is enforceable under the statute.

Further Reading:

In re Marriage of Pendleton & Fireman (2000) 24 Cal.4th 39: California's Supreme Court held that premarital waivers of spousal support are not automatically invalid. The court emphasized that couples may contract on the topics listed in *§1612(a)* as long as the agreement meets general fairness requirements. In Pendleton, the wife had waived all support but was represented by counsel, so the waiver was upheld under the applicable enforceability tests.

In re Marriage of Howell (2011) 195 Cal.App.4th 1062: The appellate court ruled that the 2002 amendment to *§1612(c)* (which imposes conditions on spousal support waivers) did not apply retroactively. Here, a 1999 agreement included a spousal support waiver. Because the agreement was signed before the amendment took effect, the waiver was found valid and enforceable under the law as it existed in 1999.

In re Marriage of Facter (2013) 212 Cal.App.4th 967: The court found that a spousal support waiver was unconscionable in its circumstances and thus unenforceable under *§1612(c)*. Nancy had far less education and no separate property while Jeffrey earned millions. Enforcing the waiver would have left her without adequate support. The court agreed with the trial court that the waiver was unconscionable, though it severed the invalid waiver and enforced the rest of the agreement.

In re Marriage of Shaban (2001) 88 Cal.App.4th 398: This case involved a one-page Arabic document intended as a premarital agreement incorporating Islamic law. The court held there was no enforceable prenup because the writing did not clearly state any substantive terms. It noted that *§1612(a)(6)* allows a choice of law (the couple wanted Islamic law), but the contract itself must be clear. Here the document was too vague, so the court applied California law to divide the community property.

In re Marriage of Miotke (2019) 35 Cal.App.5th 849: The court upheld a 1996 premarital agreement's waiver of spousal support. In this case, the couple signed a detailed prenup just weeks before marriage, waiving support and setting custody terms for their child. A private judge and later the trial court found the agreement valid. The published opinion affirms that the waiver was enforceable under *§1612* because the agreement complied with all legal requirements.

Full Text of *California Family Code § 1612*

(a) Parties to a premarital agreement may contract with respect to all of the following:

(1) The rights and obligations of each of the parties in any of the property of either or both of them whenever and wherever acquired or located.

(2) The right to buy, sell, use, transfer, exchange, abandon, lease, consume, expend, assign, create a security interest in, mortgage, encumber, dispose of, or otherwise manage and control property.

(3) The disposition of property upon separation, marital dissolution, death, or the occurrence or nonoccurrence of any other event.

(4) The making of a will, trust, or other arrangement to carry out the provisions of the agreement.

(5) The ownership rights in and disposition of the death benefit from a life insurance policy.

(6) The choice of law governing the construction of the agreement.

(7) Any other matter, including their personal rights and obligations, not in violation of public policy or a statute imposing a criminal penalty.

(b) The right of a child to support may not be adversely affected by a premarital agreement.

(c) Any provision in a premarital agreement regarding spousal support, including, but not limited to, a waiver of it, is not enforceable if the party against whom enforcement of the spousal support provision is sought was not represented by independent counsel at the time the agreement containing the provision was signed, or if the provision regarding spousal support is unconscionable at the time of enforcement. An otherwise unenforceable provision in a premarital agreement regarding spousal support may not become enforceable solely because the party against whom enforcement is sought was represented by independent counsel.

32. *Family Code section 1615* – Premarital Agreement Enforceability

Explanation:

Family Code § 1615 governs when a written premarital agreement is enforceable. A premarital agreement is not enforceable if the party against whom enforcement is sought proves either that the party did not execute the agreement voluntarily, or that the agreement was unconscionable when executed and the required financial-disclosure conditions were not satisfied.

Current *§ 1615(c)* creates a specific voluntariness framework. The court must make findings in writing or on the record addressing the statutory safeguards, including independent legal counsel or a separate written waiver after advisement, the required seven-calendar-day timing rules, the written explanation and acknowledgment required for an unrepresented party, absence of duress, fraud, undue influence, and lack of capacity, and any other factors the court deems relevant.

For agreements executed on or after January 1, 2020, the seven-day rule is not limited to unrepresented parties. *Section 1615(c)(2)*(B) requires that the party against whom enforcement is sought have not less than seven calendar days between first being presented with the final agreement and signing it, regardless of whether the party is represented by legal counsel. The rule does not apply to non-substantive amendments that do not change the terms of the agreement.

Older cases must be used with date sensitivity. *In re Marriage of Bonds* (2000) 24 Cal.4th 1 predates the 2002 statutory amendments adding detailed voluntariness safeguards. *In re Marriage of Cadwell-Faso & Faso* (2011) 191 Cal.App.4th 945 interpreted the pre-2020 version of *§ 1615(c)(2)* in a case involving represented parties. It should not be cited to avoid the current post-2020 final-agreement waiting period.

Examples:

Recent Agreement: A premarital agreement executed on or after January 1, 2020 is first presented in final form to the party against whom enforcement will later be sought only six calendar days before signing. Even if that party has independent counsel, the agreement does not satisfy the timing requirement in *§ 1615(c)(2)(B)*, unless the later change was merely a non-substantive amendment that did not alter the agreement's terms.

Older Agreement: An agreement executed before January 1, 2020 by parties represented by counsel from the outset may require separate analysis under the former statutory language and pre-2020 case law, including Cadwell-Faso. That historical rule should be described as limited to the prior statute and should not be stated as the present rule for agreements executed on or after January 1, 2020.

Unrepresented Party: If the party against whom enforcement is sought is unrepresented, *§ 1615(c)(1)* and (c)(3) require more than the seven-day final-agreement period. The party must be advised to seek independent counsel at least seven calendar days before signing, must expressly waive counsel in a separate writing if not represented, and must receive a written explanation of the agreement's terms, basic effect, and the rights and obligations being relinquished, with the required acknowledgment before or at signing.

Further Reading:

Last v. Superior Court (2023) 94 Cal.App.5th 30: Last explains that a premarital agreement is deemed not voluntarily executed unless the trial court makes the findings required by *§ 1615(c)*. A court addressing support or enforceability should not presume validity merely from the face of the agreement without the required findings.

Marriage of Clarke & Akel (2018) 19 Cal.App.5th 914: Clarke & Akel applied the seven-day review and written-advisement requirements to an unrepresented party under the pre-2020 statute and cautioned that the statutory protections cannot be avoided by recitals that are inconsistent with the actual facts.

In re Marriage of Cadwell-Faso & Faso (2011) 191 Cal.App.4th 945: Cadwell-Faso is historical authority under the pre-2020 version of *§ 1615(c)(2)*. For agreements executed on or after January 1, 2020, use the current statutory text, which requires seven calendar days between first presentation of the final agreement and signing regardless of counsel representation.

Full Text of *California Family Code § 1615*

(a) A premarital agreement is not enforceable if the party against whom enforcement is sought proves either of the following:

(1) That party did not execute the agreement voluntarily.

(2) The agreement was unconscionable when it was executed and, before execution of the agreement, all of the following applied to that party:

(A) That party was not provided a fair, reasonable, and full disclosure of the property or financial obligations of the other party.

(B) That party did not voluntarily and expressly waive, in writing, any right to disclosure of the property or financial obligations of the other party beyond the disclosure provided.

(C) That party did not have, or reasonably could not have had, an adequate knowledge of the property or financial obligations of the other party.

(b) An issue of unconscionability of a premarital agreement shall be decided by the court as a matter of law.

(c) For the purposes of subdivision (a), it shall be deemed that a premarital agreement was not executed voluntarily unless the court finds in writing or on the record all of the following:

(1) The party against whom enforcement is sought was represented by independent legal counsel at the time of signing the agreement or, after being advised to seek independent legal counsel, expressly waived, in a separate writing, representation by independent legal counsel. The advisement to seek independent legal counsel shall be made at least seven calendar days before the final agreement is signed.

(2) One of the following:

(A) For an agreement executed between January 1, 2002, and January 1, 2020, the party against whom enforcement is sought had not less than seven calendar days between the time that party was first presented with the final agreement and advised to seek independent legal counsel and the time the agreement was signed. This requirement does not apply to nonsubstantive amendments that do not change the terms of the agreement.

(B) For an agreement executed on or after January 1, 2020, the party against whom enforcement is sought had not less than seven calendar days between the time that party was first presented with the final agreement and the time the agreement was signed, regardless of whether the party is represented by legal counsel. This requirement does not apply to nonsubstantive amendments that do not change the terms of the agreement.

(3) The party against whom enforcement is sought, if unrepresented by legal counsel, was fully informed of the terms and basic effect of the agreement as well as the rights and obligations the party was giving up by signing the agreement, and was proficient in the language in which the explanation of the party's rights was conducted and in which the agreement was written. The explanation of the rights and obligations relinquished shall be memorialized in writing and delivered to the party

prior to signing the agreement. The unrepresented party shall, on or before the signing of the premarital agreement, execute a document declaring that the party received the information required by this paragraph and indicating who provided that information.

(4) The agreement and the writings executed pursuant to paragraphs (1) and (3) were not executed under duress, fraud, or undue influence, and the parties did not lack capacity to enter into the agreement.

(5) Any other factors the court deems relevant.

33. *Family Code section 2601* – Division of Community Property and Debt

Explanation:

California Family Code § 2601 allows a divorce court to give a particular community property asset entirely to one spouse, instead of splitting the asset in half, when there are sound economic reasons to do so. In such cases, the judge must make sure the overall division of property is still fair and equal by giving the other spouse something of equivalent value (for example, requiring an equalization payment or awarding additional assets). This rule gives courts flexibility to handle assets that can't be physically divided without losing value or causing harm. In plain terms, if dividing a community asset "50/50" would be impractical or would reduce its value, the court can award that whole asset to one spouse as long as the other spouse is compensated so that each ends up with the same total value in the end.

Examples:

Family Home with Children: During a divorce, suppose the couple's primary asset is the family house. Rather than ordering the home to be sold and the proceeds split, a court might award the entire house to one spouse (often the custodial parent if children are involved) under *§ 2601*. The judge would then give the other spouse assets or a payment equal to their half of the home's value. This way, the children can continue living in the house and the spouse keeping the home "buys out" the other's share, ensuring both spouses still receive equal value overall.

Small Business or Professional Practice: Imagine the spouses jointly own a small business (or one spouse's medical/legal practice). It isn't feasible to cut a business in half, and forcing a sale could destroy its value. Using *§ 2601*, a court could award the entire business to the spouse who manages or relies on it for their livelihood, and give the other spouse a collection of other community assets or an IOU (equalization payment) to make the division fair.

This lets the business continue operating smoothly with one owner, while the other spouse gets compensated for their share in its value.

(1) Unique or Indivisible Asset: If the couple owns a unique asset like a rare piece of art or a special vehicle, the court might decide it's best for one spouse to keep that item intact. For example, if one spouse has a strong personal attachment to a painting that can't be split, the court can award the entire painting to that spouse. The other spouse would then receive other property or cash equal to the painting's half-value. This approach avoids selling the artwork (which neither spouse may want) and respects the sentimental value, while still giving the other spouse something of equal worth.

Further Reading:

In re Marriage of Clark (1978) 80 Cal.App.3d 417. In this case, a divorcing couple owned shares in a closely held business (a forging company). The husband worked at the company, and the other co-owner testified he would dissolve the business if the wife became a shareholder. The trial court, citing the predecessor to *§ 2601*, awarded all of the community stock to the husband to preserve the company as a going concern. To keep the division equal, the wife received other assets to offset her half of the stock's value. The Court of Appeal upheld this decision, explaining that "economic circumstances" justified giving the entire asset to one spouse because dividing the stock between them would have impaired or destroyed the business.

In re Marriage of Brigden (1978) 80 Cal.App.3d 380. Here, a couple owned about 66,000 shares of stock in a public company (Logicon, Inc.). The trial court gave all the stock to the husband with certain conditions, rather than splitting it, but the wife appealed. The Court of Appeal reversed that part of the judgment, finding there were no special economic circumstances requiring one spouse to get all the stock. Unlike a small family business, these shares were easily divisible without loss of value. The appellate court emphasized that the exception in *§ 2601* is meant for situations where an asset "cannot be divided without impairment," and that if an asset (like publicly traded stock) can be split equally without harm, each spouse should receive their 50% share. In short, because both spouses could own their portion of the stock without undermining its value, the law did not warrant giving it all to one party.

In re Marriage of Fink (1979) 25 Cal.3d 877. This California Supreme Court case approved an "asset distribution" approach very similar to what *§ 2601* allows. The divorcing spouses had multiple assets, including the family home, the husband's law practice, and various personal items. The trial court awarded specific assets entirely to one spouse or the other (rather than splitting each item). For example, the wife was awarded the family residence (to which she was emotionally attached) and a painting she loved, while the husband was awarded his law practice, his club membership, and a painting he cherished, with a cash payment to equalize the division. The Supreme Court held that this was permissible under the law: a strictly in-kind 50/50 division of each asset was not required, so long as the overall community estate was divided equally in value. Fink confirmed that trial courts have broad discretion to allocate whole assets to one party when an equal overall result is achieved.

In re Marriage of Connolly (1979) 23 Cal.3d 590. In this Supreme Court case, the couple's community property included 10,000 shares of stock in Amdahl Corporation, a tech company where the husband was an outside director. The husband asked the court to award him all 10,000 shares so he could maintain influence as a director. The trial court did so, giving the husband the stock and ordering him to give the wife an unsecured promissory note for half of its value (about $37,500) to keep the division equal. The wife later challenged the judgment (claiming the husband should have disclosed inside information about the stock's impending public offering, which greatly increased its value). The Supreme Court ultimately found no misconduct by the husband regarding disclosure. Importantly, the court reaffirmed that awarding an asset to one spouse with an equalization payment to the other is a valid way to achieve an equal division. Connolly illustrates how *§ 2601* can be applied to stock or investment assets: one spouse can receive the entire stock holding (especially if that spouse's role in the company makes their full ownership advantageous), provided the other spouse is compensated fairly for their share.

In re Marriage of Tammen (1976) 63 Cal.App.3d 927. This case highlights the need for fair conditions when one spouse is awarded an asset under what is now *§ 2601*. The trial court had given the wife roughly 79% of the community property (including the family home), and to offset this, ordered her to pay the husband $19,820 in installments over 10 years. The Court of Appeal found that this long-term promissory note did not truly make the division equal. Due to factors like the delayed payment, lack of interest or security, and inflation, the husband's half would be worth much less in present value. The appellate court reversed that portion of the judgment, ruling that if a deferred payment is used to equalize a division, its terms must ensure the receiving spouse gets the full value of their share. In other words, when a court awards one party an asset and a note is given to the other, the note should be properly valued (with interest or other terms) so that both spouses genuinely end up with substantially equal assets.

Full Text of *California Family Code § 2601*

Where economic circumstances warrant, the court may award an asset of the community estate to one party on such conditions as the court deems proper to effect a substantially equal division of the community estate.

34. *Family Code section 2602* – Deliberate Misappropriation of Community Property

Explanation:

What It Is: *Family Code § 2602* lets a divorce court make up for one spouse's deliberate misuse or hiding of community property assets. In a California divorce, the law normally requires an equal 50/50 split of community property between the spouses. *Section 2602* is an exception to that rule when one spouse has intentionally committed "calculated thievery," in other words, taken or spent community property on purpose to deny the other spouse their share. If the court finds that one spouse deliberately misappropriated (stole, concealed, or wrongfully squandered) an asset belonging to both spouses, the judge can compensate the innocent spouse.

How It Works: Under *§ 2602*, a judge may award an extra amount or offset against the offending spouse's portion of the property equal to the value of what was misappropriated. Practically, this means the wronged spouse could receive more than 50% of the remaining community property to make up for what was taken. For example, if one spouse secretly emptied a joint bank account or sold a community asset and kept the proceeds, the court can credit the other spouse with the value of that money during property division. This ensures a fair outcome despite one party's bad behavior. The key is that the misappropriation must have been intentional and without the other spouse's consent; mere carelessness or poor investment isn't enough. California courts have emphasized that a deliberate misappropriation is required, not just negligence or mismanagement. In short, *§ 2602* allows judges to prevent a dishonest spouse from benefitting from their wrongdoing by adjusting the property split accordingly.

Examples:

Hiding Money in Secret Accounts: Shortly before a divorce, Husband transfers $50,000 of community funds into a hidden bank account in his name only, intending to keep it out of Wife's reach. In the divorce, the court discovers this deliberate hiding of assets. Using *§ 2602*, the judge can award Wife an extra $50,000 from Husband's share of other community property (or reduce his share by that amount) to offset the funds he misappropriated. Essentially, Wife will ultimately receive the $50,000 that Husband tried to squirrel away.

Unauthorized Gifts or Transfers: One spouse uses community funds to buy an expensive car for a new girlfriend without the other spouse's knowledge or any benefit to the marriage. This is a misappropriation of community property for a third party. In the property division, the court could charge the value of that car entirely to the gifting spouse's portion of assets. For instance, if Husband gifted a $30,000 car to someone else, the court can give Wife $30,000 extra from other assets off Husband's share to make up for that improper gift.

Sale of Assets and Spending Proceeds: Wife secretly sells a valuable community asset (such as stocks or a piece of real estate) and spends the proceeds on herself alone, without Husband's consent. Under *§ 2602*, the court can find that Wife deliberately excluded Husband's interest by doing so. The judge could then award Husband an equivalent amount from Wife's portion of the remaining assets. In effect, Husband gets reimbursed through an unequal division of property because Wife already got her benefit by spending the shared asset's value.

Destroying or Wasting Assets: A spouse intentionally wastes community property; for example, by gambling away large sums of marital funds in secret or deliberately destroying a valuable asset out of spite. If proven intentional, this conduct can be treated as a misappropriation. The court might grant the innocent spouse a larger share of what's left (or a judgment against the other spouse) equal to the value lost. This way, the innocent spouse isn't penalized for the other's deliberate waste of community money.

Further Reading:

In re Marriage of Schultz (1980) 105 Cal.App.3d 846: This case established the high bar for what counts as a deliberate misappropriation. The husband's mishandling of a debt (failing to show up in court, leading to a default judgment against the community) was penalized by the trial court as if he misappropriated funds. The Court of Appeal reversed, holding that mere negligence or mismanagement is not "deliberate misappropriation." The term means intentional theft, "calculated thievery," not just sloppy or negligent financial handling. Since the husband's conduct was deemed just carelessness and not an intentional attempt to deprive the wife of assets, the penalty under the predecessor of *§ 2602* was unwarranted.

In re Marriage of Partridge (1990) 226 Cal.App.3d 120: The wife argued that the husband's failure to pay certain tax obligations (and attempts to ignore a large tax debt) was a deliberate misappropriation of community funds. The appellate court disagreed. It explained that the "deliberate misappropriation" doctrine allows a court to award a greater share of property to the innocent spouse only when one spouse has intentionally deprived the community of an asset. In Partridge, the husband's conduct, while irresponsible, was aimed at benefiting the community (by hoping to improve finances) and did not permanently deprive the wife of her share. He also offered to shoulder the consequences (tax penalties). Therefore, his actions did not rise to the level of *deliberate* misappropriation, and the trial court was not entitled to make an unequal division of property under *§ 2602* in that situation.

In re Marriage of Economou (1990) 224 Cal.App.3d 1466: This case illustrates a flagrant misappropriation and the resulting remedy. The husband hid assets worldwide (in California, Georgia, and Greece) and even absconded with about $1.8 million in community funds to Europe during the divorce. He defied court orders to return the money and failed to disclose or cooperate, leading the court to enter his default. Evidence at trial showed the husband had misappropriated over $6 million of community property for his own benefit. The Court of Appeal upheld an unequal division heavily favoring the wife. It pointed out that under *Civil Code § 4800(b)(2)* (the predecessor to *§ 2602*), courts need not divide property equally when one party has deliberately misappropriated assets. In Economou, the husband's willful theft of community assets meant he forfeited the right to a 50/50 split. The wife was awarded a substantially greater share to compensate for the missing money, which *§ 2602* fully permits in such extreme misconduct. This case confirms that *egregious, intentional deprivation* of community property by one spouse justifies an unequal division in the other's favor.

Lezine v. Security Pacific Financial Services, Inc. (1996) 14 Cal.4th 56: Although not a divorce between spouses (it involved a creditor), the California Supreme Court's discussion is relevant. The husband had secretly encumbered a piece of community real estate without the wife's consent, violating her property rights. In its decision, the Supreme Court noted that the wife was not without recourse: she could seek reimbursement or credit for the husband's improper use of the community asset. The court expressly cited *Family Code § 2602* (formerly *Civil Code § 4800(b)(2)*) as a provision allowing a spouse to recover for the other's misuse of community assets. Lezine thus recognizes *§ 2602*'s role in protecting an innocent spouse when the other spouse's wrongdoing (here, an illegal transfer of property) harms the community estate. It underscores that a spouse who abuses or misappropriates a community asset can be surcharged for that loss under *§ 2602*, ensuring the wronged spouse isn't shortchanged.

Full Text of *Family Code § 2602*

As an additional award or offset against existing property, the court may award, from a party's share, the amount the court determines to have been deliberately misappropriated by the party to the exclusion of the interest of the other party in the community estate.

35. *Family Code section 2603* – Personal Injury Payments

Explanation:

California Family Code § 2603 addresses the division of community estate personal injury damages at dissolution. It does not allocate ordinary marital debts. The section applies to money or other property received, or to be received, for a spouse's personal injuries when the cause of action arose during marriage and the recovery is not separate property under *§ 781*, unless the recovery has been commingled with other community assets.

Under this provision, if one spouse receives money for a personal injury (for example, from a lawsuit or insurance settlement) and the cause of action arose during the marriage, that money is initially considered part of the community property. But unlike other community assets, these "community estate personal injury damages" are generally awarded to the injured spouse when the community property is divided. The idea is to prevent the uninjured spouse from getting a windfall from the other's personal injury compensation. The law recognizes that personal injury awards (especially for pain, suffering, or disfigurement) are personal to the injured party.

Family Code § 2603(b) says the injured spouse will receive all of these damages unless dividing them differently is necessary for fairness ("in the interests of justice"). Even if a court decides to give some of the injury award to the other spouse (for example, if the couple's economic situation makes it equitable to share a portion), the injured spouse must receive at least 50% of those damages. In deciding if an alternative split is justified, the court will consider factors like each spouse's financial needs and circumstances and how much time has passed since the injury or when the money was recovered. This ensures the division is fair, especially if the injury money was obtained long before the divorce or has been integrated into the couple's finances.

It's important to note that this rule only applies to personal injury recoveries that are community property. If the cause of action for the injury arose after the spouses were living separate (or after a divorce/legal separation was already final), then the damages are considered the injured person's separate property under *Family Code § 781* and wouldn't be subject to division at all. Also, if the injury award was commingled with other community funds to the point it can't be traced (for example, deposited into a joint account and mixed with regular savings), then it may lose its special status and be treated like general community property to be split equally.

Examples:

Traceable personal injury settlement during marriage: During marriage, Wife is injured in a car accident and receives a $100,000 settlement for pain, suffering, and related injury damages. The recovery is traceable and has not been commingled. At dissolution, *§ 2603* generally assigns the community estate personal injury damages to Wife, unless the court finds that the interests of justice require a different disposition. Even then, Wife must receive at least one-half of the damages.

Commingled recovery: Husband receives a $75,000 personal injury settlement during marriage and deposits it into a joint account used for ordinary expenses, wages, and savings. If the remaining funds cannot be traced to the personal injury recovery, the special *§ 2603* assignment rule may be lost because the statute excludes money or property that has been commingled with other community estate assets.

Post-separation injury: After the parties separate, Husband is injured and later receives a settlement for that post-separation injury. That recovery is analyzed under *§ 781* as Husband's separate property, not under *§ 2603* as community estate personal injury damages.

Interests-of-justice allocation: Wife receives a personal injury recovery during marriage, but the recovery was obtained many years before dissolution and was used to acquire identifiable assets. The court may consider the parties' economic condition and needs, the elapsed time since recovery or accrual, and all other facts. If the court assigns any portion to the other spouse, *§ 2603* still requires that at least one-half of the damages be assigned to Wife as the injured spouse.

Personal Injury Settlement Example: During the marriage, one spouse is injured in a car accident and receives a $100,000 settlement for pain, suffering, and lost wages. Under California law, that settlement is community property because the cause of action arose during the marriage. However, *Family Code § 2603* will apply to this money. In a divorce, the injured spouse will likely be awarded the majority or all of the $100,000. For example, a court might award the entire $100,000 to the injured spouse, recognizing that the funds compensate for that spouse's personal injuries and future needs resulting from the injury. The other spouse might receive little or none of that money, unless the court finds that fairness demands sharing a portion of it. Even then, the injured spouse must get at least half (so at minimum $50,000 in this example). If the accident had occurred after the spouses separated, then the settlement would be the injured spouse's separate property and the other spouse would have no claim to it.

Further Reading:

In re Marriage of Devlin (1982) 138 Cal.App.3d 804: In this case, a husband received approximately $175,000 from a personal injury settlement during the marriage, which the couple used to purchase a family home and other assets. Upon divorce, the trial court awarded the bulk of the property to the husband, tracing it all back to his injury compensation. The wife was only given a small portion of the assets. The California Court of Appeal upheld this result, affirming that personal injury proceeds (and assets acquired with those proceeds) can be allocated predominantly to the injured spouse under the law's special division rules. The fact that the money had been spent on community property (like the home) did not defeat the husband's claim, as long as those assets were traceable to the injury award, they fell under the statute's protection for the injured spouse.

In re Marriage of Morris (1983) 139 Cal.App.3d 823: Here, a wife was injured during the marriage (thrown from a horse) and received about $42,000 in a settlement. The trial court awarded 100% of that settlement to the wife, while dividing the couple's other community property equally. The husband argued on appeal that this result was unfair and that the personal injury money should be split or at least offset by giving him more of the other assets. The Court of Appeal disagreed and confirmed that *Family Code § 2603* (then *Civil Code § 4800(c)*) creates an exception to the 50/50 division rule. In other words, it's permissible for the injured spouse to receive all of the personal injury damages without an equalizing payment to the other spouse. The court found no abuse of discretion, noting the legislature's intent was to prioritize the injured spouse's recovery over an equal division.

In re Marriage of Briltz (1983) 141 Cal.App.3d 17: This case extended the special treatment of personal injury recoveries to certain disability benefits. The husband in Briltz was receiving disability payments for injuries suffered, and the question was whether those payments should be treated like personal injury damages. The court concluded that disability benefits meant to compensate for personal injury (for example, for lost earning capacity or suffering due to the injury) are akin to personal injury damages. Therefore, such benefits were subject to the same rule; they were awarded largely to the injured spouse, not split equally as ordinary income might be. This interpretation ensures that compensation for an injury (even if paid out as disability insurance or similar) is protected for the injured party under *§ 2603*.

In re Marriage of Jackson (1989) 212 Cal.App.3d 479: In Jackson, the wife (Michelle) was injured by an uninsured motorist during the marriage. She received a settlement payment from her own insurance's uninsured motorist coverage, which she used to buy a house and a car. In the divorce, the trial court characterized those insurance proceeds as "community estate personal injury damages," even though the money came from an insurance policy, it was meant to compensate her injury caused by a third party. The court awarded the entire remaining insurance money and the assets bought with it to the wife as her separate property. The husband appealed, arguing that since part of the claim against the at-fault driver was still pending at the time, perhaps the insurance money shouldn't count as personal injury damages. The Court of Appeal affirmed the trial court's decision, holding that the uninsured motorist settlement was indeed subject to *§ 2603*. The outcome meant the wife kept those funds and purchases, consistent with the rule that an injured spouse should get at least one-half, and up to all, of the personal injury recovery.

In re Marriage of Pinto (1972) 28 Cal.App.3d 86: Although decided before the current Family Code, this case addressed a related issue: what happens if a personal injury claim is still unresolved at the time of divorce? In Pinto, the court held that an unliquidated personal injury cause of action is not "community estate personal injury damages" under the statute's predecessor. In other words, if the injured spouse only has a pending lawsuit or claim (with no settlement or judgment yet received), that claim isn't divided as an asset in the divorce under the special rule. Only after the claim is resolved and money is received would the compensation become divisible, and then *§ 2603*'s allocation to the injured spouse would apply. This principle ensures that courts divide actual recoveries, not speculative claims.

Full Text of *Family Code § 2603*

(a) "Community estate personal injury damages" as used in this section means all money or other property received or to be received by a person in satisfaction of a judgment for damages for the person's personal injuries or pursuant to an agreement for the settlement or compromise of a claim for the damages, if the cause of action for the damages arose during the marriage but is not separate property as described in *Section 781*, unless the money or other property has been commingled with other assets of the community estate.

(b) Community estate personal injury damages shall be assigned to the party who suffered the injuries unless the court, after taking into account the economic condition and needs of each party, the time that has elapsed since the recovery of the damages or the accrual of the cause of action, and all other facts of the case, determines that the interests of justice require another disposition. In such a case, the community estate personal injury damages shall be assigned to the respective parties in such proportions as the court determines to be just, except that at least one-half of the damages shall be assigned to the party who suffered the injuries.

36. *Family Code section 2603.5* – Injury from Domestic Violence

Explanation:

If there is a judgment for civil damages for an act of domestic violence perpetrated by one spouse against the other spouse, and a dissolution or legal-separation proceeding is pending before final judgment, the family court may enforce that civil damages judgment against the abusive spouse's share of community property.

The statute is discretionary and share-specific. It permits enforcement against the abusive spouse's share of community property; it does not authorize taking the innocent spouse's share to satisfy the judgment, and it does not create a general unequal-division remedy for every domestic-violence allegation. The required predicate is a civil damages judgment for an act of domestic violence.

Examples:

Civil damages judgment during a pending dissolution: Wife obtains a $50,000 civil damages judgment against Husband for an act of domestic violence, and the parties' dissolution case is pending before final judgment. Under *§ 2603.5*, the court may enforce that judgment against Husband's share of community property, such as his share of sale proceeds or other community assets awarded to him.

No civil damages judgment: If there is evidence of domestic violence, a restraining order, or even a criminal proceeding, but no civil damages judgment between the spouses, *§ 2603.5* itself does not supply the remedy. Other family-law statutes may be relevant, but this section is triggered by the civil damages judgment described in the statute.

Further Reading:

Pugliese v. Superior Court (2007) 146 Cal.App.4th 1444: In Pugliese, the court held that a domestic-violence litigant may seek recovery for all acts of domestic abuse occurring during the domestic relationship, so long as the plaintiff proves a continuing course of abusive conduct and files suit within three years of the last act of domestic violence. The court granted writ relief and directed the trial court to vacate its order excluding older abuse evidence.

Full Text of *Family Code § 2603.5*

The court may, if there is a judgment for civil damages for an act of domestic violence perpetrated by one spouse against the other spouse, enforce that judgment against the abusive spouse's share of community property, if a proceeding for dissolution of marriage or legal separation of the parties is pending prior to the entry of final judgment.

37. *Family Code section 2604* – Assignment of Small Community Estates

Explanation:

Family Code § 2604 allows a court to give all of the marital community property to one spouse in a divorce or legal separation if two conditions are met: (1) the total net value of the community estate is under $5,000, and (2) the other spouse cannot be found despite reasonable efforts. In simple terms, if the couple's assets are very small and one spouse has gone missing (and can't be located with diligent search), the judge can award 100% of those assets to the spouse who is present.

How It Works: This is an exception to the usual 50/50 split of community property in California. Normally, all community property (assets acquired during marriage) is divided equally. But under *§ 2604*, when the community estate is worth less than $5,000 and one spouse cannot be located, the court can deviate from the equal division rule. The spouse asking for the property must show proof that they tried hard to find the missing spouse (for example, attempted service of divorce papers by publication, checking last known addresses, contacting relatives, etc.). If the court is satisfied that the absent spouse truly cannot be found after diligent search, and the assets are minimal, the court can award the entire community estate to the spouse who filed for divorce. The court may also impose any conditions it deems proper in the judgment when doing so (for instance, to protect the missing spouse's rights if they resurface).

Why This Rule Exists: This provision helps avoid complicated proceedings over a very small amount of property when one spouse has effectively disappeared. It allows the divorce to be finalized and the property to be distributed rather than leaving a tiny community estate in limbo. In essence, it prevents a situation where a spouse who cannot be found halts the division of a minor estate. However, because the dollar amount is very low ($5,000) and a genuine search for the missing party is required, this rule is used only in limited circumstances (typically default divorce cases where one spouse never responds or cannot be served).

Examples:

Spouse Vanishes with a Tiny Estate: John files for divorce from Jane. The only community property they have is a joint bank account with $3,500. After filing, Jane disappears — John and even a private investigator cannot locate her through any known address or contact. John serves her by publication in the newspaper, but she still doesn't respond. Because the total community assets are less than $5,000 and Jane cannot be found despite diligent efforts, the court, under *Family Code § 2604*, can award the entire $3,500 to John in the divorce judgment.

Small Assets and Missing Partner: Alice and Bob separate after a short marriage. Their community property is limited to a $2,000 savings account and some household items. Bob attempts to file for divorce, but Alice left the state and no one knows her whereabouts. Bob tries contacting Alice's family, searches public records, and even posts notice in newspapers, but Alice doesn't turn up. In granting the default divorce, the judge finds that the community estate is under $5,000 and Alice cannot be located with reasonable diligence. The judge uses *§ 2604* to award all of the community property (the $2,000 and the few assets) to Bob, allowing the case to be closed without delay.

Further Reading:

In re Marriage of Brigden (1978) 80 Cal.App.3d 380: This California Court of Appeal decision acknowledged the rule now in *§ 2604* (at that time, it was in *former Civil Code § 4800(b)(3)*). The court noted that when the net community estate is below $5,000 and one spouse cannot be found despite diligent search, the law permits awarding the entire community property to the other spouse on whatever conditions the court sees fit. In Brigden, the court discussed this provision as an exception to equal division, although it ultimately didn't apply in that case because the community estate was much larger than $5,000 and both spouses were present. The mention in Brigden confirms that California courts recognize this small-estate exception for missing spouses.

No Direct Case Dispute: It's worth noting that there are very few published cases focusing on *Family Code § 2604*, likely because it usually comes up in uncontested default divorces (where the missing spouse isn't present to appeal). The rule is straightforward, and as long as the court is convinced the spouse cannot be located and the estate's value is under $5,000, the provision can be applied. Brigden remains a key reference that explains the legislative intent behind this exception, even though the scenario was not directly at issue in that appeal.

Full Text of *Family Code § 2604*

If the net value of the community estate is less than five thousand dollars ($5,000) and one party cannot be located through the exercise of reasonable diligence, the court may award all the community estate to the other party on conditions the court deems proper in its judgment of dissolution of marriage or legal separation of the parties.

38. *Family Code section 2620* - Community Estate Debts at Trial

Explanation:

California Family Code § 2620 is the starting point for dealing with debts in a marital dissolution or legal separation. It says that debts for which the community estate is liable, if unpaid at the time of trial or if they become community obligations after trial, must be confirmed or divided under the debt-allocation rules in this part of the Family Code.

This section does not, by itself, tell the court which spouse must pay a particular debt. Instead, it directs the court to use the rest of the statutory scheme. The court must determine when the debt was incurred, whether it was incurred before marriage, during marriage, after separation, after judgment, or for a separate purpose, and then apply the more specific rules in *sections 2621 through 2626* and related provisions.

Section 2620 also helps separate two different questions. The first is whether a creditor may reach community property or a spouse personally under creditor-liability rules. The second is how the family court allocates responsibility between the spouses in the divorce judgment. A debt may be enforceable by a creditor against community property, but the family court may still assign that debt to one spouse as between the parties if another statute requires that result.

In practice, *section 2620* functions as a gateway. Once the court identifies a debt that remains unpaid at trial, or a liability the community estate will face after trial, the court confirms the debt to one spouse, divides it equally, divides it unequally, or orders reimbursement depending on the character of the debt and the timing of the obligation.

Examples:

Unpaid Joint Credit Card at Trial: Suppose spouses used a credit card during marriage to pay household expenses, and a $12,000 balance remains unpaid when the divorce case goes to trial. *Section 2620* tells the court that this debt must be dealt with in the property division. The court would then look to *section 2622* and related equal-division rules because the debt was incurred during marriage and before separation.

Community Tax Liability Discovered After Trial: Suppose a tax audit after trial shows an additional community tax liability for a year during the marriage. *Section 2620* covers debts for which the community estate becomes liable after trial, so the family court may need to divide or confirm that obligation under the applicable debt statutes.

Mortgage Balance on a Community Residence: If the parties own a community residence with a mortgage that remains unpaid at trial, the mortgage is not ignored. It must be considered with the asset it secures, so the court can divide the net equity and assign responsibility for the loan in a coherent way.

Pending Litigation Liability: If a lawsuit was filed before trial and the alleged liability may be a community obligation, *section 2620* permits the court to address that debt or reserve jurisdiction if the amount is not yet known. The ultimate allocation will depend on when the liability was incurred and whether it benefited the community.

Further Reading:

In re Marriage of Whitman (2023) 98 Cal.App.5th 456: The Court of Appeal treated *section 2620* as part of the statutory starting point for characterizing and allocating debts. The court emphasized that multiple debts arising from the same general course of conduct may need to be analyzed separately under the appropriate Family Code sections. In that case, civil penalties, criminal fines, and legal fees were not all treated as one undifferentiated debt.

In re Marriage of Feldner (1995) 40 Cal.App.4th 617: Feldner illustrates the importance of distinguishing the character of a debt from later reimbursement rights. A contract debt is generally incurred when the contract is made, but postseparation payments on that debt may raise reimbursement questions under *section 2626*. The case is useful because *section 2620* requires the court to place unpaid or later-arising community liabilities into the correct statutory category.

In re Marriage of Eastis (1975) 47 Cal.App.3d 459: Although decided under predecessor law, Eastis explains the practical problem *section 2620* addresses: the family court must dispose of obligations as well as assets. When community obligations remain after assets are divided, the court must make a just allocation rather than simply ignoring the debts.

Full Text of *Family Code § 2620*

The debts for which the community estate is liable which are unpaid at the time of trial, or for which the community estate becomes liable after trial, shall be confirmed or divided as provided in this part.

39. *Family Code section 2621* - Premarital Debts

Explanation:

Family Code § 2621 addresses debts incurred by either spouse before the date of marriage. The rule is straightforward: premarital debts are confirmed to the spouse who incurred them, and the other spouse does not receive an offset simply because the debt exists.

This means a spouse who brings a student loan, credit card balance, medical bill, tax obligation, business loan, or other debt into the marriage ordinarily leaves the marriage with that same responsibility as between the spouses. The divorce court does not make the other spouse pay half merely because the marriage later dissolves.

The phrase "without offset" is important. It prevents the debtor spouse from reducing the other spouse's share of community property just because the debtor spouse entered the marriage with a separate debt. The debt is confirmed to the person who incurred it, and the community estate is divided under the ordinary property division rules without giving the debtor spouse an automatic equalization credit.

Section 2621 is an allocation rule between spouses. It does not necessarily answer every creditor-rights question. For example, other Family Code provisions may address when community property can be reached by creditors during marriage. *Section 2621* tells the family court how to assign responsibility in the marital property judgment.

Examples:

Premarital Student Loan: One spouse enters the marriage with $35,000 in student loans. At divorce, *section 2621* confirms that debt to the spouse who incurred it. The other spouse does not owe an equalization payment merely because the loan still exists.

Premarital Credit Card Balance: A spouse has a $9,000 credit card balance before the wedding. Even if minimum payments were made during marriage, the original premarital obligation is confirmed to the spouse who incurred it, subject to any separate reimbursement issue that may arise from community funds used to pay it.

Premarital Medical Bill: Before marriage, one spouse incurs a $6,000 medical bill. The parties later divorce before the bill is fully paid. The remaining obligation is confirmed to the spouse who incurred it, without offset.

Premarital Business Loan: A spouse personally guaranteed a business loan before marriage. If that obligation remains outstanding at dissolution, *section 2621* confirms the debt to that spouse rather than dividing it as a marital debt.

Further Reading:

In re Marriage of Whitman (2023) 98 Cal.App.5th 456: Whitman did not turn on a premarital debt, but the court listed *section 2621* as one of the specific statutory rules that may govern a debt depending on timing. The case is useful because it reinforces the methodology: identify when each debt was incurred, then apply the statute that matches that timing and purpose.

In re Marriage of Feldner (1995) 40 Cal.App.4th 617: Feldner explains that the timing of a debt can be decisive. Although Feldner involved a contract made during marriage, its reasoning underscores why *section 2621* focuses on the date the debt was incurred. If the debt was incurred before marriage, *section 2621* supplies the allocation rule.

In re Marriage of Epstein (1979) 24 Cal.3d 76: See Epstein Credits (pg. 50).

Full Text of *Family Code § 2621*

Debts incurred by either spouse before the date of marriage shall be confirmed without offset to the spouse who incurred the debt.

40. *Family Code section 2622* - Debts Incurred During Marriage Before Separation

Explanation:

California Family Code § 2622 deals with debts incurred after the date of marriage but before the date of separation. As a general rule, these debts are divided under California's equal-division statutes for community property and liabilities. In an ordinary positive-asset estate, this usually means the debt is shared equally as part of the overall property division.

Subdivision (a) ties marital debts to the same basic division framework that applies to community assets. If the spouses incurred a loan, credit card obligation, tax debt, mortgage, or other liability during marriage and before separation, the starting point is that the obligation is part of the community balance sheet.

Subdivision (b) creates an important exception for a negative estate. If total community debts exceed total community and quasi-community assets, the excess debt does not have to be divided equally. Instead, the court assigns the excess debt in a way it deems just and equitable, considering factors such as the parties' relative ability to pay.

This section should also be read with *section 2625*. A debt incurred during marriage and before separation is not automatically divided equally if it was not incurred for the benefit of the community. *Section 2625* can require the court to confirm such a debt solely to the spouse who incurred it.

Examples:

Household Credit Card Debt: During marriage and before separation, the spouses accumulate $14,000 on a credit card for groceries, children's clothing, utility bills, and household repairs. Because the debt was incurred during marriage for community purposes, the court would ordinarily divide it under *section 2622* and the equal-division rules.

Car Loan for a Family Vehicle: The parties take out a car loan during marriage for a vehicle used by the family. If the loan remains unpaid at trial, it is generally treated as a community debt. The court may assign the vehicle and the related loan to one spouse and equalize the overall division with other assets or debts.

Negative Community Estate: Suppose the parties have $20,000 in community assets and $70,000 in community debts. The excess $50,000 of debt may be assigned in a just and equitable manner, considering relative ability to pay. The court is not forced to divide that excess debt exactly 50/50.

Mixed-Purpose Loan: If one spouse takes a $30,000 loan during marriage and uses $20,000 for community home improvements and $10,000 for a secret separate purpose, the court may need to separate the community portion from the separate portion rather than treating the loan as a single all-or-nothing debt.

Further Reading:

In re Marriage of Eastis (1975) 47 Cal.App.3d 459: Eastis is the leading predecessor-law case for negative marital estates. The court rejected the idea that debts standing alone must always be divided equally. When there are no assets, or when obligations remain after assets are divided, the court may allocate obligations in a just and equitable manner based on earning capacity and other relevant factors. *Section 2622(b)* reflects this same practical approach.

In re Marriage of Branco (1996) 47 Cal.App.4th 1621: See *In re Marriage of Branco* (1996) 47 Cal.App.4th 1621 (pg. 29).

In re Marriage of Whitman (2023) 98 Cal.App.5th 456: Whitman reinforces that the court must analyze the particular debt. For debts incurred during marriage, the court must still ask whether the debt was incurred for the benefit of the community, because *section 2625* may remove a non-community-benefit debt from ordinary equal division.

Full Text of *Family Code § 2622*

(a) Except as provided in subdivision (b), debts incurred by either spouse after the date of marriage but before the date of separation shall be divided as set forth in *Sections 2550 to 2552*, inclusive, and *Sections 2601 to 2604*, inclusive.

(b) To the extent that community debts exceed total community and quasi-community assets, the excess of debt shall be assigned as the court deems just and equitable, taking into account factors such as the parties' relative ability to pay.

41. *Family Code section 2623* - Post-Separation, Pre-Judgment Debts

Explanation:

California Family Code § 2623 governs debts incurred after the date of separation but before entry of a judgment of dissolution or legal separation. This is the transition period when the spouses are no longer operating as an intact marital economic unit, but the case has not yet reached judgment.

The statute separates postseparation debts into two categories. Debts for common necessaries of life of either spouse, or for necessaries of life of children for whom support may be ordered, may be confirmed to either spouse according to the parties' needs and abilities to pay at the time the debt was incurred. This rule applies only in the absence of a court order or written agreement covering support or payment of those debts.

Postseparation debts for non-necessaries are treated very differently. If one spouse incurs a debt after separation for that spouse's own non-necessaries, or for non-necessaries of the children, the debt is confirmed without offset to the spouse who incurred it.

The statute therefore asks two practical questions: when was the debt incurred, and what was it for? Rent, food, basic utilities, medical care, and necessary child expenses may be treated differently from luxury purchases, speculative investments, private litigation expenses, penalties, or other nonessential obligations.

Examples:

Postseparation Rent and Groceries: After separation and before judgment, one spouse rents an apartment and buys groceries for that spouse and the children. If there is no support order or written agreement covering those expenses, the court may assign the debt according to the parties' needs and abilities to pay when the debt was incurred.

Children's Necessary Medical Expense: A child incurs an uninsured emergency medical bill after separation but before judgment. Because the expense is a necessary expense of a child for whom support may be ordered, the court may allocate responsibility between the spouses under subdivision (a).

Luxury Vacation Debt: One spouse takes an expensive vacation after separation and charges the cost to a credit card. Because the expense is a non-necessary expense of that spouse, subdivision (b) confirms the debt to the spouse who incurred it without offset.

Postseparation Penalty or Fine: If a spouse becomes obligated after separation to pay a civil penalty or criminal fine unrelated to common necessaries, the debt is generally a postseparation non-necessary and is assigned to that spouse without offset.

Further Reading:

In re Marriage of Whitman (2023) 98 Cal.App.5th 456: Whitman applied *section 2623* to postseparation obligations arising from insider-trading proceedings. The Court of Appeal held that a criminal fine and a civil penalty imposed after separation were postseparation debts. Because they were not common necessaries of life, they were confirmed to the spouse who incurred them without offset.

In re Marriage of Munguia (1983) 146 Cal.App.3d 853: Munguia involved private investigator fees incurred after separation. The Court of Appeal held the trial court erred by treating the entire expense as a community debt. The debt was incurred after separation and was unrelated to the community, so it should have been treated as separate.

In re Marriage of Hopkins (1977) 74 Cal.App.3d 591: Hopkins, cited in Munguia, is another predecessor-law authority for the principle that a debt unrelated to the community and incurred after separation is separate. That reasoning is consistent with *section 2623(b)*.

Full Text of *Family Code § 2623*

Debts incurred by either spouse after the date of separation but before entry of a judgment of dissolution of marriage or legal separation of the parties shall be confirmed as follows:

(a) Debts incurred by either spouse for the common necessaries of life of either spouse or the necessaries of life of the children of the marriage for whom support may be ordered, in the absence of a court order or written agreement for support or for the payment of these debts, shall be confirmed to either spouse according to the parties' respective needs and abilities to pay at the time the debt was incurred.

(b) Debts incurred by either spouse for non-necessaries of that spouse or children of the marriage for whom support may be ordered shall be confirmed without offset to the spouse who incurred the debt.

42. *Family Code section 2624* - Post-Judgment Debts Before Status Termination or After Legal Separation

Explanation:

California Family Code § 2624 applies to debts incurred after entry of a judgment of dissolution but before termination of the parties' marital status, and to debts incurred after entry of a judgment of legal separation. Those debts are confirmed without offset to the spouse who incurred them.

This statute covers an unusual but important timing window. Sometimes a court enters a judgment resolving property, support, or separation issues while marital status has not yet terminated, or the parties obtain a legal separation judgment rather than a dissolution judgment. *Section 2624* makes clear that debts incurred after that judgment are not shared merely because the parties may technically still have an unresolved marital status issue.

The rule reflects the idea that once the court has entered judgment, the parties' financial affairs should generally be treated as separate going forward. A spouse who voluntarily incurs a new debt after judgment ordinarily cannot shift that burden to the other spouse through an offset in the property division.

Section 2624 is also consistent with the broader statutory structure. *Section 2623* governs the postseparation, pre-judgment interval. *Section 2624* then governs the post-judgment interval. Together, the statutes move the parties away from shared responsibility as the marital economic community ends.

Examples:

Credit Card Charges After Judgment: A dissolution judgment is entered, but marital status will terminate later. One spouse opens a new credit card and charges $8,000 for personal expenses after judgment. *Section 2624* confirms that debt to the spouse who incurred it without offset.

Legal Separation Judgment Followed by New Loan: After a judgment of legal separation, one spouse takes out a personal loan to furnish a new residence. The debt is confirmed to the borrowing spouse without offset.

Post-Judgment Business Debt: A spouse starts a new business after entry of judgment and personally guarantees a business line of credit. The debt is the incurring spouse's obligation as between the spouses.

Post-Judgment Medical Debt: If one spouse incurs medical debt after judgment, *section 2624* still confirms the debt without offset to the spouse who incurred it, subject to any separate support order, insurance obligation, or other court order that may independently apply.

Further Reading:

In re Marriage of Whitman (2023) 98 Cal.App.5th 456: Whitman noted *section 2624* as part of the debt-allocation framework for debts incurred after entry of a legal separation or dissolution judgment. Although Whitman itself focused on postseparation penalties and preseparation legal-fee debts, it demonstrates that courts must locate each debt within the correct statutory timing category.

In re Marriage of Feldner (1995) 40 Cal.App.4th 617: Feldner is useful by analogy because it carefully distinguishes the time a debt is incurred from later performance or reimbursement issues. *Section 2624* depends on that same timing analysis: if the debt is incurred after judgment, the statute confirms it to the incurring spouse without offset.

In re Marriage of Munguia (1983) 146 Cal.App.3d 853: Munguia involved an earlier timing window, but its reasoning is consistent with *section 2624*'s approach. Debts incurred after the marital economic relationship has effectively ended and unrelated to the community should not be treated as shared community obligations.

Full Text of *Family Code § 2624*

Debts incurred by either spouse after entry of a judgment of dissolution of marriage but before termination of the parties' marital status or after entry of a judgment of legal separation of the parties shall be confirmed without offset to the spouse who incurred the debt.

43. *Family Code section 2625* - Separate Debts Not Incurred for Community Benefit

Explanation:

California Family Code § 2625 is a carve-out from the ordinary debt division rules. Even if a debt was incurred during marriage and before separation, it is confirmed without offset to the spouse who incurred it if the debt was not incurred for the benefit of the community.

This statute prevents one spouse from forcing the community estate, or the other spouse in the dissolution judgment, to absorb debts that served only the incurring spouse's separate purpose. The focus is not merely whether the debt arose during marriage; the court must ask whether the debt benefited the community.

The "benefit of the community" inquiry can be fact-specific. Household expenses, family business obligations, debts incurred to preserve community assets, or loans used for community purposes will usually be community obligations. By contrast, criminal fines, penalties, attorney fees incurred primarily for personal defense, secret gambling obligations, or expenses connected to separate misconduct may be confirmed to the spouse who incurred them.

A single debt may have mixed purposes. Courts may allocate part of a debt to the community and part to the incurring spouse if the record permits a reliable division. The spouse seeking a particular allocation should be prepared to trace the purpose and amount of the debt.

Examples:

Secret Gambling Debt: During marriage and before separation, one spouse secretly incurs $20,000 in gambling debt. If the court finds the debt was not incurred for the benefit of the community, *section 2625* confirms it to the gambling spouse without offset.

Criminal Defense Fees: A spouse incurs attorney fees during marriage to defend against criminal charges arising from personal misconduct. If the fees were not incurred for the benefit of the community, the court may assign them to that spouse as a separate debt.

Debt for a Separate Romantic Relationship: One spouse charges travel, gifts, and hotel expenses connected to an extramarital relationship. Those charges do not benefit the community and may be confirmed to the spouse who incurred them.

Mixed Legal Fees: A spouse incurs legal fees in a lawsuit involving both a community business and that spouse's separate counterclaim. The community may be responsible for fees incurred to defend the community business, but not for fees incurred to pursue the separate claim, if the fees can be reasonably allocated.

Further Reading:

In re Marriage of Whitman (2023) 98 Cal.App.5th 456: Whitman is a major modern decision on *section 2625*. The Court of Appeal held that debts incurred during marriage must be analyzed to determine whether they were incurred for the benefit of the community. Legal fees arising from insider-trading proceedings could not be treated as automatically community or separate; the court evaluated each obligation and recognized that a debt may be incurred partly for community purposes and partly for separate purposes.

In re Marriage of Bell (1996) 49 Cal.App.4th 300: Bell involved debts arising from a spouse's embezzlement. The Court of Appeal treated the restitution-based civil settlement differently from attorney fees and tax liabilities. Because the embezzled funds had been used for community purposes, the settlement debt could be a community obligation; however, attorney fees for defense and tax liabilities arising from the misconduct were properly characterized as the offending spouse's separate debts.

In re Marriage of Stitt (1983) 147 Cal.App.3d 579: Stitt held that attorney fees incurred in connection with a spouse's embezzlement could be assigned solely to that spouse. The case supports the principle that one spouse should not be required to share financial consequences of the other spouse's wrongful conduct when the obligation did not benefit the community.

In re Marriage of Nassimi (2016) 3 Cal.App.5th 667: Nassimi illustrates mixed-purpose attorney fees. Fees incurred to defend claims involving a former family business could be community obligations, while fees incurred to pursue a spouse's separate property counterclaim were not. The case also shows the importance of proving the amount attributable to each purpose.

Full Text of *Family Code § 2625*

Notwithstanding *Sections 2620 to 2624*, inclusive, all separate debts, including those debts incurred by a spouse during marriage and before the date of separation that were not incurred for the benefit of the community, shall be confirmed without offset to the spouse who incurred the debt.

44. *Family Code section 2626* – Reimbursement for Debts Paid After Separation

Explanation:

California Family Code § 2626 ensures that when one spouse pays a community debt after the spouses have separated but before the divorce trial, the court can order reimbursement from the other spouse as part of the property division. In simpler terms, if you use your own money (earned post-separation) to cover what was a shared marital debt, the judge has the authority to credit you for that payment during the divorce settlement. Importantly, this reimbursement (often called an "Epstein credit" in California family law) is not automatic: the court will decide if it's appropriate based on the circumstances. The goal of *§2626* is to enforce fair division of property and debts: one spouse shouldn't be unfairly stuck paying a joint obligation alone. The law sets the time frame for these credits as after the date of separation and before the case goes to trial (final judgment), which means the issue must typically be raised and resolved during the divorce proceedings. In practice, judges use *§2626* to make sure that community debts are split equitably, reimbursing a spouse who paid more than their share, unless there's a good reason not to (for example, if that payment was essentially a gift or in lieu of support).

Examples:

A Husband continued to pay the mortgage, property taxes, and maintenance on a rental house after the couple separated. At trial, the court awarded him reimbursement for half of those post-separation payments under §2626. The Wife argued against repaying him, claiming he said he'd "take care of" the property and noting that he refused to sell it when she wanted (which later led to a drop in value). But the judge found no agreement that he waived reimbursement and no intent to make those payments a gift. Because his payments preserved a community asset without any contrary agreement, the Husband received an Epstein credit for those expenses.

Payments treated as support, no credit given: If one spouse voluntarily covers the other spouse's expenses or debts after separation (for example, continuing to pay the estranged spouse's car loan or credit cards), the court may decide not to order reimbursement. This is because those payments can be viewed as fulfilling a support obligation rather than creating a debt for the other spouse. For instance, a Wife might pay the mortgage and household bills post-separation while the Husband moves out; if those payments were effectively providing support (housing) for the family, a judge could deny her any Epstein credit, reasoning that it would be unfair to reimburse her for something that was essentially child or spousal support.

Exclusive use of property offsets debt payment: Suppose after separating, one spouse remains in the family home and uses their own income to pay the mortgage. That spouse can ask for reimbursement of those mortgage payments at trial. However, because they had exclusive use of a community asset (living in the home), the court might reduce the credit or deny reimbursement to balance out the benefit received. In practice, judges often offset an Epstein credit with a "Watts charge": a calculation of rent for the spouse's exclusive use of the home. For example, if a Husband paid $10,000 in mortgage payments after separation but also lived in the house alone, the court might find that the value of his exclusive occupancy equals what he paid. In that case, under §2626 the judge could decide it's not appropriate to reimburse him, since his payments were offset by the benefit of living rent-free.

Further Reading:

In re Marriage of Feldner (1995) 40 Cal.App.4th 617: An early post-Family Code decision highlighting that reimbursement for post-separation debt payments is discretionary, not automatic. The Feldner court noted that under *§2626* a spouse who uses separate funds after separation to preserve a community asset can request reimbursement (an Epstein credit), but the trial court must consider equitable factors before granting it. Feldner emphasized several exceptions to reimbursement: no credit should be given if the payment was effectively a discharge of a support obligation, or if the paying spouse was also using the asset and the amount paid was not substantially greater than the value of that use. This case solidified the principle that claims for Epstein credits depend on the facts. The paying spouse must not have intended a gift or agreed to assume the debt, and the request should be made by the time of property division.

In re Marriage of Boblitt (2014) 223 Cal.App.4th 1004: This appellate decision defined and applied Epstein credits in a property division dispute. The court explained that an "Epstein credit is the right to be reimbursed by the community for separate property funds used after separation to meet community expenses." In Boblitt, the wife was awarded an Epstein credit for post-separation mortgage payments she had made on a piece of real estate, but at the same time the court recognized a corresponding Watts charge (rent owed to the community for one spouse's exclusive use of that property). Consistent with *§2626*, the case illustrates the trial court's broad equitable power: it granted reimbursement for the debt payments, while also ensuring fairness by charging the benefiting spouse for her sole use of the asset. Boblitt confirms that courts can mix credits and charges to achieve an equitable division.

In re Marriage of Oliverez (2019) 33 Cal.App.5th 298: The Oliverez case underscores the discretionary nature of *§2626* and how appellate courts review Epstein credit decisions. Here, the trial court's rulings on various reimbursement claims were challenged, but the Court of Appeal affirmed them, emphasizing that a trial judge has broad discretion in deciding what is "appropriate" under *§2626*. The appellate opinion noted that it will not second-guess the trial court's decision to grant or deny Epstein credits so long as it falls within the range of reason (i.e., no abuse of discretion). Oliverez stands for the idea that as long as the family court properly considers the circumstances, such as agreements between spouses, intent, and fairness, its call on Epstein reimbursements will be upheld on appeal.

In re Marriage of Mohler (2020) 47 Cal.App.5th 788: See Mohler Pro Tanto Rule (pg. 34).

Full Text of *California Family Code § 2626*

The court has jurisdiction to order reimbursement in cases it deems appropriate for debts paid after separation but before trial.

45. *Family Code section 2627* – Education Loans

Explanation:

California Family Code § 2627 is a targeted exception to the ordinary rules for dividing community debts. It applies to two special categories: educational loans, which are assigned under *Family Code § 2641*, and certain liabilities described in *Family Code § 1000(b)(2)*, which are assigned to the spouse whose act or omission created the liability. In both settings, the statute prevents the debt from being treated as a routine community obligation simply because it arose during the marriage.

For educational loans, *§ 2627* sends the court to *§ 2641*. That means a loan incurred during marriage for one spouse's education or training is generally assigned to the educated spouse, rather than being included among the community debts for equal division. If community funds were used to pay educational expenses or repay educational loans, the reimbursement issue is also governed by *§ 2641*.

For tort-type liabilities, *§ 2627* operates with *Family Code § 1000(b)(2). Section 1000(b)(2)* deals with a married person's liability for death or injury to a person or property when the act or omission was not performed for the benefit of the community. When that condition is met, the liability is assigned without offset to the spouse whose conduct caused it.

The phrase "without offset" is important. As between the spouses, the court does not compensate the liable spouse by giving that spouse more community property merely because the debt has been assigned to that spouse. Creditor rights can raise separate enforcement issues, but in the marital property division the obligation is allocated to the responsible spouse under the statute.

Examples:

Medical School Loan Incurred During Marriage: During marriage, one spouse borrows $120,000 to attend medical school. At dissolution, the loan is not treated like an ordinary community credit card or household debt. Under *§ 2627* and *§ 2641*, the loan is assigned to the spouse who received the education, subject to the limitations and possible modifications in *§ 2641*.

Community Payments on Premarital Student Loans: Before marriage, one spouse incurred law school loans. During marriage, the couple used community earnings to make loan payments. *Section 2627* points the court to *§ 2641*, which may require reimbursement to the community for the community funds used to repay education debt, depending on the statutory substantial-benefit and fairness factors.

Personal Tort Liability Not for Community Benefit: One spouse causes a serious accident while driving for a purely personal errand unrelated to the family or community. If the liability is for injury to person or property and the conduct was not part of an activity performed for the community's benefit, the liability may be assigned to that spouse without offset.

Community-Benefit Activity: Suppose a spouse causes property damage while performing a task genuinely for the family, such as transporting children or handling a household errand. *Section 2627* may not automatically place the liability solely on that spouse because *§ 1000(b)(2)* is limited to liability not based on conduct performed for the community's benefit. The court would then analyze the obligation under the applicable debt-division provisions.

Further Reading:

In re Marriage of Whitman (2023) 98 Cal.App.5th 456: Whitman is the leading modern discussion of *§ 2627*. The husband incurred civil penalties, criminal fines, and attorney fees arising from insider trading. The Court of Appeal explained that *§ 2627* is narrower than *§ 2625*: *§ 2627* applies only to liabilities for death or injury to person or property within the meaning of *§ 1000(b)(2)*. Because the SEC penalties and criminal fines were not liabilities for death or injury to person or property, the court analyzed them under the broader debt rules instead of treating *§ 2627* as controlling.

In re Marriage of Mullonkal & Kodiyamplakkil (2020) 51 Cal.App.5th 604: Although primarily a *§ 2641* case, Mullonkal is important for the educational-loan branch of *§ 2627*. The Court of Appeal held that when community funds are used to repay one spouse's educational loans, the community may be entitled to reimbursement under *§ 2641*. The trial court did not have discretion to deny reimbursement simply because the nonstudent spouse did not personally contribute to the loan payments.

In re Marriage of Weiner (2003) 105 Cal.App.4th 235: Weiner held that *§ 2641* can apply when community funds are used during marriage to pay down educational loans incurred before marriage. The case illustrates why *§ 2627* directs educational-loan issues to *§ 2641*: the focus is not merely when the loan was incurred, but whether community property was used for education or training and whether the statutory reimbursement limitations apply.

In re Marriage of Graham (2003) 109 Cal.App.4th 1321: Graham emphasizes that reimbursement is not automatic for every educational expense. The education or training must substantially enhance the earning capacity of the spouse who received it. Where the evidence does not show a substantial enhancement, reimbursement may be denied or limited under *§ 2641*.

Full Text of *California Family Code §2627*:

Notwithstanding *Sections 2550 to 2552*, inclusive, and *Sections 2620 to 2624*, inclusive, educational loans shall be assigned pursuant to *Section 2641* and liabilities subject to paragraph (2) of subdivision (b) of *Section 1000* shall be assigned to the spouse whose act or omission provided the basis for the liability, without offset.

46. *Family Code section 2640* – Reimbursements

Explanation:

Family Code § 2640 protects a spouse who used separate property to help buy or improve marital property. It generally gives that spouse a reimbursement before division, but only for qualifying contributions, only if traceable, only absent a written waiver or valid transmutation, and only up to the property's net value. It is a reimbursement statute, not a guaranteed ownership-percentage statute.

The reimbursement cannot exceed the net value of the property at the time of division.

Common separate-property sources include property owned before marriage, inheritances, gifts, or proceeds traceable to those assets. The statute itself does not list every form of separate property in *§ 2640*, but California's community-property baseline is that property acquired during marriage while domiciled in California is community property unless another statute provides otherwise.

In practice, tracing usually means producing documents such as bank statements, escrow closing statements, inheritance records, wire confirmations, account histories, or loan-principal records showing where the money came from and where it went.

Caveat:

Subdivision (c), which addresses separate-property contributions to the other spouse's separate-property estate, was added effective January 1, 2005. For older contributions, judgments, or transactions, verify the operative version of *§ 2640* and any retroactivity limits before applying *subdivision (c)*.

Examples:

Husband contributed $100,000 separate property toward a community asset, but at divorce the asset has only $60,000 in net value. The *§ 2640* reimbursement is capped at $60,000. The statute does not create a right to recover the shortfall from other property beyond the net value of that asset.

If one spouse contributed $100,000 separate property and the property later doubled in value, *§ 2640* does not by itself give that spouse $200,000. It gives a reimbursement claim for the traceable contribution, capped by the property's net value.

Wife uses $100,000 she inherited to make the down payment on a house titled or treated as community property. At divorce, the house has $300,000 in net equity. Assuming no waiver and proper tracing, Wife generally gets a $100,000

§ 2640 reimbursement first. The remaining $200,000 is then divided as community property, typically $100,000 each.

So the result would be:

Spouse Amount
Wife's *§ 2640* reimbursement $100,000
Wife's half of remaining equity $100,000
Husband's half of remaining equity $100,000

Total Wife $200,000
Total Husband $100,000

Full Text of *California Family Code § 2640*

(a) "Contributions to the acquisition of property," as used in this section, include downpayments, payments for improvements, and payments that reduce the principal of a loan used to finance the purchase or improvement of the property but do not include payments of interest on the loan or payments made for maintenance, insurance, or taxation of the property.

(b) In the division of the community estate under this division, unless a party has made a written waiver of the right to reimbursement or has signed a writing that has the effect of a waiver, the party shall be reimbursed for the party's contributions to the acquisition of property of the community property estate to the extent the party traces the contributions to a separate property source. The amount reimbursed shall be without interest or adjustment for change in monetary values and may not exceed the net value of the property at the time of the division.

(c) A party shall be reimbursed for the party's separate property contributions to the acquisition of property of the other spouse's separate property estate during the marriage, unless there has been a transmutation in writing pursuant to Chapter 5 (commencing with *Section 850*) of Part 2 of Division 4, or a written waiver of the right to reimbursement. The amount reimbursed shall be without interest or adjustment for change in monetary values and may not exceed the net value of the property at the time of the division.

47. *Family Code section 2641* – Education and Training

Explanation:

California Family Code § 2641 addresses education and training expenses paid with community or quasi-community property. It defines "community contributions to education or training" broadly to include payments for education, payments for training, and payments made to repay loans incurred for education or training. The statute applies whether those payments were made while the spouses lived in California or elsewhere.

The central rule is reimbursement. If community or quasi-community property paid for one spouse's education or training and that education or training substantially enhanced that spouse's earning capacity, the community must be reimbursed, with interest at the legal rate. Interest runs from the end of the calendar year in which the contribution was made.

The statute also assigns educational loans. A loan incurred during marriage for one spouse's education or training is not included among the community liabilities to be divided as ordinary marital debt. Instead, it is assigned to the party who received the education or training.

Section 2641 contains important fairness limitations. Reimbursement and loan assignment must be reduced or modified to the extent the circumstances would make the result unjust. Examples include situations where the community substantially benefited from the education, where both spouses received offsetting education or training funded by the community, or where the education reduces the recipient spouse's need for support.

The statute includes a 10-year presumption. Contributions made less than 10 years before the dissolution proceeding are presumed not to have substantially benefited the community. Contributions made more than 10 years before the proceeding are presumed to have substantially benefited the community. Those presumptions affect the burden of proof and can significantly change the reimbursement analysis.

Examples:

Short Marriage and Medical Degree: A couple is married for four years. During the marriage, community earnings pay $80,000 toward one spouse's medical education, and the education substantially increases that spouse's earning capacity. Because the community likely has not yet substantially benefited from the degree, *§ 2641* generally requires reimbursement to the community, with interest.

Student Loan Incurred During Marriage: During marriage, one spouse borrows money for a nursing degree. At divorce, the loan is assigned to the spouse who received the nursing education. It is not simply divided 50/50 as a community debt.

Long-Term Benefit to the Community: One spouse earns an MBA early in a 20-year marriage using community funds. For many years afterward, the community enjoys the higher income produced by that education. Because the contributions were made more than 10 years before the proceeding, there is a rebuttable presumption that the community substantially benefited, and reimbursement may be reduced or denied.

Both Spouses Receive Education: Community funds pay for one spouse's teaching credential and the other spouse's accounting certificate. If both educational programs enhanced earning capacity, the court may offset one spouse's education against the other's in deciding whether reimbursement should be ordered and in what amount.

Reduced Need for Support: A spouse obtains training during marriage that allows that spouse to become self-supporting. Even if reimbursement might otherwise be available, the court may consider whether the education substantially reduces that spouse's support need and may reduce or modify the reimbursement obligation if justice requires.

Further Reading:

In re Marriage of Sullivan (1984) 37 Cal.3d 762: Sullivan held that a professional degree itself is not community property to be divided as an asset. The case helped frame the policy problem later addressed by the statutory reimbursement remedy: the educated spouse may leave the marriage with enhanced earning capacity, while the community may have funded the education.

In re Marriage of Weiner (2003) 105 Cal.App.4th 235: Weiner interpreted *§ 2641* to require reimbursement when community funds were used to repay one spouse's educational loans, even though the loans were incurred before the marriage. The decision rejects a narrow reading that would limit reimbursement only to loans incurred during marriage.

In re Marriage of Graham (2003) 109 Cal.App.4th 1321: Graham focused on the statutory requirement that education or training substantially enhance earning capacity. The court affirmed denial of reimbursement where the evidence did not show the spouse's legal education had substantially increased earning capacity at the time of dissolution.

In re Marriage of Mullonkal & Kodiyamplakkil (2020) 51 Cal.App.5th 604: Mullonkal held that *§ 2641* does not allow a court to deny reimbursement merely because the nonstudent spouse did not directly contribute financially to the repayment of the educational loans. Earnings during marriage are community property, and payments made from those earnings can trigger reimbursement.

In re Marriage of Dekker (1993) 17 Cal.App.4th 842: See *In re Marriage of Dekker* *(pg. 88)*.

Full Text of *California Family Code § 2641*

(a) "Community contributions to education or training" as used in this section means payments made with community or quasi-community property for education or training or for the repayment of a loan incurred for education or training, whether the payments were made while the parties were resident in this state or resident outside this state.

(b) Subject to the limitations provided in this section, upon dissolution of marriage or legal separation of the parties:

> (1) The community shall be reimbursed for community contributions to education or training of a party that substantially enhances the earning capacity of the party. The amount reimbursed shall be with interest at the legal rate, accruing from the end of the calendar year in which the contributions were made.
>
> (2) A loan incurred during marriage for the education or training of a party shall not be included among the liabilities of the community for the purpose of division pursuant to this division but shall be assigned for payment by the party.

(c) The reimbursement and assignment required by this section shall be reduced or modified to the extent circumstances render such a disposition unjust, including, but not limited to, any of the following:

> (1) The community has substantially benefited from the education, training, or loan incurred for the education or training of the party. There is a rebuttable presumption, affecting the burden of proof, that the community has not substantially benefited from community contributions to the education or training made less than 10 years before the commencement of the proceeding, and that the community has substantially benefited from community contributions to the education or training made more than 10 years before the commencement of the proceeding.
>
> (2) The education or training received by the party is offset by the education or training received by the other party for which community contributions have been made.
>
> (3) The education or training enables the party receiving the education or training to engage in gainful employment that substantially reduces the need of the party for support that would otherwise be required.

(d) Reimbursement for community contributions and assignment of loans pursuant to this section is the exclusive remedy of the community or a party for the education or training and any resulting enhancement of the earning capacity of a party. However, nothing in this subdivision limits consideration of the effect of the education, training, or enhancement, or the amount reimbursed pursuant to this section, on the circumstances of the parties for the purpose of an order for support pursuant to *Section 4320*.

(e) This section is subject to an express written agreement of the parties to the contrary.

48. *Family Code section 2650* – Jointly Held Separate Property

Explanation:

California Family Code § 2650 gives the family court jurisdiction, at the request of either party, to divide certain jointly held separate property in a dissolution property division proceeding. The property may be real or personal property, may be located anywhere, and may have been acquired at any time. The critical requirement is that the spouses hold separate property interests as joint tenants or tenants in common.

The statute matters because not everything owned by spouses together is necessarily community property. For example, spouses may have bought property together before marriage, may hold separate inheritance funds in a jointly titled account, or may have intentionally retained separate tenancy-in-common interests. Without *§ 2650*, disputes over those jointly held separate interests might have to be resolved in a civil partition or other separate action.

Section 2650 is jurisdictional and procedural. It does not automatically convert separate property into community property. Instead, it authorizes the family court, when asked by a party, to divide the parties' separate interests together with the community estate and under the same procedures and limitations used for community-property division.

The statute is especially useful when a single asset has both separate and community components. The court may need to characterize each interest, determine any reimbursement rights, and then divide the property in a way that resolves the parties' financial relationship in one dissolution proceeding.

Examples:

Premarital Cabin Held as Joint Tenants: Before marriage, the parties buy a cabin together as joint tenants. Years later, they divorce. At either party's request, the family court may divide their separate property interests in the cabin as part of the dissolution proceeding instead of requiring a separate partition case.

Tenancy-in-Common Investment Property: The spouses hold an investment duplex as tenants in common, with each claiming a separate one-half interest.

Section 2650 allows the family court to divide or allocate those separate interests along with the rest of the marital property issues.

Joint Brokerage Account with Separate Funds: Each spouse deposits inheritance funds into a brokerage account titled in both names as tenants in common. If the tracing evidence shows separate interests, the court may still divide those interests under *§ 2650* at the request of a party.

Third-Party Co-Owner: The spouses and a parent are all on title to real property. *Section 2650* may allow the court to address the spouses' interests, but the court must respect due process and cannot impair a third party's property rights without proper joinder and jurisdiction.

Further Reading:

Porter v. Superior Court (1977) 73 Cal.App.3d 793: Porter predates the Family Code but explains the jurisdictional problem that *§ 2650* addresses. Family courts generally divide the community estate in dissolution proceedings and cannot simply dispose of separate property unless a statute or proper procedure authorizes that relief. *Section 2650* supplies that authority for separate property interests held by the spouses as joint tenants or tenants in common.

In re Marriage of Rico (1992) 10 Cal.App.4th 706: Rico involved real property acquired before marriage in both parties' names as tenants in common and later converted to joint tenancy during marriage. The court approved a method for calculating separate and community interests where separate contributions and community payments both affected the property. The case is useful for *§ 2650* analysis because it deals with jointly titled premarital property and the interaction between separate interests, community contributions, and reimbursement principles.

In re Marriage of Weaver (2005) 127 Cal.App.4th 858: Weaver involved residences held in joint tenancy and discussed the court's power to divide jointly titled property in a dissolution proceeding. The Court of Appeal recognized that *§ 2650* allows a dissolution court to divide property owned before marriage in accordance with the same procedure and limitations used for community-property division, while also applying reimbursement principles where separate contributions were proven.

In re Marriage of Braud (1996) 45 Cal.App.4th 797: See *In re Marriage of Braud*: Records, Intent, and Partial Tracing (pg. 47).

Full Text of *California Family Code § 2650*

In a proceeding for division of the community estate, the court has jurisdiction, at the request of either party, to divide the separate property interests of the parties in real and personal property, wherever situated and whenever acquired, held by the parties as joint tenants or tenants in common. The property shall be divided together with, and in accordance with the same procedure for and limitations on, division of community estate.

49. *Family Code section 2660* – Real Property Held in Another State

Explanation:

California Family Code § 2660 addresses what a California dissolution court should do when the property subject to division includes real property located outside California. The statute recognizes a practical jurisdictional limitation: a California judgment generally cannot directly change title to land in another state in the same way a court in that state can. Instead, the California court should first try to divide the community and quasi-community estate in a way that avoids changing the nature of the out-of-state real property interests.

If that kind of division is not possible, *§ 2660* gives the court two tools. The court may order the parties to execute deeds, conveyances, or other documents necessary to effect the property division. Alternatively, the court may award one spouse the money value of the interest that spouse would have received if the conveyance or other action had occurred.

The statute operates through the court's personal jurisdiction over the parties. A California court may decide the spouses' rights as between themselves and may order a spouse to act, but enforcing title changes may require proceedings or recognition in the state where the real property is located.

Section 2660 prevents a spouse from defeating California community-property rights merely by investing marital wealth in land outside California. The out-of-state location affects the remedy and enforcement mechanics, but it does not automatically remove the property from the marital division analysis.

Examples:

Nevada Rental Property: During marriage, the spouses use community funds to buy a Nevada rental property. At dissolution, the California court may award one spouse other assets equal to that spouse's share so that the Nevada title does not have to change. This is the preferred approach if it can fairly divide the estate.

Required Conveyance: The only significant asset is an Oregon vacation home purchased with community funds. If the estate cannot be divided fairly without changing ownership, the California court may order a spouse to sign deeds or other documents needed to transfer the appropriate interest.

Money-Value Award: A spouse refuses to sign documents transferring an interest in Arizona real property, or a direct transfer is impractical. The California court may award the other spouse the money value of the interest that spouse would have received had the transfer occurred.

Quasi-Community Property: The parties lived outside California when they bought out-of-state real property, then later moved to California and divorced here. If the property would have been community property had it been acquired while domiciled in California, it may be treated as quasi-community property for division, and *§ 2660* supplies the remedial framework for the out-of-state real estate.

Further Reading:

Rozan v. Rozan (1957) 49 Cal.2d 322: Rozan predates the Family Code but states the foundational rule that a California court with personal jurisdiction may adjudicate the spouses' rights in out-of-state land, even though the California decree itself does not directly operate on title in the other state. The principle is reflected in *§ 2660*'s conveyance and money-value remedies.

In re Marriage of Economou (1990) 224 Cal.App.3d 1466: Economou involved extensive community and quasi-community property, including real property interests in Georgia and Greece. The Court of Appeal recognized that a California dissolution court may determine the parties' rights in out-of-state real property and may fashion orders to protect those rights, while title effects may require action in the situs state.

Muckle v. Superior Court (2002) 102 Cal.App.4th 218: Muckle involved Georgia real property that one spouse claimed was community property because it was purchased while the parties were California domiciliaries. The Court of Appeal acknowledged California's authority to adjudicate rights to out-of-state land when jurisdictional requirements are met, but held that the California court lacked personal jurisdiction over the nonresident spouse on the record before it. The case shows that *§ 2660* does not eliminate the need for personal jurisdiction.

In re Marriage of Ben-Yehoshua (1979) 91 Cal.App.3d 259: Ben-Yehoshua, a predecessor-era case, is often cited for the proposition that a California dissolution court may use in personam orders to require parties to execute documents necessary to effectuate property division involving real property beyond California's direct title jurisdiction.

Full Text of *California Family Code § 2660*

(a) Except as provided in subdivision (b), if the property subject to division includes real property situated in another state, the court shall, if possible, divide the community property and quasi-community property as provided for in this division in such a manner that it is not necessary to change the nature of the interests held in the real property situated in the other state.

(b) If it is not possible to divide the property in the manner provided for in subdivision (a), the court may do any of the following in order to effect a division of the property as provided for in this division:

(1) Require the parties to execute conveyances or take other actions with respect to the real property situated in the other state as are necessary.

(2) Award to the party who would have been benefited by the conveyances or other actions the money value of the interest in the property that the party would have received if the conveyances had been executed or other actions taken.

About the Authors

Victor VeVea

Victor VeVea received his bachelor's degree in mathematics and computer science from California State University, Bakersfield. He became interested in law after being falsely accused and facing a judge who ignored the law and the facts. Mr. VeVea was able to prove his innocence in court despite the judge ordering Mr. VeVea to proceed without an attorney, refusing to allow Mr. VeVea to compel the attendance of witnesses, and even refusing to allow Mr. VeVea to see the evidence being offered against him.

Mr. VeVea received a Bachelor of Laws and Juris Doctor degrees from Northwestern California University School of Law before passing the California Bar on the first attempt. He is an author of multiple book titles, including Handbook for the Accused, Sex Registration Guidebook, Passing Time While Doing Time, and California Criminal Defense Motions in Limine. He has also written multiple articles.

United States District Court Judge Lawrence J. O'Neill described Mr. VeVea as "an extraordinarily bright person, and… an intellectual vigilante." Despite such glowing praise, Mr. VeVea does not practice law; instead, he devotes his time to volunteer work, scholarly endeavors, helping others who have been falsely accused, assisting the self-represented with paperwork, and conducting research and investigations for attorneys on the most difficult cases.

Bakersfield Paralegal

Since its founding in 2001, Bakersfield Paralegal has grown into a trusted legal document services provider throughout California. Headquartered in Bakersfield, the firm specializes in preparing pleadings, motions, and court filings across a broad range of practice areas, including family law, evictions, criminal defense, conservatorships, guardianships, trusts, estate planning, and much more.

Operating under a client-centric model, Bakersfield Paralegal makes itself accessible to clients both locally and throughout the state. While it can meet clients in its immediate service area in person, many matters are efficiently handled by phone, video, or e-mail - allowing flexibility and convenience for parties across California.

With over two decades of experience, multiple published books on the law, and an impressive array of legal research tools, the company arrives with institutional knowledge and professionalism. Clients appreciate their thoroughness, responsiveness, and ability to explain complex legal steps clearly.

In a legal environment where the cost and complexity of representation can feel overwhelming, Bakersfield Paralegal offers a structured, affordable alternative for those navigating the court system on their own or seeking peace of mind in document preparation. Its longevity, depth of service offerings, and reputation for dependability make it a pillar in the legal support community.

www.ingramcontent.com/pod-product-compliance
Lightning Source LLC
Chambersburg PA
CBHW071438230926
51846CB00001B/270
* 9 7 8 1 9 5 0 4 1 8 0 5 3 *